Sport and Social Movements

Globalizing Sport Studies

SERIES EDITOR: John Horne, Professor of Sport and Sociology,
University of Central Lancashire, UK

Public interest in sport studies continues to grow throughout the world. This series brings together the latest work in the field and acts as a global knowledge hub for interdisciplinary work in sport studies. While promoting work across disciplines, the series focuses on social scientific and cultural studies of sport. It brings together the most innovative scholarly empirical and theoretical work, from within the UK and internationally.

Books already published in the series:

Global Media Sport: Flows, Forms and Futures
David Rowe
ISBN 9781849660709 (Hardback)
ISBN 9781849666756 (Ebook)

Japanese Women and Sport: Beyond Baseball and Sumo
Robin Kietlinski
ISBN 9781849663403 (Hardback)
ISBN 9781849666688 (Ebook)

Sport for Development and Peace: A Critical Sociology
Simon Darnell
ISBN 9781849663441 (Hardback)
ISBN 9781849665919 (Ebook)

Globalizing Cricket: Englishness, Empire and Identity
Dominic Malcolm
ISBN 9781849665278 (Hardback)
ISBN 9781849665612 (Ebook)

Forthcoming:
Globalizing Boxing
Kath Woodward

Localizing Global Sport for Development
Davies Banda, Ruth Jeanes, Tess Kay and Iain Lindsey

Sport and Technology: An Actor-Network Theory Perspective
Roslyn Kerr

Sport and Social Movements

From the Local to the Global

Jean Harvey, John Horne, Parissa Safai,
Simon Darnell and Sébastien Courchesne-O'Neill

B L O O M S B U R Y

LONDON • NEW DELHI • NEW YORK • SYDNEY

Bloomsbury Academic

An imprint of Bloomsbury Publishing Plc

50 Bedford Square	1385 Broadway
London	New York
WC1B 3DP	NY 10018
UK	USA

www.bloomsbury.com

Bloomsbury is a registered trade mark of Bloomsbury Publishing Plc

First published 2014

© Jean Harvey, John Horne, Parissa Safai, Simon Darnell and
Sébastien Courchesne-O'Neill, 2014

British Library Cataloguing-in-Publication Data
A catalogue record for this book is available from the British Library.

ISBN: HB: 978-1-7809-3414-3
ePDF: 978-1-7809-3557-7
ePub: 978-1-7809-3556-0

Library of Congress Cataloguing-in-Publication Data
A catalog record for this book is available from the Library of Congress.

Typeset by Deanta Global Publishing Services, Chennai, India

Contents

Globalizing Sport Studies
Series Editor's Preface

There is now a considerable amount of expertise nationally and internationally in the social scientific and cultural analysis of sport in relation to the economy and society more generally. Contemporary research topics, such as sport and social justice, science and technology and sport, global social movements and sport, sports mega-events, sports participation and engagement and the role of sport in social development, suggest that sport and social relations need to be understood in non-Western developing economies, as well as in European, North American and other advanced capitalist societies. The current high global visibility of sport makes this an excellent time to launch a major new book series that takes sport seriously, and makes this research accessible to a wide readership.

The series **Globalizing Sport Studies** is thus in line with a massive growth of academic expertise, research output and public interest in sport worldwide. At the same time, it seeks to use the latest developments in technology and the economics of publishing to reflect the most innovative research into sport in society currently underway in the world. The series is multi-disciplinary, although primarily based on the social sciences and cultural studies approaches to sport.

The broad aims of the series are to *act* as a knowledge hub for social scientific and cultural studies research in sport, including, but not exclusively, anthropological, economic, geographic, historical, political science and sociological studies; *contribute* to the expanding field of research on sport in society in the United Kingdom and internationally by focusing on sport at regional, national and international levels; *create* a series for both senior and more junior researchers that will become synonymous with cutting-edge research, scholarly opportunities and academic development; *promote* innovative discipline-based, multi-, inter- and trans-disciplinary theoretical and methodological approaches to researching sport in society; *provide* an English-language outlet for high-quality non-English writing on sport in society; *publish* broad overviews, original empirical research studies and classic studies from non-English sources; and thus attempt to *realize* the potential for *globalizing* sport studies through open content licensing with 'Creative Commons'.

Sport and Social Movements: from the Local to the Global offers a good illustration of the international collaboration that contemporary social scientific research into sport in a globalizing world requires. Three of the five authors, including the series editor in the United Kingdom and Harvey and Safai in

Canada, have been discussing this work for several years. Collectively the five of us have been interested in exploring challenges to the economic and political order of sport. More specifically, the book explores the relationship between sport and wider social movements; those influencing sport, using sport and movements within sport contributing to bigger causes. As we note, the forms of resistance to the sport social order are various – including protests, boycotts, demonstrations, campaigns, coalitions and other counter-initiatives – and they have been around for a long time, and with varying degrees of success. Arguably though, contentious forms of collective action are now more visibly present in various forms at the local, the national and the global levels.

In this book, the focus is on how and why sport connects with five broad social movements – workers, women's, rights, peace and environmental – and it charts the shift in these social movements through what Touraine (1981) called 'new social movements' to global social movements associated with sport. The contention is that social movements have not yet received enough attention in the scholarly analysis of sport and that given trends in social and political life, such analyses of sport and social movements are now required. As the literature on various specific protests, activist campaigns and social movements in sport grows, this book is the first to provide a systematic and comprehensive overview of sport and social movements, as well as pointers to where future research might focus.

John Horne, Preston and Edinburgh 2013

Acknowledgements

The authors would like to thank their families, friends, colleagues and students for contributing in many different ways to this book, the referees who commented extensively on the original submitted manuscript and members of the editorial team at Bloomsbury Academic.

The book has been produced collaboratively, including a symposium hosted by the Research Centre for Sport in Canadian Society at the University of Ottawa in May 2012, where the authors were able to present early drafts and exchange ideas about their contributions and the shape of the book. Initial authorial responsibility was as follows: Introduction, Chapter 1 and Chapter 2, Harvey; Conclusion and Chapter 4, Horne; Chapter 3, Safai; Chapter 5, Darnell; and Chapter 6, Courchesne-O'Neill. Horne and Darnell completed editing work on the entire manuscript.

Finally the authors would like to extend special thanks to Professor Jacques Defrance, University of Paris-Nanterre, who acted as discussant for the initial versions of the chapters during the Ottawa symposium and provided most valuable comments and suggestions that have helped improve the book in many ways.

List of Tables

A Chronology of Sport and Social Movements: From the Local to the Global

Year	Major Historical Events	Workers	Women	Rights	Peace	Environment	Sport-related Developments
1848	Publication of the *Manifesto of the Communist Party*						
1859							*Deutsche Turnerschaft* founded
1864	First meeting of the International Working Men's Association, (The 'First International')						
1888			International Council of Women founded				
1889–1914	The 'Second International'						
1892					The Interparliamentary Union founded; International Peace Bureau founded		
1896							First Modern Olympic Games held in Athens (men only)

Year					First (Western) women take part in the Olympic Games
1900					
1913		Lucerne Sport International (LSI) founded			
1914–1918	World War I	'Fédération sportive du travail' (FST) inaugurated (1914)			1916 Berlin Olympics cancelled due to WW1
1917	Bolshevik Revolution, Russia				
1919	Third (Communist) International				
1921		Red Sport International (RSI) founded, Moscow	Fédération Sportive Féminine Internationale (FSFI) founded		
1922			First 'Women's Olympic Games'		
1923		British Workers' Federation for Sport founded			
1925		First 'Workers' Olympics', Frankfurt			

(continued)

(Continued)

Year	Major Historical Events	Workers	Women	Rights	Peace	Environment	Sport-related Developments
1926			Second 'Women's Olympic Games'				
1931		Second 'Workers' Olympics', Vienna					
1936							Summer Olympic Games, Berlin ('The Nazi Olympics')
1937		Third 'Workers' Olympics', Antwerp					
1939–1945	World War II						1940 Tokyo Olympics cancelled
1941	Japanese attack on Pearl Harbor; start of the 'Pacific War'						
1945	Nuclear bombs dropped on Hiroshima and Nagasaki; Japan surrenders and accepts terms of Potsdam Proclamation						
1946		'Comité sportif international du travail' (CSIT) founded	UN establishes 'Commission on the Status of Women'				

Year							
1948					The United Nations adopts the Universal Declaration of Human Rights (UDHR); the 'apartheid' regime established in South Africa		London hosts the Summer Olympic Games; Stoke Mandeville hospital stages the first Stoke Mandeville Games for disabled patients
1949				International Association of Physical Education and Sport for Women and Girls (IAPESGW) founded			
1960					Sixty-nine demonstrators are killed by South African police during the 'Sharpeville Massacre'		
1961					Amnesty International Founded		
1962						Rachel Carson's *Silent Spring* is published	The South African Non-Racial Olympic Committee (SANROC) is formed

(continued)

(*Continued*)

Year	Major Historical Events	Workers	Women	Rights	Peace	Environment	Sport-related Developments
1963				'March on Washington', D.C.			
1965				UN International Convention on the Elimination of All Forms of Racial Discrimination (CERD)			
1966					Muhammad Ali refuses draft into US military service		
1968				'Olympic Project for Human Rights' (OPHR); 'The salute' by Smith and Carlos; first (World) Special Olympics, Chicago, USA.			Mexico City, Mexico hosts the Summer Olympics
1969				The 'Gay Liberation Front' develops following protests against policing at the Stonewall Inn in Greenwich Village, New York City			
1970						'Earth Day' celebrated in the USA	

Year						
1972				The first 'Center for Independent Living' established in Berkeley, California for people with disabilities; Union of the Physically Impaired Against Segregation (UPIAS) founded in the United Kingdom.		
1974						Women's Sport Foundation (WSF) founded
1975	'Helsinki Accord' recognizes the post-World War II borders of Europe			UN stages 'International Women's Year'		
1976						Montreal, Canada hosts the Summer Olympics
1977				The 'Gleneagles Agreement' on withholding sporting contact with apartheid South Africa is signed; the General Assembly of the UN adopts a similar declaration		

(continued)

(*Continued*)

Year	Major Historical Events	Workers	Women	Rights	Peace	Environment	Sport-related Developments
1978				The International Lesbian and Gay Association (ILGA) is founded			
1979			UN Convention on the Elimination of All Forms of Discrimination Against Women (CEDAW)				
1981				British Council of Organisations of Disabled People (BCODP) founded; 'Disabled Peoples' International' (DPI) holds First World Congress			
1982							First Gay Games, California
1984			Women's Sports Foundation (WSFUK) founded				
1986				The UN launches 'The International Year of the Special Olympics'			

Year						
1988	Clean Clothes Campaign (CCC) founded, The Netherlands					Seoul, South Korea, hosts the Summer Olympic Games and the Paralympics in the same venues
1989		European Women and Sport (EWS) network founded				
1990					'Surfers Against Sewage' founded	
1991	Demolition (Fall) of the Berlin Wall					
1992					UN Conference on the Environment and Development (UNCED), Rio de Janeiro, Brazil	Albertville Winter Olympic Games, France
1993			'Let's Kick Racism out of Football' campaign started in the United Kingdom			
1994		WomenSport International (WSI) founded; the 'Brighton Declaration on Women and Sport'				Lillehammer Winter Olympic Games, Norway

(continued)

(Continued)

Year	Major Historical Events	Workers	Women	Rights	Peace	Environment	Sport-related Developments
1997			Anita deFrantz elected as IOC Vice President				
1999	Demonstrations against the World Trade Organization (WTO), Seattle			'Football Against Racism in Europe' founded			
2000	Thousands of French farmers and anti-globalization protesters support Jose Bove in Milau, France, as he stands trial for attacking the local branch of McDonald's				UN 'International Year for the Culture of Peace'	Ten thousand residents of Rio de Janeiro, Brazil, protest against rising sewage level in the sea	
2001	First World Social Forum (WSF), Porto Alegre, Brazil with 11,000 activists; under the banner of 'another world is possible', acts as an alternative to the World Economic Forum, held in Davos, Switzerland; '9/11' – terrorist attacks on the World Trade Center in New York City and the Pentagon in Washington, DC.					The Denie Indians of Manaus in the Amazon, Brazil, win the right to protect their land from illegal logging and industrial practices	

Year						
2002	Second WSF, Porto Alegre; a final statement declares the WSF as a 'global movement for social justice and solidarity'			The International Criminal Court (ICC) is established in The Hague, empowered to prosecute individuals anywhere in the world for genocide, war crimes and crimes against humanity		Launch of international campaign to promote migrant workers' rights in Japan and South Korea at FIFA Football World Cup
2003	Third WSF in Porto Alegre; attended by 100,000					
2004	Fourth WSF held in Mumbai, India; Mumbai Resistance 2004 held opposite the main forum is critical of the WSF process		First 'Play Fair' campaign launched			Athens hosts the Summer Olympic and Paralympic Games
2005	Fifth WSF in Porto Alegre; attended by 155,000; 225,000 demonstrators travel to Edinburgh, Scotland, to join the 'Make Poverty History' march ahead of the G8 Summit in Gleneagles, coinciding with 10 Live 8 Concerts around the world; '7/7' – terrorist attacks on the London transportation system		Sister Dorothy Stang is murdered after working for 30 years working for sustainable development with the Landless Workers Movement	The European Court of Human Rights rules that two British environmental campaigners (the 'McLibel Two') were treated unfairly when the British government refused them legal aid for their defence against a libel case brought by McDonald's		UN 'International Year of Sport and Physical Education'

(continued)

(*Continued*)

Year	Major Historical Events	Workers	Women	Rights	Peace	Environment	Sport-related Developments
2006	Sixth WSF opens in several venues in Africa, South America and Asia			International Conference on LGBT Human Rights, Montreal, produces the 'Declaration of Montreal'; UN International Convention on the Rights of Persons with Disabilities (CRPD)	UN action plan on sport for development and peace		First World Outgames, Montreal
2007	Seventh WSF opens in Nairobi, Kenya		International Women's Day (8 March) is marked by 500 events in 49 different countries, including a Right to Play campaign in Tanzania to promote female inclusion in sport	Anti-racism events are held in cities around the world to mark 'International day for the Elimination of Racism' on the anniversary of the Sharpeville Massacre that killed 69 anti-apartheid demonstrators in 1960; the UN adopts the Universal Declaration of the Rights of Indigenous People			

2008	A global day of action takes place instead of a WSF under the banner of 'another world is possible'	As an alternative to the Olympic torch, a virtual torch relay is launched in the Netherlands by the Play Fair coalition of labour rights organizations	Protests take place in many countries where the Olympic torch relay comes over Chinese government's human rights record and calls are made to boycott the Beijing Olympics	The Olympic torch world relay in advance of the Beijing Summer Olympics is started in Olympia, Greece. During the torch lighting ceremony members of 'Reporters without Borders' breach security to express their support for the Free Tibet campaign
2009	A meeting of G20 leaders and finance ministers to discuss the global financial downturn in London attracts mass demonstration		A Global Day of Action for Human Rights in Iran held in more than 110 cities around the world	
2010	The tenth WSF begins in Porto Alegre with further events occurring elsewhere throughout the year			

(continued)

(Continued)

Year	Major Historical Events	Workers	Women	Rights	Peace	Environment	Sport-related Developments
2011	9.0 magnitude earthquake hits northeastern Japan, subsequent tsunami and nuclear crises						
2012			Olympic Games Opening Ceremony features performances referring to the suffragettes	Paralympic Games Closing Ceremony features performances referring to the UDHR			London Summer Olympic and Paralympic Games

Sources: See references in Chapters 2–6 of this book plus J. Timms (2012) 'Chronology of Global Civil Society Events – A Yearbook Retrospective'. In M. Kaldor, S. Selchow and H. Moore (Eds), *Global Civil Society 2012: Ten Years of Critical Reflection*. London: Sage, pp. 204–17.

List of Acronyms

AAM	Anti-apartheid Movement
AI	Amnesty International
ANC	African National Congress
ANTENNA	Asian Tourism Network
APPEN	Asia-Pacific People's Environmental Network
BCODP	British Council of Organisations of Disabled People
BOCOG	Beijing Organising Committee of the Olympic and Paralympic Games
BWB	Basketball Without Borders
CAAWS	Canadian Association for the Advancement of Women and Sport
CAT	Convention against Torture and Other Cruel, Inhuman or Degrading Treatment
CCC	Clean Clothes Campaign
CED	International Convention for the Protection of All Persons from Enforced Disappearance
CEDAW	Committee on the Elimination of Discrimination against Women
CERD	International Convention on the Elimination of All Forms of Racial Discrimination
CIL	Center for Independent Living
CMW	Convention on the Protection of the Rights of All Migrant Workers and Members of Their Families
CNN	Continuous News Network
COHRE	Centre on Housing Rights and Evictions
CONI	Italian Olympic Committee
CORE	Congress of Racial Equality
CRC	Convention on the Rights of the Child
CRM	Civil Rights Movement
CRPD	International Convention on the Rights of Persons with Disabilities
CSIT	Comité sportif international du travail (also known in English as the 'International Workers and Amateurs in Sports Confederation')
CSW	Commission on the Status of Women
DAW	Division for the Advancement of Women
DAWN	Development Alternatives with Women for a New Era
DPI	Disabled Peoples International

DRM	Disability Rights Movement
ECOSOC	Economic and Social Council
EHRC	Equality and Human Rights Commission
EPA	Environmental Protection Agency
EU	European Union
EWS	Working Group for European Women and Sport
FARE	Football Against Racism in Europe
FGG	Federation of the Gay Games
FIBA	Fédération Internationale de Basketball Amateur
FIFA	Fédération Internationale de Football Association
FOE	Friends of the Earth
FSAT	Fédération sportive athlétique du travail
FSFI	Fédération sportive féminine internationale
FSGT	Fédération sportive et gymnique du travail
FST	Fédération sportive du travail
GAGM	Global Anti-Golf Movement
GLF	Gay Liberation Front
GLISA	Gay and Lesbian International Sports Association
GNAGA	Global Network for Anti-Golf Course Action
GSM	Global Social Movements
HRW	Human Rights Watch
HWC	Homeless World Cup
IAAF	International Amateur Athletic Federation
IAPESGW	International Association of Physical Education and Sport for Women and Girls
ICC	International Coordinating Committee of National institutions for the Promotion and Protection of Human Rights
ICCPR	International Covenant on Civil and Political Rights
ICESCR	International Covenant on Economic, Social and Cultural Rights
ILGA	International Lesbian and Gay Association
IMF	International Monetary Fund
INGO	International Non-governmental Organizations
IOC	International Olympic Committee
IOSD	International Organization of Sport for the Disabled
IPC	International Paralympic Committee
ISA	International Sociological Association
ITGLWF	International Textile, Garment and Leather Worker's Federation
ITUC	International Trade Union Confederation
ITWC	International Women's Tribune Centre
IWG	Working Group on Women and Sport

IWY	International Women's Year
LCFO	Lowndes County Freedom Organization
LGBT	Lesbian, Gay, Bisexual and Transgender
LOCOG	London Organising Committee of the Olympic and Paralympic Games
LSI	Lucerne Sport International
MAI	Multilateral Agreement on Investment
MDG	Criticism of the Millennium Development Goals
NAACP	National Association for the Advancement of Colored People
NATO	North Atlantic Treaty Organization
NBA	National Basketball Association
NGO	Non-governmental Organization
NHL	National Hockey League
NHRI	National Human Rights Institutions
NIMBY	Not in My Backyard
NOC	National Olympic Committees
NSM	New Social Movement
NYAC	New York Athletic Club
OPHR	Olympic Project for Human Rights
PAC	Pan-Africanist Congress
PCF	Parti Communiste Français (French Communist Party)
PFC	Perfluorinated Compounds
PMO	Peace Movement Organizations
POW	Protect our Winters
RC	Research Committees
RSI	Red Sport International
SAN-ROC	South African Non-Racial Olympic Committee
SAPs	Structural Adjustment Policies and Programs
SAS	Surfers Against Sewage
SCLC	Southern Christian Leadership Conference
SDP	Sport for Development and Peace
SFIO	Section of the Socialist Party
SNCC	Student Non-violent Coordinating Committee
SOCOG	Sydney Organising Committee of the Olympic and Paralympic Games
TAN	Transnational Advocacy Network
TGR	Teton Gravity Research
TOP	The Olympic Programme
UDHR	Universal Declaration of Human Rights
UISP	Unione Italiana Sport per Tutti (Italian Sport for All Union)
UN	United Nations
UNEP	United Nations Environment Program

UNESCO	United Nations Educational, Scientific and Cultural Organization
UN HRC	UN Human Rights Council
UPIAS	Union of the Physically Impaired Against Segregation
USOC	United States Olympic Committee
USSGT	Union des Sociétés Sportives et Gymniques du Travail
WB	World Bank
WCED	United Nations World Commission on Environment and Development
WEF	World Economic Forum
WIDF	Women's International Democratic Federation
WISC	Women's International Sports Coalition
WSF	World Social Forum
WSF-UK	Women's Sports Foundation, UK
WSF-US	Women's Sport Foundation, USA
WSI	Women Sport International
WTO	World Trade Organization
WUNC	Worthiness, Unity, Numbers and Commitment

Introduction

In 1921 French woman Alice Milliat took the lead in setting up the Fédération sportive féminine internationale (FSFI; in English, the International Women's Sports Federation). This was an organization designed to lobby and fight against the International Olympic Committee (IOC) and the International Amateur Athletic Federation (IAAF) for the inclusion of women's events in the Olympics and other international sports competitions, particularly in track and field events. Baron Pierre De Coubertin and his fellow members of the IOC and IAAF were well aware of FSFI feminism but were firmly against what they then saw as its abuses and deviations, let alone the whole-scale participation of women in the Olympics' most popular events. In response to the IOC's and IAAF's denial of women's participation, the first Women's Olympics were held in 1932 with great success, and were followed by three other Games that turned the attention of the world to women's athleticism. By 1934 the IAAF – and by extension, the IOC – came to the conclusion that the Women's Olympic Games were not going to disappear as they had hoped and began to incorporate women, in controlled and controlling ways that were not genuinely reflective of their capacity to participate in sport, into the Olympic Games (see Chapter 3 for further discussion of the FSFI).

In what is considered by many to be the best-known public protest in a sports arena, at the 1968 Mexico City Summer Olympic Games, Tommie Smith and John Carlos, raised their black-gloved fists during the playing of the US national anthem on the medal podium, in solidarity with the civil rights movement in the United States. In support of their protest, the silver medallist from Australia, Peter Norman, wore a human rights badge. All three athletes were criticized – in fact, vilified – for their actions. Smith and Carlos were condemned immediately by the United States Olympic Committee (USOC), the IOC and most of the international press for their 'politicization' of the Games, and they were expelled from the Games. Norman was reprimanded by the Australian Olympic Committee and media and was never allowed to compete again in the Olympics despite successful qualification times at subsequent Olympic trials (see Chapter 4 for further discussion of rights movements and sport.

More recently, large portions of the 2008 Beijing Olympic Games torch relay itinerary became the site of political protests – in favour of Tibet's autonomy from China, against exploitative working conditions in sporting goods manufacturing industries, against child labour and for the promotion of human rights in China and around the world. On the eve of the London 2012 Olympic

Games, hundreds of NGOs, global unions, and human rights and workers' organizations worldwide coalesced into a Play Fair campaign to protest against, among other issues, the poor working conditions in the subcontracting factories where clothing, souvenirs and apparel for the Games were to be produced (see Chapter 2 for more on the labour movement and sport).

What does each of these events have in common? They were all challenges to the economic and political order of sport. More precisely, they were all inspired by wider social movements: movements of resistance influencing sport, movements that use sport as an instrument to support their cause, or movements from within sport contributing to larger causes. Protests, boycotts, demonstrations, campaigns, petitions, town hall meetings, coalitions, lobbying, counter-initiatives, the forms of resistance to the sport social order are various and have been around for a long time, and with varying degrees of success. Indeed, historically, modern sport as an institution has always been challenged for sustaining different forms of discrimination and negative social impacts. In turn athletes, sport and social activists, engaged intellectuals and citizens have organized against these. From neighbourhood coalitions organizing against the building of a sport facility for professional sports teams subsidized by public funds, to global campaigns for equity for women in sport, to worldwide bans of apartheid regimes, sites and levels of protest, resistance and activism have been present throughout the history of sport. Contentious forms of collective actions are now ever more present in various forms at the local, the national and the global levels.

In this book, we focus on how and why sport connects with social movements. Conceptually, like Bourdieu (1984), we are interested in exploring the relationship between the political (field) and the sports (field). We recognize that political protest in sport is not new; social movements' involvement with sport is not new either. That said, we further recognize that sport is a field in which progressive social movements face serious difficulties, for two connected reasons. First the apolitical ideology that pervades sport often means that people interested in and involved in sport are often less concerned with, and sometimes actively resistant to, getting involved in the politics of sport to improve the social circumstances within which it takes place. This can be seen, for example in Chapter 2 where we discuss the labour movement and sport. Second and related, the ideology of sport's political neutrality reinforces the position of the dominant power holders in sport. Rhetorical tropes such as 'for the good of the game' and the 'Olympic family' espoused by the leading international sports organizations FIFA and IOC, respectively, help sustain the apolitical hegemony of the dominant sports order. Nonetheless we attempt in this book to demonstrate how this is contested. Sports mega-events such as the men's Football World Cup Finals and the Olympic Games, for example, continue to channel the energies of both the 'boosters' of the current order and the 'sceptics', critics and activists challenging it.

Hence we chart in this book the shift in social movements through what Touraine (1981) called 'new social movements' (NSMs) to global social movements associated with sport. Our contention is that social movements have not received enough attention in the scholarly analysis of sport and that given trends in social and political life, particularly around globalization in which one specific form of contentious political action or collective behaviour, global social movements have emerged, such analyses of sport and social movements are now necessary. Moreover, as an emerging literature focusing on various specific protests, activist campaigns and social movements in sport is now slowly growing, we developed this book as the first of its kind to provide a systematic and comprehensive analysis of sport and social movements.

It may be useful to clarify what we mean by social movements here. Examples of institutions and organizations from the world of sport that are sometimes considered to be social movements, but are not in our view, include the Olympic 'Movement', as underpinned by the IOC and the Sport for Development and Peace (SDP) sector. As the stewards of the Olympic Games and its brand, the IOC has often presented itself as the leader of a social movement named the 'Olympic Movement', underpinned by the philosophy of 'Olympism' as an approach to and a philosophy of life. Principle 3 of the IOC Charter (http://www.olympic.org/Documents/olympic_charter_en.pdf [accessed 14 May 2012]) declares for example:

> The Olympic Movement is the concerted, organized, universal and permanent action, carried out under the supreme authority of the IOC, of all individuals and entities who are inspired by the values of Olympism. It covers the five continents. It reaches its peak with the bringing together of the world's athletes at the great sports festival, the Olympic Games. Its symbol is five interlaced rings.

However in social scientific terms, 'Olympism' and the 'Olympic movement' cannot be considered a social movement. While it is true that the Olympics, at least in the eyes of its modern founder de Coubertin, sought to effect change in social life by promoting the practice of sport which itself is described as a social good, the IOC is not, nor has ever been, a *dominated* actor which resisted marginalization and called for foundational social and political change. In fact, the historical evidence suggests that just the opposite is true (Horne and Whannel 2012, pp. 27–46). The IOC is an elitist, self-selecting club and one of the pre-eminent institutions that today governs a global sport order based on commodified sport (Perelman 2012). In turn, the IOC and the Olympic movement have no identifiable or dominant adversary nor is the IOC the bearer of a new progressive form of society or sport system. Indeed today, the IOC is a powerful force for the sporting status quo; as such we cannot consider the Olympic movement a social movement.

A second example of a recently popular 'movement' in sport that does not fit our definition of a true social movement is the burgeoning Sport for Development and Peace (SDP) sector comprised of organizations that coordinate and mobilize sport to meet the goals of international development. The popularity of SDP, and its transformative ethic, has led to it being termed a social movement (see for example Kidd 2008). Its identification as such is undoubtedly more nuanced than in the case of the Olympics and IOC given that some initiatives that fall under the umbrella of SDP and 'sport-for-development' may be viewed as inspired by current issues and events that connect to other global social movements. The Homeless World Cup (HWC) football/soccer tournament is a good example of this. This initiative emerged out of the housing rights movement and was established by the International Network of Street Papers in 2003 (Sherry 2010). The HWC aims to 'promote social opportunities, including access to support services and interaction with others, for participants experiencing homelessness and social disadvantage' (Sherry 2010, p. 63). While the HWC has been found to benefit participants through the development of social capital (Sherry 2010) and to positively affect the attitudes of spectators towards homelessness (Sherry et al. 2011), like many sport-for-development initiatives, it has now become more institutionalized, slowly losing its emancipatory and resistive dimension.

Other initiatives within SPD are even more remotely connected to social movements. For example, the Fédération Internationale de Basketball Amateur (FIBA)'s and National Basketball Association (NBA)'s 'Basketball Without Borders' (BWB) initiative describes itself as a global basketball development and community outreach programme that unites young basketball players to promote the sport and encourage positive social change in the areas of education, health and wellness. However, workshops organized under this programme serve in many respects to identify new talent for the NBA and support the globalization of its brand and corporate outreach. As Millington (2010, p. 3) has argued, 'BWB sits at the intersection of the emerging trends of SDP, and corporate philanthropy' and therefore *aligns* with the dominant order and logic of global capitalism rather than resisting it or calling for reform. Indeed, SDP initiatives tend to eschew the identification of a dominant force or opponent against which they organize and campaign (Darnell 2012, p. 18/19); as such, we consider that it is inaccurate to theorize, identify or define SDP initiatives like BWB as social movements.

So, what do *we* mean by social movements and global social movements? As we shall see in the next chapter there is considerable debate in the social science literature about what social movements are. We find Diani's (1992, p. 13) definition most useful: social movements are '. . . networks of informal interactions between a plurality of individual groups, or associations, engaged in a political conflict, on a basis of a shared identity'. Social scientists recognize that different types of social movements emerged at different historical stages: hence, there are old social movements, NSMs and finally global social movements. Global social movements we argue in this book, following

•

Wieviorka (2005) and others, are the latest forms of social movements, which are engaged in political conflicts of a global nature. They are mainly in conflict with the so-called neo-liberal 'Washington consensus', the most recent hegemonic model of economic globalization. They strive for more humane forms of globalization and coalesce around a larger movement, the 'movement of movements' or alter-globalization. Indeed, as we shall see in later chapters, alter-globalization refers to a large spectrum of global social movements supporting new forms of globalization based upon values of democracy, justice, environment and human rights rather than upon purely economic concerns (Pleyers 2010).

In other words, in this book, we are interested in investigating the relationships between sport and global social movements as a new and underdeveloped but important area of study. As we argue here, global social movements are the latest and growing form of contentious political action in our globalized world that pervades numerous areas of social life, including sport. Hence, this book addresses several key contemporary research questions. How are social movements and alter-globalization influencing the current sport order as well as the wider world order? How do the different forms of political actions spurred by these movements differ from previous forms in their reach and goals for change? Are there existing sporting forms or sport organizations whose goals participate or are in line with global social movements and alter-globalization? What actual or potential influences do these organizations have on the sport global social order?

Since the initial call for the study of global social movements and sport by Harvey and Houle in 1994, and a subsequent article (Harvey et al. 2009), an emerging literature addressing different aspects of social movements and sport has slowly begun to emerge. For example, Sage (1999) published a landmark paper on coalition advocacy groups protesting against working conditions in Nike's factories. Wilson (2002) published a study of the 'anti-jock' movement in the age of internet, and another one on new media and social movements (Wilson 2007). More, recently Wilson (2012) published a book focusing on sport and peace, with reference to the peace movement. Taking up an engaged academic stance, Lenskyj (2000; 2002; 2008) has published a series of books on different aspects of the 'power, politics and activism' against the Olympics, providing a participant overview of coalitions and movements resisting what she calls the current hegemonic 'Olympic industry'. From a different perspective, Davis-Delano and Crosset (2008) provide a discussion of the use of social movement theory to study local protests in sport, while Boykoff (2011) provided an assessment of the Vancouver 2010 anti-Olympics protests as a form of 'event coalition'. Most recently, framing her study within the social movement literature, Cornelissen (2012) offered an analysis of the forms of activism connected to the global workers movement that took place around the 2010 FIFA Men's Football World Cup Finals in South Africa.

One reason why there has not been much attention paid to global social movements in sport is the complexity and variety of forms of organizations that make simple classification difficult. Another may be that while sport scholars often prescribe radical social change in order to improve social conditions in sport, most of the movements focusing on sport in consumer culture tend to be pressure groups interested in achieving reformist goals or simply 'value for money' rather than wholesale social or political transformation. Just as there are multiple reactions to globalization and sport, a working typology of different organizations, groups and networks that directly or indirectly pose a challenge to the hegemonic global sport order under the alter-globalist paradigm will be similarly diverse (see Harvey et al. 2009 for a first attempt at this). There is a clear need for more studies of the most prominent global social movements, as well as the relationship between sport and movements. This book aims precisely at a wider examination of social movements in sport, through an analysis of what we consider the most salient global social movements today challenging the world sport order or having the most potential to influence it in the near future, and also challenging the wider world social order, from within or from outside sport.

Necessarily this book can only cover a number of possible social movements – workers, women's, human rights, peace and the environmental movements – partly in order to keep the project manageable but also because these are the leading social movements involved with sport. Hence our selection, although apparently limited in number, actually covers a wide scope of social life. Moreover as we will show, they intersect with each other and often act together on various issues that they are concerned with. First, the movements discussed in detail in this book illustrate the shift from the local to the national and to transnational organizing and campaigning in the development of global social movements. Second, the movements are the most prominent ones in the study of the politics of sport. Third, the movements were selected for pragmatic reasons; there was ready availability of data and documentation for these movements in the languages in which we conducted our research (English and French). Fourth and finally, these movements were ones for which we shared a collective research interest and expertise. Here in brief is an outline of the contents of the book.

The first chapter elaborates on definitions and theoretical trends in the study of social movements. The idea of alter-globalization as the 'movement of movements' is also discussed and the general theoretical framework structuring the empirical studies that follow is outlined. Chapters 2–6 constitute the core of the book. Each chapter focuses on one of the social movements selected for this book and follows a similar structure with small variations. In each chapter there is an introduction briefly outlining the relations between the movement and sport; a discussion of the relevant movement including the historical development of the movement and the politics of the movement's cause; and then discussion of the relationship it has to sport and the relation of sport to the movement. A major focus of each chapter is to explain the development of their current forms of activism as global social movements in order to assess their potential for transforming the politics of sport in a globalized world. While each chapter is dedicated to one specific social movement, we have made a point of underlining the various intersections between these movements as they are interconnected in networks of different sorts as their form of activism has developed.

Chapter 2 deals with the labour movement. There are several reasons behind that choice. As will be explained in Chapter 1, social movements evolved over time and took several forms, aimed at different levels of society. From the mid-nineteenth century onwards, the labour movement was the most prominent social movement and became a challenging force in the industrializing capitalist societies (Hobsbawm 1969; Thompson 1968). The labour movement was the first major social movement to become a challenging force in the industrializing capitalist societies from the mid-nineteenth century onwards (Hobsbawm 1969; Thompson 1968). The labour movement was at first mostly concerned with working conditions in factories and mining, but it grew extensively to be concerned with all aspects of workers' lives as capitalist social relations expanded. As arguably one of the oldest social movements, the labour movement is the best example to demonstrate the evolution of social movements as capitalism developed over time. Today, worker sport may be less prominent than it was but, in some countries, especially France and Italy, its organizations continue to provide an alternative to the mainstream sport order.

Chapter 3 is dedicated to the global women's movement whose antecedents draw from the activities of individuals and organizations at the national and international level but which, arguably, only became genuinely transnational with the United Nations' dedication of 1974 as the International Women's Year and 1975–85 as the Decade for Women (in concert with the actions and efforts of a wide variety of non-governmental organizations or NGOs). While often not a central focus of the global women's movement, advocacy for and activism around women's sport has enjoyed parallel development around with the broader movement; yet, today, women are still fighting for equal rights in sport and in society at large. The global women's movement intersects with other key social movements; as shown in Chapter 2, for example, women working in the clothing industry started what has become today the 'Clean Clothes Campaign' in coalition with the global workers movement. On the sports field, women's coalition groups are still questioning the current sport order and yet also trying to solidify their participatory and leadership space in the hegemonic sports model.

Chapter 4 expands on the previous one through an examination of the ramifications of other human rights movements, namely anti-racism and the civil rights movement, the disability rights movement and the Lesbian, Gay,

Bisexual and Transgender (LGBT) rights movement. Again while focusing on these three movements, this chapter provides another demonstration of the common roots and interconnections between what we here have divided into discreet movements.

Chapter 5 focuses on the peace movement and organizations associated with it, outlining the shifting goals and approaches of the movement since the late nineteenth century. It also provides an analysis of the ways in which some peace activists and peace movement organizations (PMOs) have connected to, and shaped sport, and how various athletes and sports organizations have come to approach and support struggles for peace. Most importantly the chapter makes special reference to the recent shift in focus in the peace movement towards generating a 'culture of peace' that has potential consequences for the transformative power of peace as a social movement.

Chapter 6 deals with the environmental movement. The chapter first outlines the history of the movement and the evolution of various forms of activism associated with environmentalism. The chapter then focuses on examples of organizations having a connection between sport and environment, including Surfers Against Sewage (SAS), and the Global Anti-Golf Movement (G'AGM).

Finally, in the concluding chapter, we review the most salient points of the book in a discussion of the potential transformative power of each of these movements under the current hegemony of the global sport social order. We also indicate the great potential for further research into (global) social movements and sport. Such research will enable us to better understand how global social movements operate in relation to sport and also to identify the global forces, connections and imaginations that underpin contemporary global social movements.

1

Analysing Sport and (Global) Social Movements

As noted in the introduction, the term 'social movement' has been used quite loosely in both academic and popular discourse. In this chapter we discuss how the concept of 'social movement' has been understood and debated in academic literature in order to contextualize our use of the term in this book. For us, 'movement' implies a change over space and time; a relocation from one place to another and talk of social movements refers to the historical agency of social classes and other social collectivities in the shaping of society. Simply put then for us a social movement combines the idea of change with the notion of a strategy or intentionality and the coming together of dominated or minority social groups in efforts at social transformation (Bennett et al. 2005, pp. 224–5).

Some writers about sport and society, for example, Jarvie with Thornton (2012, pp. 381ff), have suggested that sport itself should be considered as a social movement. From their viewpoint, in its organized form, it has characteristics such as informal interaction networks, shared beliefs and organizational goals that can be found in other social movements. We argue that such a broad and inclusive definition is too imprecise to help understand the differences between movements that have a progressive social agenda and those that do not, which includes several so-called 'movements' within sport. As we demonstrate in this book, rather than positioning sport itself as a social movement, it is more accurate to state that sport has often had a connection to social movements and social movements have influenced sport. For example, in Chapter 3 we show how various forms of the women's rights movement and of feminism have influenced the development of a global women's sport movement. It is not analytically helpful therefore to simply conclude that sport itself can be described as a social movement.

With this in mind, the remainder of the chapter consists of two main sections. First, we explore definitions of the concept of social movements through an examination of two major theoretical traditions in the study of social movements – the so-called school of 'contentious politics' and 'the theory of action' – and attempts by scholars to find a synthesis of them. In so doing, we pay attention to different forms of activism and resistance, or in Charles Tilly's words, different forms of 'contentious politics'. We do this in order to identify the forms of action specific to social movements in contrast to, for example, local ad hoc protests and political pressure groups. Drawing on the work of Touraine and other theorists, we develop a blended theoretical model by which to grasp the developmental trajectories of the different social movements we focus on in this book. This also serves to outline the conceptual underpinning of the book. In the second section we use this theoretical framework to revise a typology, as well as a periodization, of the history of social movements that was first discussed in Harvey et al (2009). This section also discusses the specifics of the contemporary phase of global social movements, including the different political responses to neo-liberal globalization and to more recent forms of 'alter-globalization' (Pleyers 2010).

Competing approaches to the study of social movements

While there are several approaches to the study of social movements in the literature (see Chesters and Welsh 2011) according to Wieviorka (2005), there are broadly two main competing theoretical approaches for understanding social movements in sociology and social theory. These approaches have come to define the field and we have utilized them to underpin the research in this book. While the differences between them have been so profound that the International Sociological Association (ISA) established two separate research committees (RC) on social movements in the 1990s (RC 47 and 48), we will adopt a blended model drawing from each of them to frame the analysis of social movements and sport, since they are not entirely incompatible as they focus on different levels of societal functioning (Wieviorka 2005).

ISA RC 48 has been closely associated with the theoretical approach of social historian Charles Tilly and is often referred to as the 'contentious politics' school that evolved from the theory of the 'mobilization of resources' pioneered by economist Mancur Olson (1965). Wieviorka (2005, p. 1) states that the contentious politics school defines social movements as 'the rational behavior of collective actors attempting to establish themselves at the level of the political system, maintaining this position and extending their influence by mobilizing all sorts of resources including, if necessary, violence'.

Indeed for Tilly and Woods (2009, p. 3), social movements 'are a distinctive form of contentious politics – contentious in the sense that movements involve collective making of claims that, if realized, would conflict with someone else's interests'. Politically speaking, the claims put forward by social movements often involve, in one way or another, governments. Governments (at local, regional, federal or national levels) can be the object of the claims, or the allies, claimants or the monitors of the point of contention (Tilly 2004, p. 3). The process by which social movements are formed is thus, in Tilly's view, intimately linked with the political apparatus, and its role can be detached or involved, depending on the specific social setting.

Also of importance for Tilly is the need for a deep understanding of the historical setting pertaining to the social movement(s) studied: (1) it explains why social movements have incorporated important features enabling them to be separated from other form of politics; (2) it identifies significant changes in how they operate; and (3) it makes possible the singling out of particular political conditions that made the appearance of social movements possible (Tilly 2004). For Tilly, 'the rise and fall of social movements mark the expansion and contraction of democratic opportunities'. (2004, p. 3). More precisely, in their extensive detailed history of social movements, Tilly and Wood (2009) argue that it is between 1765 and 1830 in England and in the United States that the historical elements crystallized which made possible the emergence of social movements as a distinctive form of contentious politics. For them, the elements that constitute (and define) the distinctive features of social movements are (1) an organized public effort put forward in order to stake a variety of claims on specific, targeted forms of authority (i.e. a campaign); (2) the use of different forms of political action (i.e. performances); (3) and a concerted display of Worthiness, Unity, Numbers and Commitment (WUNC) (Tilly 2004, pp. 3–4). WUNC is, by any standards, the bread and butter of social movements as it involves direct representation on the street coupled with pragmatic factors like headcounts at a demonstration or the chanting of slogans during a march. Tilly argues that it is only by a combination of the three above-mentioned elements that a social movement may arise and have a concrete impact on any given social cause.

The combination of all these factors, together with the importance of a thorough historical investigation of the social setting, defines the broader spectrum of a social movement. Upon revisiting the definition in one of his last books on the subject, Tilly clearly stated that the term 'social movement' was still very much up for debate. However, taking into account his extensive work on the subject, he adopted the following definition:

> . . . a distinctive way of pursuing public politics began to take shape in Western countries during the later eighteenth century, acquired widespread recognition in Western Europe and North America by the early nineteenth century, consolidated into a durable ensemble of elements in the middle of the same century, altered more slowly and incrementally after this point, spread widely through the Western world, and came to be called a social movement. That political complex combined three elements: 1) campaign of collective claims on target authorities; 2) an array of claim-making performances including special-purpose associations, public meetings, media statements, and demonstrations; 3) public representations of the cause's worthiness, unity, numbers, and commitment. I am calling that historically specific complex a social movement. (Tilly 2004, p. 7)

Finally, Tilly's overall research agenda is to develop a detailed historical account of the evolution of the widest possible range of social movements. He suggests that (1) from their beginnings, social movements were interactive campaigns rather than ad hoc events; (2) they combine three kinds of claims: programme, identity and standing; (3) the relative salience of the former varies significantly among and within social movements, as well as over time; (4) democratization helps the formation of social movements; (5) social movements promote people's power; (6) social movements depend on political entrepreneurs; (6) once established, social movements collaborate and get accepted in other settings; (7) social movements evolved in forms and personnel; and (8) social movements can evolve in other social forms (Tilly and Wood 2009, pp. 12–14). In this book we take from Tilly the emphasis on the importance of historical accounts of the evolution of social movements, although our focus is on a much more modest range of movements.

By contrast, the other main approach to the study of social movements found in ISA RC 48 is associated most closely with the French sociologist Alain Touraine and his 'theory of action'. This approach 'sees in a social movement the action of an actor who is dominated and challenges the order by opposing a social adversary in an attempt to appropriate the control of historicity, that is to say the main orientations of community life' (Wieviorka 2005, pp. 1–2). Tourainian analysis is thus more interested in understanding the wider social conditions under which social movements develop than the mechanisms by which they develop. Crossley (2002), for example, suggests that Touraine developed the theory of NSMs at a time when the conventional Marxist approach to social change and social movements was being supplanted. NSMs would be the new 'revolutionary vanguard' once the proletariat had been incorporated into consumer capitalism.

Another major distinction between the two approaches is that for Tilly, reforms within the existing political system have specific, defined goals, whereas for Touraine, the action is aimed at a higher and more abstract social level or what he terms 'historicity'. 'Historicity' refers to the entire mode or structure of social organization at any one time in a social formation. Touraine identifies three specific components of historicity: the system of knowledge (by which society can act and reflect on itself), the system of accumulation and the dominant cultural model (for a detailed exploration of the concept, see Touraine 1977, Chapter 1). While for Tilly action in a social movement can take any direction – from emancipatory, to self-interested or even reactionary – in Touraine's collective action definition, social movements can only take the direction of emancipation towards a better society, a characteristic that suggests an ethical dimension to the conceptualization of social change. Hence for Touraine, counter-emancipatory groups, such as neo-fascists and terrorists, cannot be considered as social movements, but rather constitute 'anti-movements' (Wieviorka 2005). Put differently, while for the contentious politics approach, social movements may arise from either dominant or dominated actors, in Touraine's definition social movements emerge *only* from and among the efforts of *dominated* social actors. Acknowledging that social classes are no longer the principal collective agents that will bring about fundamental social transformation, for Touraine the search is to understand the single social movement that epitomizes the struggle against historicity at any one period of time. In turn, for Touraine, if social movements become dominant, they can no longer strictly be defined as social movements as they become part of a new hegemonic social order. Indirectly distancing himself from Tilly, Touraine (1988, p. 63) argues that:

> Most of all, the empiricist illusion must be clearly rejected: it is impossible to define an object called social movements without first selecting a general mode of analysis of social life on the basis of which a category of acts called social movements can be constituted.

In other words, Touraine defends a much more restrictive definition of what should be understood as a social movement than Tilly. He proposes to call 'collective behaviors' all those '. . . conflictual actions that can be understood as attempts to defend, to reconstruct, or adapt a sick element of the social system' (Touraine 1988, p. 64). He continues 'when conflictual actions seek to transform the relations of social domination that are applied to the principal cultural resources, they will be called social movements' (p. 64).

While the distinction between these two schools of thought has remained significant and even steadfast, some bridges have been identified. Diani (1992; Diani and Bison 2004), for example, has attempted to find common ground between these two traditions, as well as to identify the forms of collective action specific to social movements. Diani (1992) helpfully defines social movements as 'networks of informal interactions between a plurality of individual groups, or associations, engaged in a political conflict, on a basis of a shared identity' (p. 13). There are several dimensions to Diani's definition that are compatible with our view of social movements in relation to sport. First is the idea of 'networks of interactions' between different types of organizations. We agree that social movements are recognized for possessing a constellation of organizations acting at different levels – sometimes very locally, in a city or even a neighbourhood, and sometimes at an international or global scale. As a result, we consider that there is no single organization that is *the* social movement; organizations, coalitions and initiatives all contribute to the formation, direction and maintenance of a social movement. Second, Diani shares with Touraine the idea of a 'shared identity'. From this perspective, social movements regroup a diversity of collective actions around a specific cause that serves to constitute the identity of the group. In other words our understanding of social movements is that they

> can most usefully be seen as a network of groups and organizations that are unified by a shared conception that they *do* form part of a single "movement" with

specific goals, by deliberate attempts on the part of the groups and organizations to ally themselves with one another through joint action, coalitions, umbrella groups and so forth, and by shared beliefs and ideals among the members of the groups and organizations. (Scott 2012, p. 154)

While we embrace Diani's definition and Scott's elaboration of it, we follow Touraine's (1977) recognition that social movements have three interconnected dimensions: (1) they have a collective identity; (2) they have a clear social adversary; and (3) they are the bearers of a new social model that they strive for. Hence in our discussion of social movements and sport in the following chapters, we will discuss the three components that underpin their formation: their identity, their opponent and an alternative conception of social order (or 'totality'). Touraine defined these principles as follows. First, '. . . the principle of identity is the definition the actor gives of himself. A social movement cannot be organized unless this definition is conscious . . . it is conflict that constitutes and organizes the actor'. (Touraine 1977, p. 311). The principle of opposition was defined in the same manner: a movement 'cannot be organized without being able to name its adversary. . . . The conflict causes the adversary to appear, as it shapes the consciousness of the actors confronting each other' (Touraine 1977, p. 312). Thirdly, all social movements possess what Touraine (1977) calls a principle of 'totality', the latter being a new 'system of historical action' that the social movement wishes to implement. Hence, as an example, as we shall see in the next chapter, throughout its long history the labour movement has always identified itself as *the* movement of workers; a social movement opposed to capitalism as a social and economic system based on the exploitation of all workers. The movement struggles either for major reforms to capitalism or for its overthrow and replacement by a socialist system. In each of the subsequent chapters we will attempt to demonstrate how these three principles are present in other social movements.

Nonetheless we also embrace criticisms of the social movement literature itself. As noted by a number of key writers in the area (e.g. Ferree and Mueller 2007; Rupp and Taylor 1999; Taylor 1999; Taylor et al. 2001), and in a two-part special issue on gender and social movements in *Gender & Society* (1998; 1999), scholarship on social movements has tended to neglect sex and gender despite the fact that political protest – from inception to mobilization, leadership, strategies, culture, symbols, narratives and ideologies – is profoundly gendered. As part of the cultural turn in social movement theory, and as studies on women's and feminist movements grew among scholars, social movement theory was criticized for 'operating with gender-neutral terms, for assuming the men as the normative political actor and for conspicuously failing to examine the role of women in political protest' (Yulia 2010, p. 629). Feminist scholarship on the state, discourse and identity (in particular, looking at the ways identity is intersected by sex, gender, race, ethnicity and class) challenged existing conceptualizations of all social movements, not just those that pertained to or involved women. For example, researchers began paying more careful attention to the division of labour within mixed-sex movements – the ways in which women tend to be allocated auxiliary roles (e.g. secretarial roles) aside male leadership and/or are excluded from leadership positions altogether in spite of the fact that, in some cases, women initiate the movement and constitute the clear majority during the movement's infancy (see Fonow 1998).

Scholars studying women and social movements emphasize the need for multi-level analytical frameworks that take into account the structural, cultural and interactional dimensions of mobilization and protest. Such frameworks emphasize the interaction of broader sociocultural conditions, referred to as the 'opportunity structures', within which social movements grow or die, the characteristics and processes of mobilization (e.g. the social movement organizations, collective identity), as well as the meaning-making, often referred to as interpretative framing, that underpins social movements and social movement organizations (Pelak et al. 1999; Taylor et al. 2001). For example, it should be unsurprising that social movements draw on gender framing, such as images of femininity and masculinity, to mobilize, legitimize and inspire collective action. Emotionality (often ascribed to the feminine) is often understudied and undervalued in social movement theory. Without positing women as any more emotional than men, studies of women's movements have challenged the idea that emotions interfere with reason. The association of emotion to femininity (and, in turn, rationality to masculinity) and view of emotion as subversive to knowledge has often served as a discursive source for the delegitimization of women as political actors and, consequently, of women's movements such that some female activists often intentionally frame their political messages in less emotional, more rational terms (Einwohner et al. 2000; Taylor 1999; Taylor and Whittier 1996).

A significant contribution put forward by scholars studying the impact of gender on opportunity structures has been in highlighting women's tendency to mobilize in grassroots settings either as a function of being more linked to the domestic sphere than men or by being more often marginalized from formal political settings dominated by men (Yulia 2010). The open or closed nature of political systems around the world, the presence or absence of allies for protest groups, or even the state's capacity or inclination for repression impact women's ability to challenge inequity (Antrobus 2004). The act of social or political protest by women in Canada or the United Kingdom, for example, carries different risks and consequences when compared with such protest by women in some regions of the world where state oppression of dissenting opinions and voices, broadly, and of women's rights, specifically, is more overt, omnipresent and dangerous. Some social movement theorists, however, point out the irony that in some cases, 'the political opportunity for mobilizing women may be distinctively advantageous, as in Chile . . . where women's domestic networks offered them greater protection and moral leverage in challenging dictatorships in power than did men's' (Ferree and Mueller 2007, p. 579; see also Yulia 2010). Basu (1995, p. 2) adds that '. . . a much more important influence on women's movements than the level of [socio-economic] development is the extent of state control'. Women's movements tend to be weak where state control permeates civil society and strong where state control has been relaxed. Bringing gender squarely into the analysis of social protest leads us to ask whether the forms of organization that characterize women's protest groups may, in fact, be more diffuse and local? With regard to sport, some contend that the exclusion of women from meaningful leadership positions in high-performance sport leaves women no choice but to mobilize and participate at the grassroots/community level (Hargreaves 2001; Hayhurst 2011). In terms of the so-called 'women and sport movement', as will be discussed in Chapter 3, the most organized and politically visible organizations dedicated to advancing women's sport have tended to originate within and among nations where the political opportunity structures are more amenable to women's rights and advocacy work.

Having briefly discussed the main theoretical perspectives, and considered the cultural and gender turn, in social movements studies, we now focus our attention on identifying the main types of social movements historically.

From old to global social movements and alter-globalization

Individually, social movements can be seen to go through a series of phases in their development – formation and problem identification, activism in search of solutions and dealing with the aftermath of new policies and practices that emerge as a result (Blumer 1971). However, irrespective of their singular history, social movements evolved within larger historical contexts and therefore take different forms accordingly.

Table 1.1, 'A Periodization of Social Movements', outlines significant shifts in the evolution of social movements according to the development phases of modernity. The table is partly derived from Raymond Williams' (1977) identification of different hegemonic phases in the development of cultural forms (see also Gruneau 1983) and also Wieviorka's (2005) analysis of social movements. In each phase in history, dominant, residual and emergent cultural practices have been present and active. That is, for each major shift in the social development (in Touraine's language, 'historicity') of capitalism, dominant, residual and emerging forms of social movement have existed. Accordingly, and as summarized in the table, it is possible to identify three major phases in the evolution of social movements.

The first period, from the mid-nineteenth century to the late 1960s, was marked by the emergence and prominence of the workers' or labour movement. Although Tilly points to the existence of several workers movements before

Table 1.1 A periodization of social movements

Historicity	Period	Forms		
		Dominant	Residual	Emergent
Industrial	Nineteenth century to 1960s	Workers	Suffrage (e.g. First wave feminism)	Peace
Post-industrial	1960s–late 1990s	New social movements (NSMs) (e.g. Women's'; Civil rights)	Workers	Human rights
Global	Mid-1990s–to date	Global	NSMs	Environmental

Source: Adapted from Harvey et al. 2009.

then (Tilly and Woods 2009), arguably, the birth of that phase can be traced to the formation of the First International Meeting of the International Working Men's Association in London in 1864, the Second International from 1889 to 1914, and its continued dominance well into the twentieth century. While it can be argued that it is no longer as central to social and political life as it once was, the labour movement (and its influence on sport) is still apparent and influential today (as will be discussed in the next chapter). It is also important to recognize that it was during this same time period that the first phase of struggles for civil rights emerged. For example, we see the emergence of struggles for women's rights in different countries that coalesced in 1888 with the founding of the International Council of Women. Hence the dominant social movement in this period was the labour movement, while the movements for suffrage, civil and political enfranchisement were either residual (because women obtained the right to vote after men in most nations) or emergent, such as the human rights and peace movements.

Drawing directly from Touraine's work, Wieviorka (2005, p. 4) lists five major characteristics that are at the basis of the labour movement as the dominant form of social movements in industrial society: 'it operates within the framework of the nation-state, it challenges domination, the actions associated with it are genuinely social, it rarely rises to the political level of its own accord, and it is impelled by a subject which is also social'. In other words, despite the fact that early in its development the workers' movement put in place international networks of solidarity, their main level of action was at the nation-state level. Where the movement was challenging the relations of domination stemming from the workplace, a strong local, and sometimes regional, working-class culture often animated it. Finally, the worker's subjectivity 'was defined in social terms on the basis of the relationships of production and domination . . . in which they have of been deprived of the control of productive activity, or of any control over what is produced' (Wieviorka 2005, p. 4). The subjectivity of the workers was also social in the sense that workers were conscious of belonging to the working class with its culture and organizations.

The second period of social movement activity was primarily initiated by economic transformations after World War II that eventually led to the prominence of 'new social movements' at the end of the 1960s and beginning of the 1970s as the Western world entered into a new phase of historicity, labelled by Touraine as the post-industrial (or programmed/technocratic) society. NSMs were concerned with a wide range of issues, from civil rights, to feminism, human rights and ecology. Camilleri (1990, p. 35) suggests that NSMs 'articulate [d] new ways of experiencing life, a new attitude to time and space, a new sense of history and identity. Indeed, it may not be far-fetched to suggest that they [were] in the process of redefining the meaning and boundaries of civil society'. These NSMs should be recognized as different from the previous phase of social movements in so far as they did not hold economic concerns as their central focus nor did they advocate, as their main goal, the radical change of society through radical measures or proletarian revolution. In this sense, and drawing on the work of Touraine, Melucci and Habermas, Crossley (2002, p. 151) concluded that the recognition of NSMs was related to 'the shift in the modes of historicity in western societies and the corresponding shift in the central struggles of those societies. It is the mode of historicity and its fault lines which lends NSMs their "newness"'. In other words, NSMs aimed at changing society not only in economic terms, but also in various social, cultural, identity and political ways.

Returning to Touraine and Wieviorka (2005), the characteristics of NSMs were significantly different than in the previous stage although not entirely so. Like the labour movement, NSMs continued to define themselves in the context of the nation-state, although some of their attributes started to show global reach. For example, the ecology movement was concerned with the fate of the whole planet. Contrary to the workers' movement, the social adversary of the NSMs was less easily identifiable (i.e. technocratic structures in general). However, these movements had a high degree of cultural awareness, as they 'had no qualm about challenging the cultural orientation of the societies in which they lived' (Wieviorka 2005, p. 6). Proclaiming that everything is political, their aim was to eliminate various forms of institutionalized forms of power relations such as unequal gender relations. Finally, NSMs were mainly interested in the subjectivity of actors. Contrary to the labour movement, NSM mostly invested their energies in cultural rather than social issues. Also, compared with the labour movement, they were not proposing a whole new model of society. Their claims remained specific to their singular identities. Some critics have argued that NSMs failed to produce a significant impact on the historicity of the time as the 1980s witnessed an increase in individualism (Wieviorka 2005).

Following the fall of the Berlin wall and the end of the Cold War, the 1990s marked what we consider, along with several authors (e.g. Wieviorka 2005; McDonald 2006) to be a third period of global social movements, connected to specific responses and resistance to the hegemonic nature and aspects of contemporary globalization. Adapting Crossley's (2002) logic of argumentation and modifying his account of current 'historicity', we argue that a response to the application of the 'Washington Consensus' and the spread of neo-liberal globalization has led to the emergence of *global social movements* (GSM). These in turn have coalesced into what some call the 'movement of movements' or alter-globalization (de Jong et al. 2005; McDonald 2006; Pleyers 2012). The expression 'Washington consensus' originates from a 1989 document by economist John Williamson listing ten recommendations for developing countries facing debt problems. The World Bank (WB) and the International Monetary Fund (IMF) decided that loans to these countries would be subject to conditions such as budget discipline, fiscal reform, financial liberalization, privatization of public corporations, deregulation of markets and the elimination of barriers to foreign investments (Beaudet et al. 2010).

In our terms, global social movements differ from the NSMs discussed above in three ways: (1) they represent a shift in scale from the state level to multiple levels, including the global; (2) they are characterized by new forms of social interactions, often devoid of hierarchical structure, that regularly embrace alternative forms of affective and embodied organization and practice (Pleyers 2010); and (3) they take up a specific principle of 'totality' (Touraine 1977) aimed at no less than developing more humane forms of globalization and humanity (although as we shall see later that identity is loosely defined). Referring back again to Wieviorka (2005), GSMs present a shift in scale from previous movement stages as their struggles no longer are limited to the framework of the nation-state. They confront international spheres of negotiations, worldwide economic regulation and justice, as well as the governance of transnational institutions. This shift in scale results from a recognition that under neo-liberal globalization the nation state has lost some of its sovereignty over transnational institutions, like the World Trade Organization (WTO) and the IMF, for example. While many of the protest are fought at the local level, they are nevertheless global also in the consciousness of actors thinking globally and acting locally. Finally, while GSMs do exist by themselves, they coalesce in alter-globalization.

According to Johnston and Laxer (2003), the seeds of alter-globalization are to be found in the resistance that emerged against the North American Free Trade Agreement (e.g. by groups like the Zapatistas in Chiapas, Mexico), the successful campaigns against the Multilateral Agreement on Investment (MAI), and the infamous Seattle demonstrations against the WTO in 1999. However, it is important to remember that the crowds that converged on Seattle were composed of various individuals and organizations – from religious groups to anarchists – with different, sometimes opposing, views of society. Notably, the Seattle activists in 1999 included two Brazilians who eventually visited the office of the journal *Le monde diplomatique* in 2000. Out of the discussions with journal staff emerged the idea of organizing a World Social Forum (WSF) as a counter forum to the World Economic Forum (WEF) organized each year in Davos, Switzerland, during which heads of state and of multinational corporations meet to discuss economic and social policy. As a result, in 2001, the first WSF was held in Porto Allegre with the goal not to reject globalization outright, but to discuss and promote the idea that another form of globalization was possible (Mertes 2003).

With 20,000 participants, the first WSF forum was successful in attracting participants and was followed by several follow-up forums, even better attended. WSF are still today organized on a regular basis. The recognition of the WSF eventually led to the organization of numerous regional forums across the globe and, in January 2008, a global call for action. As its point of departure, the WSF (and the regional social organizations that operate more locally and which feed into and out of the WSF network) champions 'the new global social movements of the oppressed that include indigenous peoples, peasants, sexual minorities and women as well as working classes' (Scholte 2005, p. 45). The organization and direction of the WSF has not gone without criticism – ranging from accusations of its vague idealism devoid of real-world application, its incorporation of popular grassroots movements and its ineffective decision-making structure – seen by some as too centralized while, ironically, seen by others as too diffuse (Curran 2007). Still, to date, the WSF remains one of the few established worldwide entities explicitly committed to struggle and resistance against social exclusion as fostered under neo-liberal globalization and stands as an important illustration of the alter-globalization ethos (Grzybowski 2006; de Sousa Santos 2006; see also Pleyers 2010).

Clearly then, the concept of alter-globalization is important for under-standing global social movements. Often now described as the 'movement of movements' (Grzybowski 2006; Mertes 2003), alter-globalization is characterized as a multifaceted form of resistance to neo-liberal globalization active at the local and the global levels in advocating for more humane globalization. Most important is that where proponents of anti-globalization tend to resist any and all forms of globalization, alter-globalization refers to a large spectrum of global social movements that support new and reformed modes of globalization based upon values of democracy, justice, environmental protection and human rights.

The championing of alter-globalization connects with global social movements since a key feature of the concept of alter-globalization is the principle that alternatives to neo-liberal globalization do exist and that 'another world is possible': 'a fairer world, with greater solidarity and greater respect for differences'. (Pleyers 2010, p. 5). Importantly, alter-globalization can have both reformist and transformist tendencies; the 'alternative' ethic of alter-globalization can either support current forms of globalization in a reformed manner or the replacement of current globalization by an alternative one. Hence, a distinctive feature of alter-globalization is its diversity.

Alter-globalization can be understood to be concerned with the question of what to do about current hegemonic neo-liberal globalization. The position taken in response to this question is what separates alter-globalization advocates from other political and social actors. While 'neo-liberals' tend to accept globalization as a means of expanding market exchange and promoting capitalist relations of production, 'rejectionists', who might also be considered to support anti-globalization, tend to look to local, or rather national, responses to it. Only 'reformists' and 'transformists', among whom the global social movements we consider here take their place, can be understood as proposing alter-globalization itself as a response. Drawing from Held and McGrew (2007) and Scholte (2005), we define 'reformist' as the position of actors who assert that globalization can be reshaped to encourage economic efficiency, stability equity and ecological sustainability.

'Transformists' are actors guided by the principle that a more global world is an opportunity for large-scale, wide-reaching social change in order to build a fundamentally different global society. These two responses focus either on harnessing the force of globalization for carrying out institutional reforms within a mixed economy via public policy initiatives or on utilizing globalization as a means of stimulating social change, fighting for human security and protection of the environment, as well as for a wide range of human rights. Indeed, while this book focuses more specifically on the development of global movements rather than on alter-globalization itself, developing a better understanding of reformist and transformist types of alter-globalization responses as they connect to sport is also one of our main interests in this book.

For Pleyers (2010), alter-globalization is a movement concerned with the struggle for alternate and progressive forms of globalization. Alter-globalization is recognizable in the ways that it believes in, and proposes, legitimate alternatives to current forms of economic and corporate-led globalization. According to Pleyers (2010), in this way, alter-globalization is underpinned by diverse stakeholders and participants who propose, celebrate and attempt to strengthen a 'global consciousness'. Here lies the unity of GSM and alter-globalization as there is neither a central organizational structure nor any form of hierarchy among the components of the movement as their relationships are network-like and fluid, constantly evolving as events are organized. It is not uncommon that protest events regroup under various coalitions of actors from different horizons, such as was the case with resistance against the Vancouver Winter Olympics (Boykoff 2011).

Pleyers (2010) situates the alter-globalization movement as the (often difficult) convergence between two forms of contemporary political action – subjectivity and reason – creating different organizations and objectives for social change and the potential for structural tensions to underpin alter-globalization. In the subjectivity and creativity approach, the aim of alter-globalization activists is to experiment with different forms of social and political existence and 'feel' these alternatives in daily life. Such objectives do not stand in linear relation to activism – neither do they preclude action – but are co-constitutive with it. From this perspective, alter-globalization activity aims to 'unlearn' the experiences and citizenship of neo-liberal globalization and to assert new autonomies of subjectivity.

In the second form of alter-globalization, based on reason and expertise, activists seek to propose alternative forms of social and political organizing that are more egalitarian, environmentally responsible and ethical towards fellow (global) citizens. As opposed to experience and feeling, the terms of debate in this form of activism are, for example, the ever-widening income gap between rich and poor or the numbers of people across the world forced to live without regular food, water, shelter or health care. Exposing the limited success of neo-liberalism in bringing prosperity to the world, and proposing alternative approaches to and policies for economics and politics becomes the focus of this form of alter-globalization.

Alter-globalization movements are thus recognizable by the ways in which they seek to exploit the possibilities of globalization while recognizing the challenges this entails. According to Scholte (2005), the possibilities include technological and organizational developments; greater public awareness of global problems; larger transnational solidarities among people; and an increased receptiveness among political and economic elites to refer to policies on globalization. Moreover, we argue that alter-globalization movements rely on a consciousness that each and every human being is part of a single world, a world that has been fragmented by a neo-liberalism that exacerbates individualism and, as a result, is in need of a re-articulation of the social, the political and the economic through new, more legitimate and democratic forms of global governance. The challenges that remain are not inconsiderable: the continuing force of neo-liberal economic ideology at key levels of government; the power of large capital; attachment to the idea of state sovereignty; and the underdeveloped institutional capacities of alternatives. Another major problem remains the lack of a strong and distinctive alternative economic strategy to free trade and foreign direct investment.

Still, alternatives are regularly put forth by social movement actors and by scholars. Literature on globalization and alter-globalization covers developments around such issues as democracy from below (Dallmayr 1999), global civil society (Germain and Kenny 2005; Holton 2005), cosmopolitanism (Beck and Sznaider 2006), global governance (Held 2007) and global citizenship (Cabrera 2011). Of note is Appadurai's (2006) discussion of 'grassroots globalization'. In the midst of the development of an 'international civil society', which exists in the shape of networks of activists, civil society institutions, transnational organizations and popular social movements converge to form transnational NGOs. Appadurai refers to Keck and Sikkink (1998) and their idea of transnational activist networks involved in (1) new forms of international bargaining; (2) global social movements; and (3) the creation of a 'third space', outside the market and the state. Appadurai suggests that there are thus two types of transnational activity: (1) visible street protests and (2) less publicized advocacy and coordination in pursuit of policy change at local, national and global levels. This second form of transnational activism attempts both to slow down neo-liberal processes – force greater transparency, put pressure on states and circulate information more rapidly in order to mobilize protest, for example – and to form partnerships – 'the David and Goliath leverage through which such networks have become effective' (Appadurai 2006, p. 133). This activity can foster the creation of 'deep democracy' (Appadurai 2006, p. 134) by moving away from agitation-based politics and towards an emphasis on the capacity building of poor and disadvantaged people through the setting of goals, the development of expertise, the sharing of knowledge and the generation of commitment. This new transnational activism builds solidarity not from the declaration of broad universal principles alone (as in socialism) but 'from smaller convergences of interest . . . in a more ad hoc, inductive, and context-sensitive manner' (Appadurai 2006, p. 136). In this way, 'global networking is put at the service of local imaginings of power' (Appadurai 2006, p. 136) creating 'utopian cellularities' of 'new transnational organizational forms' (Appadurai 2006, p. 137).

For our purposes, this theorizing suggests that we could place examples of alter-globalization movements into at least two camps – 'visible' and 'less visible'. In relation to sport, some sport initiatives may reside more in the less visible, inductive and ad hoc, while others may be linked with more visible transnational organization (e.g. UNESCO). To make better sense of this, though, requires a scholarly commitment to understanding the complex, and sometimes contradictory, relationships between sport and social movements. In the next section, therefore, we turn our attention to the need to understand the place of sport in relation to global social movements and struggles for alter-globalization.

The importance of studying sport and social movements within alter-globalization

As noted in the Introduction, since the late 1990s, the intersections of sport, identities and cultures, at both the local and global level, as well as local reactions to hegemonic global forces in sport, have been well documented. In recognizing the importance and salience of these phenomena and, indeed, arguing for more comprehensive conceptualizations of global-local resistance, Harvey and Houle (1994) argued that research on sport and globalization should pay close attention to NSMs and their potential impact on sport. Harvey and Houle (1994, p. 344) highlighted how these movements go beyond traditional categories of nation, state and class:

> The emergence of such new political identities, transcending the self and national space, is not only the product of globalization but also a contribution to the global reconfiguration of space.... This means ... that we must adapt our conceptions of the relationships between the nation-state and civil society, and between political authority and political community.

To our knowledge, besides Jarvie's (2003) passing reference to the existence of an anti-globalization movement, only three contributions (from Wilson) have so far answered this call for studying sport and global social movements. Wilson (2002) provided a foundational study of the 'anti-jock' movement and its organization and dissemination through the internet. Of particular relevance was his positioning of online communication as a forum for community building, information sharing and a portal for interventionist/activist practices by sport scholars. Wilson (2007, p. 472) called for more nuanced and theoretically informed analyses of the internet as a communication tool and conduit for 'the potentially changing nature of local responses to global forces' within the sociocultural study of sport. Most recently Wilson (2012, Chapter 5 especially) has explored the role of social movements and activists more generally and it is worth briefly considering his contribution.

Wilson suggests that there is a range of activist responses to social injustice within sport, as well as activism conducted by sports people themselves. These forms of political activism are heterogeneous, ranging from formal organizations (like feminist advocates for women in sport) to more loosely formed cultural groups that nonetheless seek change in and through sport. He draws attention to three ways in which social movements in sport might be identified in sociological terms. The first is through subcultures, groups that identify and organize around a particular cultural (or sporting) practice and use this group formation as a platform for collective action. The second is 'alter-globalization' or the movement of movements. The third, according to Wilson, is the notion of life or lifestyle politics, as understood through the work of Giddens (1991). In opposition to the transformist and reformist ethos of alter-globalization, lifestyle politics are more concerned with lifestyle and consumer choices that construct and reflect a political perspective. The choice to purchase sporting apparel that is not made using sweatshop labour would fit into this category of sport-related political activism.

In his analysis of the topic of social movements and sport, Wilson gives significant attention to the question of evaluation and success. How might analysts and researchers conclude that a social movement (in sport) has been successful in effecting social change? Drawing on Davis-Delano and Crosset (2008), he suggests that the mobilization of resources, the leveraging of existing political opportunities and the establishment of frames of collective action are important criteria by which to assess social movements and political action in sport. Importantly, though, Wilson suggests that much more research is possible, and needed, in this area in order that scholars have a detailed and nuanced understanding of the efforts, successes and even failures of sport-related social movements. In his words (Wilson 2012, p. 98):

> With the exception of Davis-Delano and Crosset (2008), little attention has been paid to . . . sport-related activism, or to the theories that help explain the success of social movements in particular contexts. In light of the attention that is consistently paid to protests around hosting the Olympics in particular . . . it would seem that this area deserves more attention.

In sum, Wilson argues for the importance of recognizing that all social movements (sport-related or otherwise) are not successful, nor do they all approach the issue of social change in a uniform manner. Indeed, it is possible to identify forms of 'ironic activism' in sport (Wilson and Hayhurst 2009) in which sport-focused social movements, through the negotiation of hegemonic power formations, may actually serve to re-inscribe neo-liberalism and the very social injustices they seek to challenge.

We agree with Wilson that is necessary to investigate (global) social movements in more detail in order to better understand the contemporary global sport order. At the start of the twenty-first century, this order continues to be one based on fully commodified sport, that is a form where sport is prominently an exchange value, monopolized by multinational corporations of the manufacturing and professional sectors of the sport industrial cluster and governed by supra-national authorities, like the IOC and the largest international federations' globocracy (Nelson 2002). To some extent, this global sport world order constitutes the sport branch of the current supranational 'Empire' described by Hardt and Negri (2002). And yet, as we have noted, since the 1990s, contestation and resistance to globalization has expanded to form a vast, loosely connected, international network of resistant groups that have coalesced around the notion of alter-globalization. We aim to demonstrate the way that these developments relate to sport, athletes and sports organizations.

In this chapter, we have discussed the concept of social movements and proposed a periodization of their evolution, from the labour movement, to NSMs and global movements. We have also discussed alter-globalization and the two types of responses to globalization that it carries. Hence, we have outlined the theoretical framework that underpins the following empirical chapters, which present a selection of case studies of social movements in relation to sport. While subsequent chapters focus on the history of these movements as they interact with sport, making a particular emphasis on their last phase as global social movements, less attention is paid to their relationship with alter-globalization. Nonetheless, this chapter has attempted to situate global social movements within the development of alter-globalization since this is the historical trajectory that global social movements have been taking. It is possible that alter-globalization will grow in importance as various forms of contentious politics take shape in sport in the future.

2

From Workers' Sport to Alter-Sport and Global Workers' Rights

As we saw in Table 1.1 in the previous chapter, the labour movement – the focus of this chapter – can be considered as one of the oldest social movements and the dominant one for a large part of the twentieth century. As we shall demonstrate in this chapter, its influence on sport today is still strong in certain countries but also complex and shifting. The labour movement is now global and since its emergence, has advocated for the improvement of the lives and employment conditions of working people, as well as for the transformation or even overthrowing of capitalism worldwide. Applying Touraine's (1977) three key characteristics of social movements, its identity is that of the movement of workers under capitalism, its adversary is capitalism as a system of worker exploitation, and as for its social project or totality, the movement has seen divisions along political and strategic lines, ranging from the goal of reformist state socialism to revolutionary communism. As we shall see, consistent with Tilly's claims about the evolution of social movements, it has also gone through major changes in its overall orientation and forms of activism over time.

The sphere of labour movement activity has historically been wide, covering almost all areas of workers lives including their leisure and sports: consequently, the labour movement is the first social movement to be discussed in this book. Moreover, it is the best example by which to illustrate the historical transition of social movements developed in the previous chapter. The history of the labour movement also demonstrates how social movements have been transformed as the history of capitalist societies evolved through different stages of 'historicity' (Touraine 1981). Finally, as Riordan (1996) argued worker sport as an emanation of the larger labour movement is by no means insignificant for sports history and the history of the overall labour movement. In the 1930s it united more than four million workers worldwide: '. . . making it by far the largest working-class cultural movement', (Riordan 1996, p. vii). Worker sport comprised sport and gymnastic clubs which were linked to the labour movement, designed in order to provide workers and their families opportunities for sport participation with their fellow workers outside of (and against) 'bourgeois' amateur sport. Worker sport was also a site for the reproduction and promotion of the ideals of socialism and communism among workers participating in these initiatives. Worker sport was therefore both a sport initiative and a political instrument for the promotion of a post-capitalist society.

Why and how did the labour movement get involved in sport? How, accordingly, over time, have the forms of activism of the labour movement in sport evolved? What are its current forms of activism and what influence does this movement have on sport? How does it intersect with other global social movements and on what types of issue? These are the questions that will be addressed in this chapter. In the first section, we outline in broad strokes the origins and developments of the labour movement and sport up until the beginnings of the Cold War in the 1950s; this corresponds roughly to the first phase of our periodization of social movements in Table 1.1. Analysing the evolution of the labour movement worldwide and of worker sport within it during such a long period is well beyond what is possible to cover in this chapter (for a broad view of the history of the labour movement see Fantasia and Stepan-Norris 2004 and for an overview of the history of worker sport in several countries see Krüger and Riordan 1996). Our discussion here is centred on the study of one specific case, the Fédération sportive et gymnique du travail, (FSGT) based in France. Indeed, its almost 100-year history provides a useful lens through which to study worker sport not only in France, but also at the international level, because of its extensive relationships with sister organizations in other countries such as the Unione Italiana Sport per Tutti (UISP; the Italian Sport for All Union) and its involvement within international workers organizations. In the second and third sections of the chapter, we focus our attention on the contemporary period in order to sketch a picture of the impact of the labour movement in sport, with special attention paid to its influence on alter-globalization and sport. The second section continues with our analysis of the FSGT in order to illustrate what became of what was once called 'worker sport' and is now labelled 'sport populaire' or 'sport travailliste'. In the third section we introduce another facet of the relationship between the labour movement and sport: the new forms of global activism for the rights of workers worldwide, and particularly those working in manufacturing industries supplying sports equipment, clothing and footwear. To illustrate this aspect, we discuss the example of the Play Fair campaign organized around sports mega-events, such as the Olympic Games and the FIFA Men's Football World Cup Finals.

Uniting workers through sport or providing sport for workers

Arguably, the origins of the international labour movement can be traced to the formation of the First International in 1864, an international organization aimed at regrouping socialist, communist and other leftist groups, and of the Second International from 1889 to 1916, which resumed the tasks of the first one and whose strong influence continued well into the whole twentieth century. During the same period, the first phase of struggles for civil rights emerged with, for example, the beginnings of women's rights in different countries that coalesced in 1888 with the founding of the International Council of Women. The international labour movement's 'emergence' phase lasted up until the early twentieth century. This was due to the fact that, from one country to another, the evolution of industrialization and of democratic reforms that shaped the historical conditions for the formation of working class consciousness and consequently the rise of labour movements in specific nation states occurred at different times and thus took different forms in different places. As is well known, the history of the labour movement and of the political parties they created in support of their cause is replete with divisions, factions and groups of many political stripes, which can be divided into two broad camps. On the one hand, Socialists, also called reformists, considered that in democratic states socialism could be achieved by gaining power through winning elections. On the other hand, for communists or revolutionaries, socialism could only be achieved by overthrowing capitalism through revolution lead by the working class. In this chapter, the term reformism specifically refers to socialist movements and parties, and therefore bears a slightly different meaning from that in chapter 1.

In several countries, the evolution of worker sport followed similar lines. For example, the *gymnastics* society in *Germany*, better known as the *German Turner* movement or *turnverein*, became crucial to the development of the *German* nation-state. In 1859, the *Deutsche Turnerschaft* was created, regrouping close to 2,000 clubs including social democratic organizations (Krüger 1996). In the early 1890s, members of different social democratic organizations discussed the creation of workers' Turner associations. From 1895 until 1911, the young *Arbeiter Turner-Bund* membership grew significantly (Kruger 1996). According to Kruger (1996), the political life of the nascent German worker sport organizations – such as *Solidarity*, a Leipzig-based national worker association created in 1893 – were subject to anti-association legislation that prevented them from flourishing. Nevertheless, German worker sport grew rapidly until banned under the Nazi regime in the 1930s. German worker sport did not reappear after World War II.

In England, by contrast, socialist workers' organizations were already numerous by the end of the World War I and worker sport was then adopted by organized labour (Jones 1996). For example, the Clarion Cycling Club, created in 1894, had a clear socialist character. One of its aims was '... to propagate Socialism and Good fellowship' (Jones 1996, p. 99). At the initiative of the Clarion club and members of the Labour Party, the British Workers' Federation for Sport was created in 1923 in order to 'further the cause of peace between nations'. (Jones 1996, p. 101). The workers' sport movement in England was indeed strongly influenced by the presence of the socialist reformist inclined Labour Party which became prominent at the beginning of the twentieth century.

In Canada, by contrast, immigrant groups such as Finns and Ukrainians as well as Jewish people were the front-runners of worker sport as they reproduced institutions from their country of origins. These served as a means to socialize among fellow immigrants as much as to practice sport and gymnastics (Kidd 1996). In Italy, on the other hand, worker sport did not emerge until after World War II, as a result of the condemnation of sport as a bourgeois institution by the Italian left (Pivato 1994). In France, the roots of worker sport reached back to the birth of the first national worker sport organization in the country, the Fédération sportive athlétique du travail (FSAT), a section of the socialist party (SFIO). One of its founding members published a short manifesto in the leftist newspaper *l'Humanité* revealing the vision behind its creation:

> . . . [the organisation] will recruit its members among those of the Party, as well as their children. There are numerous advantages to this creation. Here are some: to develop the muscular force and to purify the lungs of the young proletariat; to give youth healthy and joyful entertainment which will be a palliative to alcoholism and bad acquaintances; to bring young comrades to the party; to advertise for the party (quoted by Borrel 1999, p. 29; our translation).

In short, the goal of the initiative was to provide healthy pursuit opportunities to members of the Party, but also to attract new members. Soon after other socialist-inclined sport initiatives saw the light of day and united into a new organization, the Fédération sportive du travail (FST) inaugurated in 1914. The FST affiliated with the socialist-inclined (reformist) Lucerne Sport International (LSI), established a year earlier, and which was the first international organization for worker sport to be created. For a detailed account of the birth of the two main international worker sport organizations, see Gounot (1994).

The Bolshevik revolution in Russia in 1917 and the creation of the Third international (Communist) in 1919 created a major schism over the leadership of the labour movement and resulted in an open war between socialists and communists. As far as worker sport was concerned, the schism materialized with the creation in 1921 of the Moscow-based Red Sport International (RSI) whose mandate was to attract workers to the communist party through sport and to use sport as an instrument to transform workers into soldiers for class struggle and communism (in contrast with the LSI whose mandate was first to provide sport for workers and after that try to get them involved in the socialist movement). With the RSI, Moscow wanted to create '. . . a worldwide worker sport and gymnastic organization in charge, to spread the experiments of the Russian proletariat to all countries, and to form, with the help of these experiments, a sufficient reserve of revolutionary combatants for the decisive struggles'. (International Communist congress, 1920, quoted by Gounot 1994, p. 236). In France, in 1923, under the leadership of Jacques Doriot, a former socialist militant converted to communism as well as former secretary of RSI, communists took over the FST, which then switched affiliation from the LSI to the RSI (Gounot 1999). As a result of the takeover, socialists created a new organization, the Union des Sociétés Sportives et Gymniques du Travail (USSGT) in 1926. Ironically, after years of confrontations and divisions, the two competing organizations merged in 1934 to create the FSGT, as around the industrialized world leftist parties regrouped in order to fight fascism in Europe. From 1936 the FSGT benefited from the newly elected Front Populaire government in France, most especially from Léo Lagrange the Minister of Sport, who channelled significant state funding into the organization. As a result, the FSGT thrived and its membership grew significantly up until the occupation of the country by Nazi Germany.

The period between the two world wars can thus be seen as the golden age of worker sport (Riordan 1996). As shown above, during that period, worker sport was divided along the same lines as the larger labour movement. On the one hand, socialist organizations were mostly interested in social reforms in order to create more democratic and equal societies. Their peaceful internationalism was most importantly inclined towards a solidarity among workers for economic and democratic reforms and solidarity with colonized peoples. On the other hand, under the strong hold of Bolshevism and later Stalinism, communist parties and their affiliated organizations were striving for the universalization of the communist revolution. Their pacifism and internationalism was motivated by a solidarity with workers worldwide against capitalist imperialism and in favour of a communist world order under the guidance of the USSR.

The internationalism of each of these two leftist opponents manifested itself through their global initiatives. One of the prominent events organized by the LSI was the Workers Olympics, an anti-bourgeois sport initiative (i.e. against the games of the 'bourgeois' IOC). Games were held in Frankfurt in 1925, which attracted some 1,000 athletes and 40,000 spectators, and in Vienna, in 1931, which attracted even more athletes and spectators (Gounot 1994). Opening ceremonies included a parade of 100,000 worker athletes in the streets, some of them holding banners 'for world disarmament and universal peace', while others raised their fist making an anti-fascist salute. These games were strongly condemned by the RSI, because of the exclusion of all non-socialist organizations. The Communists replied with the creation of their own Workers Olympics, the Moscow 'Spartakiads' which were staged only once in 1928. Since then, several forms of sports have gathered under the name of 'Spartakiads' with many still organized, but none have had the same goal of forming a counter-Olympics (Edelman 2006). A 'Peoples' Olympics' was also planned for Barcelona in 1936 but was cancelled because of the Spanish civil war. Although they both fought each other up until 1936, the LSI and RSI joined forces in their strong opposition to the IOC's bourgeois Olympics and were particularly active in the campaign to boycott the Olympic Games in Berlin (often referred to as the Nazi Olympics). As a result of their alliance, organizations affiliated with both the LSI and RSI participated in a third and final Workers Olympics held in Antwerp in 1937.

During World War II, worker sport largely ground to a halt as attentions turned to the global fight against fascism. The victory of the allies led to the dawn of a new world order. After the war, economic and democratic transformations eventually led to the emergence and prominence of NSMs. Post-war reconstruction in Western industrialized countries led to new forms of government intervention in the economy and society, often heralded as the 'welfare state'. The development of welfare states resulted in the democratization of mass education and increased opportunities for workers in numerous areas of social life, including state-funded universal health services and leisure and sport facilities, especially at the local level. Workers' conditions of living improved as they reaped some of the benefits of the nascent consumer society.

The end of World War II also marked a major shift in international politics that impacted severely upon workers sport. Indeed, the two main allies that defeated Nazi Germany became enemies virtually as soon as the war ended. The Cold War between Western capitalist countries and the Eastern Bloc associated with the USSR lasted from the early 1950s until the fall of the Berlin Wall in 1989 and the demise of the USSR in 1991. During the Cold War, mass organizations of the communist parties in most Western industrialized countries became treated with suspicion by democratic capitalist governments. From one country to another, depending on the composition of the political spectrum and class divisions, labour-associated organizations had a different fate. For example, in the United States in the 1950s, under McCarthyism, all left leaning organizations were automatically assumed to be agencies of communist propaganda for the USSR and came under attack from government, federal agencies and the police. However, in several European countries where the labour movement had been historically stronger, workers' sport organizations were able to survive and grow as mass organizations of communist or socialist inclined political parties.

Such was the case with the FSGT, which had suffered during the Nazi occupation of France. After liberation, several of its leaders who had been complacent during the occupation were removed and communists took back control of the organization. The FSGT became a mass organization again attached to the Parti Communiste Français (PCF; French Communist Party) and would remain so until the mid-1970s (Sabatier 2011), despite renewed claims of the 'neutrality' of the organization by the leaders of FSGT, themselves members of the PCF (Borrel 1999). During the Cold War, as a result of its links to the PCF, FSGT's state financial support was cut for several decades and the organization went into a long period of stagnation as the communists' social capital, gained by their participation in the resistance against German occupation, slowly declined (Borrel 1999). Another major factor that influenced worker sport after World War II was the complete change of strategy by the USSR, in the context of the Cold War, as it decided to join the 'bourgeois' Olympics in 1955. On the one side, the USSR and other countries of the Eastern Bloc embraced the Olympics in order to show the world the supremacy of their revolutionary regimes through the performances of their state-funded athletes. On the other side, through its affiliated communist parties and worker sport organizations in Western countries, Moscow continued to use sport as a tool through which to attempt to export the communist revolution to the Western world. The influence of the Communist parties progressively declined however.

In sum, there were three major factors that influenced worker sport, both at national and international levels. First, the history of worker sport was strongly influenced by the divisions within the labour movement between socialists and communists. These divisions resulted in the creation of several organizations competing to attract workers within their ranks, a situation that arguably prevented worker sport from growing. In addition to these internal divisions within the labour movement, worker sport was not the only type of organizations competing to attract workers. In France and Québec in Canada for example, as well as in other countries where Roman Catholicism was strong, church-run sport organizations were put in place in order to keep youth under control (Harvey 1988). In the Protestant religious world, organizations like the YMCA and YWCA played a similar role. At the beginning of the twentieth century, nascent professional sport started to attract working-class youth. Moreover, from the 1920s onwards, several business leaders put in place sport and leisure opportunities for their workers and their families in order to ease their relationships with their employees and prevent them from getting involved in organized labour (Melchers 1988). Finally, as the Olympic Games became more and more prominent, amateur sport federations progressively opened their doors to working-class athletes – as a way to gain more Olympic medals, a way to compete against worker sport successes and a way to fight against the development of professional sport. Given this context of intense competition to attract workers, the huge successes of workers' sport in attracting workers between the two world wars are notable. However, despite the impressive number of participants, mostly in European countries, workers' sport was never a successful tool through which to recruit militants for their larger political projects, since most of the workers who became involved did so mostly for the sport participation opportunities provided, rather than for anything else. (Borrel 1999; Kidd 1996). Nevertheless, worker sport formed a thriving vehicle for the extension of workers' rights to participate in sport as well as a means to foster the larger rights of the working class and, therefore arguably, has constituted a significant part of labour movement history.

From sport for all to alter-global sport

Despite the fact that the golden age of worker sport was the interwar period, the movement survived in many countries outside of North America and, from the 1970s onwards, it strove to maintain a significant membership worldwide. A measure of this trend is the revival of the former LSI in 1946 under a new name, the Comité sportif international du travail (CSIT) – an organization that still exists today with 43 union members in 32 countries, boasting some 230 million individual members worldwide (CSIT 2012). We return later in the chapter to consider the most recent actions of the CSIT. Hence, worker sport is still alive today, although in new clothes. Worker sport has become an '. . . international multi-sport organization based on the ideas of the international labour movement: equality and solidarity in sport' (CSIT 2002). Moreover, CSIT defines itself as an organization that aims at broadening workers' sport worldwide and thus developing into a world-wide movement. (CSIT 2012). While heralding its inheritance from workers sport, since the 1970s CSIT and its union members often use different words to describe their social project with labels like 'sport populaire' (sport for the people) and 'sport for all'. The 'sport for all' objectives of CSIT and its fellow members are mainly to provide positive and healthy sport experiences for people who normally do not have access to sport, encouraging openness and human understanding despite their skill levels and giving importance to the pleasurable aspects of sport and its health-related benefits. (CSIT 2012) In order words, the CSIT sought to find new ways of doing sport in less competitive and more recreative ways. These objectives are carried out through promoting '. . . sport activities for the sake of social, cultural and healthy aims with no or little regards for results' (CSIT 2012).

One way to see more concretely how this general social project is carried out locally by CSIT member organizations is to return to our earlier example, the FSGT, which is today an active member of CSIT. FSGT still defines itself as a multisport 'fédération affinitaire' (a federation of clubs sharing common social values, our translation) with a 260,000-person strong membership and a presence in 75 of the 96 French administrative departments. On its website, FSGT promotes its new motto: 'from a sport gathering to a human gathering'. FSGT defines 'sport populaire' as:

> **Quality sport:** through a critique of elite sport and the adaptation of rules to foster collaboration in competition
> **Affordable:** through extensive involvement of volunteers
> **Democratic and secular:** through non-hierarchical civic governance
> **Conviviality:** by the cultivation of human relationships and an ethic of sharing and caring in the activity. (FSGT 2012; our translation).

The philosophy of the FSGT according to its statement of goals and beliefs is:

Involvement in solidarity against social inequalities
Rejection of hierarchy in the organisation of the sport governing body itself
Refusal to limit oneself to the technical aspects of sport
Against the domination of the weak by the strong
Rejection of commodified sport
Building of a more humane world and heightened citizenship
Solidarity in the perspective of universality. (FSGT 2012; our translation)

FSGT's vision is to develop an alternative to current hegemonic competitive and commodified sport. In a recent special issue of its periodical *Sport et plein air* entitled 'Another competition is possible', FSGT further explained its social project. Competition is now synonymous with elimination sport. Another form of competition would be one without losers, a competition becoming a '. . . form of co-operation within a team and with its opponents that would connect back to its Latin etymology *cum petere*, "researching together"' (FSGT 2011, p. 16). In the same issue, FSGT identified seven key conditions for 'alter-competitions': extensive play time for each; equality of chances to win; democratic play (i.e. no elimination); socialization through convivial sport; players taking on responsibilities with regard to the organization and unfolding of the game; opening up the rules to participants to adapt; and minimal cost – human and financial (FSGT 2011, p. 16). Finally, FSGT argues that '. . . as long as the central issue remains play for the sake of play, competition can be educational and formative for all' (FSGT 2011, p. 17). This vision of alter sport offers an explicit criticism of commodified sport where cheating, violence, exclusion and doping are considered to be widespread. It takes several forms that we discuss below.

One concrete example of such an alter-sport form is 'alter-foot' or 'foot at 7'. This alternative form of football is played on a half-size soccer pitch with the following rules: there are a maximum of five replacement players per team; sides are permitted the unlimited changeover of players; there are no off-sides; no tackling is allowed; and the match is self-refereed (i.e. the players themselves referee the game). The sport is now spreading quickly and, in 2012, there were 350 teams alone in Paris (Seckel 2012). At the core of FSGT, life is a constant reflection on how to develop a more inclusive and healthy sport within its affiliated clubs: this is thus one of the forms of activism of the contemporary FSGT.

A second form of FSGT activism is its constant efforts at lobbying the state, for recognition of its activities as a public service that deserves state funding, as well as for sport reform. The strategy here is to try to reform sport from inside. In line with this form of action was the campaign of the FSGT to earn election onto the CNOSF (the French National Olympic Committee), which it succeeded in doing in 2009.

A third form of FSGT activism is its open international peace solidarity campaign for oppressed people around the world. The internationalism of the FSGT has manifested itself through involvement in Palestine since 2000. Here among other sport development projects, they have exported 'foot at 7'. International exchanges of players are organized from year to year, sport leaders are trained, and specific initiatives to provide girls with sport participation opportunities are conducted in refugee camps.

A fourth form of FSGT activism is its involvement in the global diffusion of 'sport populaire' through its membership and participation in CSIT along with its Italian sister organization UISP and others. UISP also has deep roots in the labour movement. Like the FSGT, at the end of the 1970s, UISP went through a process of detaching itself from the political parties it was affiliated with. It was recognized in 1974 by the Italian Olympic committee (CONI) as a sports promotion organization. In the 1990s, UISP also reoriented itself as a 'sport for all' association. At its 50th anniversary in 2008, UISP claimed over one million active members and 14,000 affiliated clubs (UISP 2008). UISP actively works for 'alter sport' and, in 2004, it organized a conference under what it now claims is the core of its mission: 'Un altro sport è possibile' or 'another sport is possible'. The UISP co-organized two workshops within the 2006 World Social Forum held in Nairobi, Kenya, as well as a 'marathon race among the slums for human rights'. One of the two workshops was entitled 'Sport of Peace: Playing against War' where the role of sport as a mediator of conflicts or as a way to re-create dialogue between different cultures was discussed. The other workshop was entitled 'Champions of Freedom or Slaves of the Millennium' and touched on the dual role that sport can play for youth. UISP (2008b, para. 1) argues that sport can make people free but can also bring about new forms of slavery: '. . . managers without scruples explore the poorest areas of the world for finding possible talents to bring to Europe. A real draft of human persons' (see, for example, Darby 2012). UISP is also active in different networks of organizations and specifically with Libera, an anti-mafia organization, the World Wildlife Organization and Amnesty International. Most recently, in May of 2011, UISP – in collaboration with a variety of national and international organizations – presented the European Charter of Women's Rights in Sport to the European Parliament as part of its involvement in the Olympia Project, an initiative designed to encourage women's participation in sport and to provide 'equal opportunities via and within sport' (retrieved from http://www.olympiaproject.net/?p=187#more-187 [last accessed 13 January 2013]).

Both FSGT and UISP have become deeply involved in an alternative form of sports event under the umbrella of CSIT, the 'World Sport Games'. Indeed, the first World Sport Games were in Rimini (Italy) under the leadership of IUSP. They were followed by a second Games in Tallinn, Estonia, in 2010, and a third Games in Varna, Bulgaria, scheduled for June 2013. The Rimini Games were attended by 2800 participants from 20 different countries. Included in the programme were such disciplines as gymnastics, football, tennis, athletics, as well as 'sport for all' activities. These games distinguished themselves from the Olympics and single sport world championships by their inclusiveness and their lack of commercialism. Indeed, following the 'sport for all' objectives of the CIST and its affiliates, the Rimini games were heralded as the 'non-commercial games of the people' ('sportif populaires et amateurs').

A fifth and final form of activism of the FSGT is participation in the larger labour movement campaigns for the rights of workers worldwide and in particular in the sport manufacturing industry, such as the Play Fair campaign, which will be discussed in the next section. Indeed, the June 2008 issue of *Sport et plein air* featured articles both about the exploitation of workers in Chinese manufacturing and about the larger issue of human rights in China by Amnesty International. Moreover, in the streets of Paris during the pre-2008 Olympic Games torch relay, the FSGT participated in the demonstrations against workers exploitation in the sport manufacturing industries (Renou 2012).

In this section, through a historical overview of the examples of the CSIT, the FSGT and the IUSP, we have sketched a picture of one aspect of the contemporary action of the labour movement as it connects to sport. We noted how worker sport before World War II gradually transformed from an instrument of communist and socialist parties into a reformist practice. In the next section, we examine more contemporary struggles for workers' rights within the sports industry.

Sports mega-events as a platform for promoting workers' and human rights

Arguably the most visible aspect of the presence of the labour movement in contemporary global sport today is the campaigns against the exploitation of workers in the sports manufacturing industry. What began in the 1990s as global union and NGO campaigns against worker exploitation aimed specifically at a small number of major sports brands, such as Nike (Sage 1999), has progressively grown larger to target sports mega-events such as the Olympic Games and the FIFA Men's Football World Cup Finals, as well as governments in order to halt the exploitation of workers worldwide.

As we argue in the following pages, several campaigns for the rights of workers have emerged in the last 20 years using the visibility of the Olympics and other sports mega-events. Some of these campaigns are interconnected and reinforce each other, as they bring together networks of organizations that have workers' rights as their overall goal. They also interconnect with other rights groups concerned with, for example, women's rights, children's rights and the rights of indigenous peoples (see also Chapter 3). The struggle against exploitative working conditions in manufacturing industries dates from the beginnings of the labour movement but under contemporary neo-liberal globalization these campaigns have become global. Arguably, one of the first organized networks was the transnational advocacy network ('TAN') that began in 1994 in protest against working conditions in Nike factories (Sage 1999). Today, new coalitions and networks link human rights NGOs, global unions, women's groups, religious groups, consumers, as well as citizens groups, fighting against capitalist exploitation and for a better form of globalization. Here, we will briefly discuss the Play Fair Campaign as a concrete example of those actors that have used sports mega-events as a platform to fight for their cause, alongside human rights NGOs like Amnesty International and environmental groups like Greenpeace. The Play Fair campaign illustrates network-like coalitions between diverse actors acting both at the local and at the global levels. Through these coalitions, we see how several global social movements (workers, women, human rights, etc) intersect with each other and form alliances around specific struggles.

In the context of the then forthcoming Athens Olympics, the first Play Fair Campaign was officially launched on 4 March 2004 (Play Fair 2004). A press release entitled 'Betraying the Olympic Spirit' called for 'sportswear companies to clean up their act'. The main argument put forward was that indeed: 'Giant sportswear brands are violating the rights of millions of workers around the world in order to fill shops with the latest and cheapest sports shoes, clothes and accessories in time for the Athens Olympics'. (Play Fair 2004). The press release spelt out the main claims of widespread denials of basic workers' rights (such as long hours, unpaid forced overtime, below living wages, non-recognition of union rights and no maternity leave). The campaign was aimed at the sportswear brands Fila, Puma, Nike, Adidas and Lotto, as well as at their subcontractors, but also called on the IOC to challenge the abuses of its sponsors and licensees. Finally, the campaign called on governments to resist the pressure from the companies and ensure labour legislation was enforced to protect the rights of the workers. In short, the first Play Fair campaign sought to challenge injustices in the global labour supply chains that underpin sporting events, to improve conditions for workers and eliminate exploitation and abuse in the global sporting goods industry.

The first Play Fair Campaign was spearheaded by the Clean Clothes Campaign (CCC), global unions, and Oxfam, along with a myriad of associated local coalitions such as, for example, in Canada, the 'Coalition québécoise contre les ateliers de misère' (the Quebec Coalition Against Sweatshops). Based in Amsterdam but active worldwide, CCC lies at the core of a network of more than 250 organizations according to Sluiter (2009). It began in 1988 with a demonstration by women picketing in front of a C&A store in protest against the production of clothes using sweatshop labour. This, in turn, illustrated that the CCC has also had a strong connection to the women's movement (Sluiter 2009). Rapidly, the campaign that started in the Netherlands went global with, according to Sluiter (2009), two goals in mind. First, the clothing and garment industry is highly mobile mainly composed of leading brands (such as Nike, Puma, Adidas, etc.) and a myriad of subcontracting companies. Second, the majority of the workers in the industry were poorly paid women (Enloe 1995). The strategy of the CCC has four targets: brands and retailers, consumers, governments and workers themselves (Sluiter 2009, p.17). In this grand strategy, brands are held responsible for the way their merchandize is produced (i.e. according to the CCC code of conduct); consumers are educated in the hope they will adopt responsible buying behaviour, governments and politicians are lobbied for the development of transparent laws and regulations that protect the rights of workers; and garment workers in the industries of the Global South are supported financially and through actions of solidarity between the North and the South (Sluiter 2009). Thus, the first Play Fair campaign displayed a wide range of tactics organized both at the global and at the local levels by affiliated local groups and coalitions. These included demonstrations in the streets, particularly during the Athens Olympic torch relay, press releases, posters and meetings with policy-makers.

A second Play Fair campaign was organized around the Beijing Summer Olympics in 2008 and addressed 'four hurdles' faced by workers: limits to freedom of association; insecurity as a result of the high mobility of the industry; forms of abuse in the work place; and wages paid below the cost of living (Play Fair 2012). In preparation for the campaign, the CCC investigated workers' rights abuses by four Chinese companies licensed to produce Olympic goods (Sluiter 2009). Again the second campaign was structured as a coalition led by CCC, the International Trade Union Confederation (ITUC) and the International Textile, Garment and Leather Worker's Federation (ITGLWF). Additionally, it was connected to a wide variety of organizations worldwide ranging from trade unions, women's groups, North-South solidarity networks and it included the FSGT. The FSGT, as mentioned earlier, organized protests to coincide with the Olympics Torch Relay itinerary in France, displaying a series of white tables with faceless humans dressed in white in front of white sewing machines in Paris as a gesture of solidarity with workers in the South.

Such campaigns have continued. A third Play Fair campaign targeted the 2010 World Cup in South Africa with a special focus on the working conditions of construction workers. Most recently, the Play Fair campaign was organized around the 2012 London Olympic Games in order to challenge the London Organising Committee of the Olympic and Paralympic Games (LOCOG) to '. . . ensure that the Games are not tainted by the exploitation of workers' (Play Fair 2012, p. 7). This campaign again regrouped a renewed wide coalition of global and local actors, including War on Want, a British NGO created in 1952 that focuses on the global fight against poverty. Collectively, this coalition argued that sportswear and athletic footwear companies, the IOC, National Olympic Committees (NOCs), as well as national governments should take steps to eliminate the exploitation and abuse of workers in the global sporting goods industry. They urged these organizations to act in the spirit of the Olympics and demonstrate to the world how the principles of *fair play* can and should be extended to the workplace (Play Fair 2008). In this latest campaign, Play Fair convinced LOCOG to adopt a code of conduct in the procurement of goods and services for the Games, as well as to sign an agreement to act on the protection of workers' rights (Play Fair 2012). In its report, Play Fair recognized that LOCOG had taken unprecedented steps to protect the rights of workers, but also argued that much more still needs to be done. Indeed, Timms (2012, p. 365) outlines the difficulties facing the implementation of this code of conduct. First, it was difficult for the suppliers to respect the code for the LOCOG merchandize in factories that otherwise do not live up to these standards for the rest of their production. Second, without knowing where the factories are located, it is difficult for the suppliers to verify if the standards are protected. Third, it is difficult to monitor whether the new standards in these factories will be upheld after the manufacturing of Olympic merchandize is completed. Fourth, there is no official mechanism of complaint attached to the code. Nevertheless, despite these challenges, the fact that this code was adopted by LOCOG speaks to the relative success of the previous campaigns and London 2012 in particular for drawing attention to the rights of workers. As Price noted (2008, pp. 100–1), the Play Fair campaign before the 2008 Olympics in Beijing skilfully used the rhetoric of the Olympic Movement and has 'appropriated an officially proclaimed narrative of Olympic decency and then sought to hold those involved to their articulated high standards'.

The question remains, why did the CCC and its coalition allies choose the Olympics and other sports mega-events as platforms for protest? According to Timms (2012, pp. 358–9), 'the garment industry represent a significant portion of the global labour market . . . including some of the poorest and less organized and protected workers, who are disproportionally women'. This fact, combined with the high profile of the Olympic Games, makes such events an effective target for coordinating labour activism. Additionally, 'ethical campaigning on supply chains has had some success in establishing responsible governance as an issue companies have to address'. (Timms 2012, p. 359). Finally, Timms (2012, p. 359) adds, 'its global reach, its system of procurement and its ethos' make the Olympics not only a prime site for international marketing of its sponsors, but also at the same time an ideal opportunity to promote workers' rights.

Conclusion

As we have seen in this chapter, the labour movements' relationship to, and influence on, sport has a long and complex history. While the workers movement no longer plays the role of the dominant social movement in the world, it still represents a significant force. Some of the worker sport national organizations regrouped under the CSIT remain very active and represent a significant challenge to dominant sporting forms and offer an alternative voice that questions the current hegemonic world order of sport based on neo-liberal philosophy and organized by groups like the IOC. Sport organizations such as the FSGT and UISP are still connected to a form of international solidarity and linked to alter-globalization as a 'movement of movements'. According to these groups, the IOC has sacrificed the original philosophy of the Olympic Games on the altar of global capitalism and global media conglomerates. Are these workers' sports groups likely to be able to exert significant influence over the IOC? It is interesting to note that while they have defined themselves against the domination of IOC, most of these organizations have also sought, or have become organizations recognized by national Olympic committees and the IOC. Can we deduct that these movements are in the process of being institutionalized? As a result are they progressively losing their emancipatory potential? Although a clear answer to this question would require further investigation, one possible hypothesis is that recognition by the IOC and National Olympic Committees could add new opportunities for reforming sport, this time from inside the system. Indeed, their recognition has not stopped organizations like the FSGT and UISP continuing to fight for alternatives to the dominant sport order.

3

Women's Movements and Sport

Following the 2012 London Olympic Games, the UN Secretary General's Special Adviser on Sport for Development and Peace, Wilfried Lemke, praised the Games for promoting social change in a number of areas including the fight against gender inequality: 'In particular, the inclusion of female athletes in all delegations, including Saudi Arabia [as well as Qatar and Brunei], will help change mentalities and is a very encouraging step in the fight for gender equality and women's empowerment in and through sport' (UN Daily News 2012). His words echoed Jacque Rogge's comments during the opening ceremony of the Games as well as comments from spectators, journalists (e.g. CNN's reference to the 2012 Games as the 'Women's Games'; Brown 2012) and pundits from around the world, all of who saw the inclusion of female athletes in every national team for the first time ever, women's competition in every event, the introduction of women's boxing as an Olympic discipline, and the first-ever (knowingly) pregnant Olympic competitor as examples of improved gender relations in international sport. Approximately 45 per cent of the nearly 11,000 athletes were women and some countries, most notably the United States, sent more female athletes (269) than male (261) for the first time ever.

Yet, despite the increased participation of women athletes in the Olympics, greater representation of women in the IOC and significant improvements in policy, leadership, advocacy and participation for women in sport outside of the Olympics, gains for sporting women have been uneven globally and still are not fully on par with the participation and leadership opportunities for men in sport (see Donnelly and Donnelly 2013; Lenskyj 2012). The gains that have been achieved are the result of the concerted efforts of women (and their male allies) who have banded together to advance sport for women globally, and this chapter will focus on select milestones of the global women and sport movement. This chapter is not and cannot be an exhaustive and complete review of the global women's movement and the women and sport movement: the scope of that endeavour goes well beyond this book and even what is explored in this chapter is limited by accessibility of information. In other words, the developments explored in this chapter may not (and most likely do not) necessarily represent what is happening 'on the ground' all over the world with regard to the fight for gender equity in sport. The chapter is organized in three sections, the first of which traces the historical evolution of the global women's movement.

The second section of the chapter explores the development of the global women and sport movement. Lastly, the chapter examines the limitations of the women and sport movement around the world with a focus on continuing unresolved tensions within the movement. As will be demonstrated in the chapter, and in keeping with the theoretical framework of this book, the general principles of the global women's (and sport) movement can be identified arguably in the following ways. The collective identity of the global women's (and sport) movement centres on womanhood (although, as will be explored in the final section of this chapter, a notion of universal womanhood as collective identity is highly contested) and the movement operates in opposition to patriarchy. The totality of the women and sport movement, then, is directed towards the fight against sex/gender discrimination and the fight for equity in all areas of social, cultural and political life, including sport.

The complex contours of studying the global women's movement

Much like the other social movements in this book, we recognize that a full and all-encompassing examination of the historical development of the global women's movement falls well beyond the scope of one chapter (even beyond the scope of one book). Our intent here is to describe the historical milestones of the global women's movement and identify, in broad brush strokes, the features that have framed and informed (and which continue to do so) the movement. In so doing, we recognize, *a priori*, the impact and potential consequences of the choices we make in highlighting (or not) certain individuals, groups or factors over others. For example, even our depiction of a global women's movement in the singular (rather than global women's movements) carries risk in downplaying the significant plurality of women's activism and advocacy around the world. Furthermore, while we recognize that the historical development and current social organization of the global women's movement is comprised of complex linkages/interactions between local/regional NGOs and the UN (see Chen 1995), this chapter does not attempt to provide an exhaustive list of such organizations (see Eschle and Maiguashca 2010). That said, the historical milestones identified in this chapter are not arbitrarily selected; numerous women scholars, activists and policy-makers recognize them as pivotal to the global women's movement. Although the historical evolution of the global women's movement can be periodized in a variety of ways, we will explore the movement in two broad phases: in the period of time leading up to and including the UN Decade for Women (1975–85) and the developments following the Nairobi conference up to the present post-Beijing conference period (1985 onwards).

The early years of the global women's movement

For many scholars, the roots of the global women's movement can be traced back to the emergence of the United Nations and the signing of the UN Charter in 1945. This is to suggest not that women were not engaged as activists prior to World War II but, rather, that women's efforts to improve the social, political and economic conditions of their lives tended to be more local or regional/ national in scope than global. Examples abound of initiatives undertaken collaboratively by women from different parts of the world (e.g. Alice Milliat's efforts with the IOC is one such sport-specific example) prior to 1945. But, such initiatives would not be as far-reaching and as consequential for the global women's movement as the inscription of women's rights in the UN Charter and, eventually, the development of various bodies within and outside the UN focused on the status of women globally. Although Snyder (2006) goes so far as to call the UN the 'unlikely godmother' of the global women's movement, it is important to avoid equating the global women's movement solely with the UN (cf., Antrobus 2004; Basu 2000). While the UN figures pivotally in the emergence and solidification of the global women's movement, broader sociocultural (e.g. the various waves of feminism), political and economic forces as well as the mobilization of non-governmental women's and feminist networks and organizations from both the Global North and South, as noted above, have played equally important roles.

The issue of women's rights was an agenda item at the inaugural meeting of the UN General Assembly in February 1946. A sub-commission dedicated to the status of women was established and situated under the Commission of Human Rights under the auspices of the Economic and Social Council (ECOSOC). However, many women delegates and representatives felt that this sub-commission was not enough and, by 1947, 'the sub-commission formally became the Commission on the Status of Women (CSW), a fully-fledged Commission dedicated to ensuring women's equality and to promoting women's rights' (UNWomen.org n.d., p. 2). The CSW was to provide recommendations and reports directly to ECOSOC on 'women's rights in political, economic, civil, social and educational fields' and make recommendations 'on urgent problems requiring immediate attention in the field of women's rights' (UNWomen.org n.d., p. 2). From the start, the CSW enjoyed close ties with numerous non-governmental women's organizations and, between the late 1940s and the early 1960s, the Commission focused on promoting women's equal rights through the development of international conventions (e.g. the Universal Declaration of Human Rights), attempts to change discriminatory legislation, increasing knowledge of and research on women's experiences around the world, and the fostering of global awareness of women's issues (UNWomen.org n.d.). By the early 1960s, the Commission's efforts exceedingly focused on the role of women and socio-economic development as evidence documenting the disproportionate rate of poverty among women especially in, but not limited to, developing countries grew (see Antrobus 2004; Snyder 2006).

Antrobus writes that, much like many other social movements, the 'social and political ferment of the 1960s' represented the start of the women's movement as we know it today:

> The anti-imperialist and anti-Vietnam War movements, civil rights struggles, challenges to social and sexual mores and behaviour, and above all the rising of young people, brewed a potent mixture from which emerged many of the social movements of the succeeding decades worldwide. What was specific to the women's movement among these was its call for recognition of the personal as political. (2004, p. 23)

The famous slogan, 'the personal is political', speaks to the feminist politics that have and continue to interweave throughout the global women's movement, but it is very important to distinguish that not all women's movements are feminist movements. Feminist movements, in both ideology and action, focus on challenging patriarchy and transforming gender relations that subordinate women to men. Women do, however, organize as women to confront or promote other aspects of social life. Ferree and Mueller (2007, p. 577) highlight the utility of a broad definition of women's movements – women banding together as women to confront any form of inequity – by suggesting that it allows us to take 'into account that many mobilizations of women as women start out with a non-gender directed goal, such as peace, environment, social justice or anti-racism and gradually acquire explicitly feminist components; other, originally feminist mobilizations, expand their goals to challenge racism, colonialism, and other oppressions'. To narrow women's movements to just those that address gender inequity would be to neglect the fluid and dynamic nature of wide-scale political action. Women do not, however, live in social vacuums. Rather, women live in temporal and spatial contexts that have their own gendered and gendering regimes, therefore 'all women's movements are rooted in gendered structures of oppression and of opportunity' and 'all have some actual or potential relation to feminism, whether this is currently a primary goal for them or not' (Ferree and Mueller 2007, p. 579; see also Gamble 2001; Hall 1996; Hooks 1984; Kemp and Squires 1997; Scraton and Flintoff 2002).

While the exact antecedents of the designation of 1975 as the *International Women's Year* (IWY; since then 8 March has been designated International Women's Day) are not clear, it is recognized by many that the 'UN's receptivity to the idea owed a great deal to the efforts of women's organizations that were part of the CSW as well as to women on the delegations of member countries' (Antrobus 2004, p. 34). The observance of the IWY was intended to remind all that discrimination against women was persistent in the world and to encourage governments, NGOs, networks and individuals to increase their efforts to promote equal rights for women and recognition of their contributions to socio-economic development.

The Commission called for the organization of an international conference to coincide with the IWY and the *World Conference of the International Women's Year* was held in Mexico City, Mexico, in 1975. Delegates from over 133 governments took part in the UN conference, while over 6000 representatives participated in a parallel non-governmental tribune (or forum). In total, over 8000 people participated in the joint conferences (70% of whom were women and the majority of whom were with the NGO tribune), the IWY conference was the first official occasion where women – some familiar with UN and governmental settings and some not – from around the world gathered together to speak of issues specific to their lives and experiences (Antrobus 2004). A major theme at the conference was the fostering of better understanding of the experiences of women from developing and industrialized countries and the debates at the conference tended to focus women's basic concerns (e.g. health, literacy, education, employment, nutrition) as supported by the majority of member governments. The role played by government officials at the IWY, many of whom were men and thus lending support to Morgan's (1996/1984, p. x) assertion that the 'UN is a notorious old boys network', resulted in the notable silence around such issues as violence against women, sexuality and sexual orientation (Antrobus 2004); the silence on such issues would be lifted by the end of the Decade.

The debates occurring in the parallel NGO forum were more far-ranging as there were no restrictions on the topics discussed among participants and few formal presentations structuring the tribune. Fierce debates over feminism and feminist politics, particularly along North-South lines, characterized the conference: 'women from post-colonial states worried that feminism represented yet another form of cultural imperialism, while Western women felt they were the only feminists' (Basu 1995, p. 18; see also Antrobus 2004). The assumption of the struggles of women around the world and of sameness among women, a global sisterhood (cf. Morgan 1996/1984), spurred the resentment of many from the Third World/Global South, and women participants at the conference and tribune were deeply divided around what was seen as the ethnocentric and middle-class bias of the West and of Western women (Basu 1995). Despite the deep contestations around feminism that punctuated the IWY (and the Decade), these debates were widely recognized as being vitally needed and the conference represented the first occasion for women from around the world to engage in collective reflection and action that would be eventually sustained through the identification of the UN Decade for Women.

The conference defined a *World Plan of Action for the Implementation of the Objectives of the International Women's Year*, a key feature of which was the designation of 1975–85 as the *UN Decade for Women: Equality, Development and Peace* (UNWomen.org n.d.). In so doing, a powerful legitimacy was brought to the women's movement and to women's issues internationally. One key indicator of this was the surge in the number of research institutes, women's studies programmes at universities around the world, NGOs and lobby/advocacy groups, national women's commissions and interregional governing and advocacy bodies following the IWY conference and throughout the Decade; simply put, the IWY and the Decade ushered in a period of institution- and network-building as it pertained to the women's movement (Snyder 2006; see also Antrobus 2004). Sen and Grown (1987, p. 15) add: 'The United Nations Decade for the Advancement of Women (1975–85) made many of these experiences possible, prodding virtually every development body – United Nations agencies, national governments, and private organizations – to develop projects and programs that would improve the economic and social position of women'.

Two additional conferences comprised the UN Decade for Women: a mid-decade *World Conference of the UN Decade for Women* in Copenhagen, Denmark, in 1980 and a *World Conference to Review and Appraise the Achievements of the UN Decade for Women* in Nairobi, Kenya, in 1985. Both conferences saw exponential growth in the women's movement, and the mid-decade conference saw the beginning of more critical attention being paid to root causes for women's inequality including unjust economic, social, political and cultural structures (Antrobus 2004, p. 50). This greater critical attention to structural issues on inequality can be attributed to, in part, the role played by an ever-growing number of women's organizations, rather than just by governments, in generating political will and in promoting self-reliance (Antrobus 2004; Chen 1995).

While deep divisions among women based on nationality, race, class, religion, region, language and sexual orientation characterized the 1975 and 1980 conferences, 'better communication between these groups of women at the 1985 Nairobi conference occurred once they abandoned the myth of global sisterhood and acknowledged profound differences in women's lives and in the meanings of feminism nationally' (Basu 1995, p. 3). This was aided in large part by the growing presence and influence of women activists, researchers, political leaders and networks from the Global South (Antrobus 2004; Basu 2000; Sen and Grown 1987; Snyder 2006). The North-South divide did not completely disappear but there was a new sense of confidence from women of the Global South that pushed forward the global women's movement in ways not seen earlier. Third-World women's influence, as individuals, groups and as part of advocacy networks, on the conference and parallel non-governmental forum helped to facilitate even more critical dialogue on the structural roots of disparity in women's lives and the articulation of alternative development strategies (Basu 2000; Chen 1995).

From Nairobi to Beijing and beyond

Despite the tremendous gains achieved by women as part of the UN Decade for Women and the welcomed addition of the *Nairobi Forward-Looking Strategies for the Advancement of Women*, there was growing evidence from researchers and activists that 'rather than improving, the socio-economic status of the great majority of Third World women has worsened considerably throughout the Decade' (Sen and Grown 1987, p. 16). The emergence of conservative governments in the United States (under Reagan) and Britain (under Thatcher), the adoption of the Washington Consensus (see Chapter 1), the introduction of structural adjustment policies/policies (which helped the IMF/WB to supplant the UN as the centre of international policy debates) and the disastrous social and human consequences of such initiatives for countries of the Global South combined with continuing and pervasive 'traditional cultural attitudes and prejudices regarding women's participation in economic and social life' (Sen and Grown 1987, p. 16). Women in developing countries were particularly disadvantaged by the politico-economic shift of the 1980s as the structural adjustment policies and programmes (SAPs) that emphasized economic growth depended on women's unpaid labour as caregivers (i.e. social reproduction) and underpaid (exploited) labour in the marketplace (Tinker 1990; see also Bezanson and Luxton 2006). Despite the clawbacks of the 1980s, the global women's movement – as represented by the work of the UN, international NGOs and a multitude of the local/regional/transnational networks and alliances – continued to advance forward. While the UN Decade for Women, and events leading up to it, put 'women's issues' on the global map, the developments following the Nairobi conference (1985 and onwards) – in particular, women's participation in the UN world conferences of the 1990s – succeeded in establishing 'women's perspectives on global issues (Chen 1995).

By the late eighties, the CSW, as part of a larger shift among women activists and women's organizations, shifted its attention to locate and promote women's equal rights as an interlocking and cross-cutting theme in economic development, human rights, political, cultural as well as social policy issues (UNWomen.org, n.d.). The activism of women in the lead up to and at these global conferences was essential for influencing governments to see that '*all* issues are women's issues' (Morgan 1996/1984, p. x; emphasis in original). The different tack taken to women's involvement in the world conferences of the 1990s is a testament to the international meetings of the 1975, 1980 and 1985 conferences, the tens of thousands of smaller local and regional meetings of women that grew in and amidst the Decade for Women (many of which were organized at the regional level by women activists from the South, independent of both the UN and national governments, Basu 2000). These developments additionally speak to the increasing sophistication of women activists, throughout this period of time, as savvy political negotiators and lobbyists/strategists both within and outside of the UN (Chen 1990).

It was amid this energy that the Fourth World Conference on Women was held in Beijing, China, in 1995. The conference itself boasted the largest gathering of government and NGO delegations (6,000 delegates from 189 governments, more than 4,000 accredited NGO representatives, and about 4,000 journalists and media representatives) and the preparatory process in the lead up to the conference was the most extensive it had ever been. The negotiations for the draft *Platform for Action* were contentious given diverging views on women's rights around the world yet, by the end of the conference, women's human rights and equal rights were advanced significantly by the unanimous adoption (by 189 countries) of the *Beijing Declaration and Platform for Action*. As the strongest official statement on women internationally to date, the Declaration: 'set new benchmarks for the advancement of women and the achievement of gender equality . . ., [consolidating] five decades of legal advances aimed at securing the equality of women with men in law and in practice' (UNWomen. org, n.d. p. 16). The women's movement can be said to have become truly global in their appeal to universal principles of human rights (Basu 2000; Rao 1996; Ruppert 2002).

Beyond Beijing, there have no other UN-sponsored world conferences specific to women to date although, on 8 March 2012, the President and Secretary General of the General Assembly jointly proposed convening a fifth UN World Conference on Women in 2015. Within the UN, a series of review and appraisal special sessions were called for by the General Assembly, on the recommendation of the CSW, to bring together governmental representatives and NGOs to assess progress on the Platform worldwide. Convened at the UN headquarters in New York, Beijing +5 was held in 2000, Beijing +10 was held in 2005 and Beijing +15 was held in 2010. These special sessions were consistently the largest ever held at the UN headquarters. Each session assessed the implementation of the Platform's action items at the local and regional level, reaffirmed the *Beijing Declaration and Platform*, and reached consensus on further actions and initiatives to further women's status in all aspects of social, cultural, political and economic life. Furthermore, in 2010, the UN created UN Women, the United Nations Entity for Gender Equality and the Empowerment of Women (retrieved from http://www.un.org/womenwatch/daw/daw/index.html).

These developments attest to the strength of the global women's movement and the vibrant energies of women from all levels of government, inter-government (i.e. UN) and civil society (i.e. local/regional groups, NGOS, networks, etc) working collaboratively together. By Beijing, many saw a smaller divide between women of the Global North and South and greater consensus around issues that reached across North-South lines (Basu 2000; Bunch and Fried 1996). This was due in part to greater awareness of and sensitivity towards the 'local origins and character of women movements cross-nationally' and the widespread recognition that 'women's movements must be situated within the particular political economies, state policies, and cultural politics of the regions in which they are active' (Basu 2000, p. 68). Such a message was more readily accepted by the mid-1990s in part due to the changing global order, changes in the forms of women's activism internationally, and complicated (at times conflicting) interchanges between local and global feminism (Basu 1995). While the tenets of second-wave, particularly liberal, feminism continue to inform women's groups both within and outside of government, third-wave feminism, including post-colonial feminism, emerged in the late 1990s in response to the assumption of the universal female identity – one grounded in and emphasizing white, upper-middle-class women's experiences (Mills 1998) – ensconced in second-wave feminism. Third-wave feminists pushed for greater understanding of the discursive construction of woman and womanhood, the intersectional realities of women's lives and the need to attend to and mobilize in ways that resist the homogenization of women's experiences (Mohanty 1985; 1997; 2002). Third-World feminists, furthermore, criticize research and advocacy that positions marginalized women (often women of colour) as victims or social dupes arguing that such a position ignores or minimizes women's agency amidst local and global forces (e.g. Mohanty 2003; Narayan 1997; Spivak 1988; 1996; 2003; Sandoval 2000). In other words, we must recognize and embrace the diversity of womanhood as part of the collective fight against patriarchy.

Furthermore, some suggest that the very growth of the transnational women's movement is erasing the local face of women's inequality. While some argue that transnational networks have more far-reaching impact than local initiatives (cf., Moghadam 2000; 2005), others argue that as transnational women's movements have grown, 'commitment to grass roots mobilization and cultural change has diminished' (Basu 2000, p. 69; see also Alvarez 1998). It would be inaccurate to suggest that all local women's movements have been absorbed into global ones or that they only act now to resist global influences:

> Rather what prevails is a more complex and varied situation in which local and transnational movements often exist independently of one another and experience similar challenges and dilemmas. Furthermore, while transnational ideas, resources, and organizations have been extremely successful around certain issues in some regions, their success with these issues is more circumscribed elsewhere. (Basu 2000, p. 69–70)

Linked closely to these concerns is the critique that the global women's activism has been co-opted into and diluted (depoliticized) by the international state apparatus as part of larger shift towards gender mainstreaming. By the late 1980s, the CSW's approach to dealing with women's issues was as part of the mainstream rather than as a separate issue, and the word 'gender' was used in place of 'women'. As Khan (2002, p. 39) argues, however, 'the problem with the notion of 'gender' is that it can mean *both* men and women or *either* man or woman. The specificity of women's oppression disappears' (emphasis in original). While activists and scholars recognize that men are also locked into destructive constructions of masculinity and that long-lasting and sustained social transformation around sex/gender relations cannot happen without transformation of male privilege, the neutralized language of gender and gender equality (i.e. gender mainstreaming) is seen to only deflect attention away from women's oppression and subjugation by men (Khan 2002; Tripp 2006). Criticism of the Millennium Development Goals (MDGs) focuses squarely on the deflection of attention from women, specifically, and even of gender, more broadly. Whereas the Beijing Declaration and Platform is seen as more far-reaching, the MDGs reduce gender to just one of eight points and commitment to some rights (e.g. reproductive) has been dropped completely (Barton 2004).

An understanding of the historical evolution of the global women's movement is vital to better understanding the global women and sport movement as many of the determinants and embedded issues of the former – the emergence and legitimatization of the global women's movement, as supported by the UN, many (but not all) governments and the burgeoning and increasingly sophisticated NGO network/global civil society; the growing critical attention to both structural and cultural issues (including sport) that impact women's lives around the world; the impact of feminism(s) on the global women's movement including challenges to notions of universal womanhood; shifting relations of relations along North-South and local-global lines; and gender mainstreaming and the fear of the co-optation of the women's movement into government state apparatus – inform and contextualize the development and current status of the latter. In concluding this section of the chapter, how can we characterize the status of the global women's movement and the status of women around the world? We recognize that progress in the betterment of women's lives has been made in a number of sociocultural, politico-economic and legal areas, yet progress remains uneven around the world and girls and women continue to experience profound inequalities and discrimination amplified by their geographical location, economic status, sexual orientation, race/ethnicity, age, ability and other factors. Why do such challenges remain? A number of cross-cutting issues limit progress, including women's under-representation (or lack of) in key decision-making bodies at all levels of governance; continued violence (particularly sexual) against girls and women; the continued heavy reliance on girls and women for domestic and caregiving work; and continuing and pervasive social and cultural sex/gender stereotypes that constrain women's opportunities and choices. These issues are exacerbated by the inadequate allocation of financial resources for the effective implementation *and* reinforcement of laws and policies dedicated to gender equality and the empowerment of women, a situation that is only worsening with the major global economic downturn and uncertainty of the past few years. Political will and leadership is vital for sustaining action around women's right. It is on this note that we turn our attention to better understanding global women and sport movement.

The women and sport 'movement'

The study of the global women and sport 'movement' is not an easy one given its complexity, breadth and depth. In fact, the very way in which we identify this as a 'movement' (i.e. the women and sport movement vs. the women's international sport movement vs. the international women's sport movement vs. women in the global sport movement) represents the first of many challenges in conceptualizing what has occurred around the world over time with regard to women and sport. Distinguishing between these terms (including between women's sport and women and sport) is not an attempt to be pedantic with language but rather sensitive to the ways in which language frames the actions of individuals, processes, organizations and movements. Comprehensive analyses of the topic require us to negotiate the global women's movement(s) generally, and global women's sport (or women and sport) movements specifically. This is further compounded by our need to recognize the complex synergies and distinctions between: (1) movements/ networks/organizations that have focused on women's sport (i.e. the focus of this section; (2) political action that uses sportswomen/women's sport as a strategy for broader sociopolitical mobilization in areas of social life other than gender (e.g. Věra Čáslavská's protest, while on the medal podium, of the Soviet-led invasion of Czechoslovakia at the 1968 Olympic Games); and (3) women's social movements that use sport as a site of change in broader gender relations (e.g. the London 2012: Justice for Women protest of the allowance of the hijab in competition or the challenge put forward by Egyptian feminists to the ultras in efforts to secure women's rights to unrestricted protest; see Wolff 2012 and Dorsey 2012, respectively).

As Taylor (1999) notes, the emergence and maintenance of a social movement rests on the ability of mistreated groups to develop organizational solidarity; thus, we must attend to the mobilizing processes – that is, the organizing practices and intra-movement dynamics – of these collectivities (cf., Della Porta and Diani 2006). With regard to the women and sport movement, this requires us to pay close attention to the individuals and groups, particularly those in key decision-making positions, involved in international women and sport organizations. This section does not offer an exhaustive mapping (chronological or otherwise) of the movement but, rather, offers an identification of select groups and milestones that have framed the current status of the women and sport globally. This section draws from Jennifer Hargreaves' extensive work in this area (1999, 2001), Darlene Kluka's unpublished doctoral dissertation, as well as the promising work coming out of the Anita White Foundation at the University of Chichester (see Matthews et al. 2012). Following this description of the mobilizing processes of the women and sport movement, the final section will delve further into the continuing concerns and constraints of the global women and sport movement.

As noted earlier, the 2012 Games mark significant developments for women and sport globally, developments that stand in dramatic contrast to the first modern Olympic Games where no female competitors participated and where, in fact, Pierre de Coubertin, the founder of the modern Games, refused to even consider women's participation in sport, let alone in the Olympics. Repeatedly referring to women athletes as inappropriate, unattractive and wrong, de Coubertin argued that 'a woman's glory rightfully came through the number and quality of children she produced, and that where sports were concerned, her greatest accomplishment was to encourage her sons to excel rather than seek records for herself' (Spears 1972, p. 63). His beliefs on women's incapacity for and in sport were not remarkable given societal attitudes towards women at that historical moment in time but, as Wamsley and Schultz (2000, p. 113) note, 'were significant considering the influence he held on the calculated emergence of international sport'. Yet neither he nor the IOC nor the international sport federations, particularly the International Association for Athletics Federation (IAAF), could completely resist the tide of women's participation in sport broadly and in the Olympics specifically.

The inclusion of women in the Olympic Games came about as a result of the actions of key women sport leaders, most notably France's Alice Milliat, engaged in concerted international political action against gender discrimination in sport. At risk of understating the importance of the suffrage movement for women and women's physical activity opportunities (see Kay 2007; 2008) and neglecting the tremendous developments happening in women's sport in the late nineteenth and early twentieth centuries within different nations around the world (e.g. see Kidd 1996 or Hall 2002 for discussion of the role of early women's sport organizations in Canada), a brief examination of the rise and eventual decline of Milliat's Women's Olympic Games in the 1920s and 1930s is warranted given that it represents, in many ways, the most cogent example of an early international feminist social movement on women and sport.

In response to the IOC's and IAAF's opposition to women's official inclusion in the Olympic track and field events, Milliat established the Fédération Sportive Féminine Internationale (FSFI) in 1921 and, in the following year, organized the first-ever Women's Olympic Games (Kidd 1996). Up to this point in time, women had participated in some Olympic events (e.g. tennis, golf, gymnastics, swimming) but these were informally held at the behest of sympathetic event organizers and/or sport federations (Kidd 1996). These events never enjoyed official status and, despite the growing numbers of women participating in track and field, women were unequivocally disallowed participation in the most prestigious of Olympic events, track and field. Milliat – an avid rower, professional translator and a committed feminist – perceived an intimate link between women's right to vote and women's participation in sport:

> Women's sports of all kinds are handicapped in my country by the lack of playing space. As we have no vote, we can not [sic] make our needs publicly felt, or bring pressure to bear in the right quarters. I always tell my girls that the vote is one of the things they will have to work for if France is to keep its place with other nations in the realm of feminine sport. (as cited in Leigh and Bonin 1977, p. 76).

For Milliat and her contemporaries, suffrage was as vital to bringing about acceptance of and recognition for women's sports as sport was for advancing women's rights in society more broadly. This chapter does not offer a comprehensive examination of first-wave feminism given its focus on the global women's movement, but the importance of first-wave feminism cannot be overlooked as, 'in their buoyant, post-suffrage enthusiasm for new frontiers' (Kidd 1996, p. 113), women fought for their rights to participate in sport as athletes using, in this case, bloomers, track shoes and shot puts as tools of protest rather than marches in the streets or sit-ins (Riegel 1963; Schweinbenz 2000). Schultz (2010, p. 1135) goes so far as to describe the suffragists' incorporation of physical activity into their protestations as 'physical activism, or the articulation of physical activity and political activism'.

Although distasteful to some now, women's sport leaders during the suffrage movement and post-suffrage period often advocated for women's sport separate from that of men's – for 'women's sport run by women' (Kidd 1996). Even though, at times, reproducing the feminine apologetic and problematic discourses of women's supposed physical frailty (Lenskyj 1986), many first-wave feminist sport leaders mobilized to ensure that women gained the right to sport. As Kidd writes sympathetically, '. . . rather than capitulate to the reigning definitions of 'feminine', they reworked them to include the right to vigorous physical activity under their own leadership' (1996, p. 141; see also Hargreaves 1985). We can critique individuals such as Alice Milliat or organizations such as the FSFI (and their national counterparts) for not questioning and reproducing the centrality of male-dominated sport but we must not allow our current sensibilities to dim their accomplishments – they, within the confines of the (more overt) patriarchal society and male-privileged sport of the late nineteenth and early twentieth centuries, offered an opportunity for women to network together in organizations dedicated to women's sport and helped to legitimate women as serious, able and competitive athletes in (elite and otherwise) sport (Kidd 1996).

The 1922 and 1926 Women's Olympic Games witnessed record-breaking performances by female athletes from all over the world in a variety of events and attracted record numbers of spectators (including the Swedish royal family). The growing presence of Milliat's Women's Olympics and the success of women athletes in track and field could not be overlooked by either the IOC or the IAAF, and negotiations ensued between the FSFI, the IOC and the IAAF around women's inclusion in the Olympics. By the 1928 Olympics, Milliat had secured five events for women in track and field – despite being promised 10 events – a move that 'disgusted' the British Women's Athletics Association and prompted the only feminist boycott of an Olympic Games (Adams 2002, p. 144) – in exchange for renaming the Women's Olympics to the Women's World Games (Kidd 1996; Wamsley and Schultz 2000). However, by 1935, women were still denied a full programme of events in the Olympics and full representation on the IOC despite repeated calls for advancement by Milliat and the FSFI. Through a series of IOC-IAAF political manoeuvrings (see Leigh and Bonin 1977), by 1936, the FSFI ceased to exist as the IAAF took over complete control of women's track and field cementing its position as the international governing body for track and field for men and women as endorsed by the IOC. While the early years of Milliat's and the FSFI's work was sustained by the victories of first-wave feminism, its decline was hastened by the changing global geo-political atmosphere of the late 1930s and early 1940s including a world-wide depression, the growing rise of fascism in Europe and, eventually, World War II (Kidd 1996).

In their concerted and global political action against the IAAF, the IOC and the Olympics, and despite the staunch opposition of such sport leaders as de Coubertin, Milliat and the FSFI did advance international women's sport and we must applaud their efforts in doing so. However, we must also acknowledge that the IOC and IAAF succeeded in 'monitoring, regulating, and controlling significant aspects of women's sport' (Adams 2002, p. 143). In giving women five events in the 1928 Games, the IAAF effectively placated the FSFI and in assuming control of international track and field for all women and men, the IAAF and the IOC conceded that women's sport participation was 'inevitable' but also ensured that it would be 'strictly supervised by qualified individuals, namely men' (Adams 2002, p. 145). The introduction of gender testing or sex verification by the IAAF and the IOC in the late 1960s is but another example of efforts to monitor, control and contain women in sport (see Ritchie 2003 and Wrynn 2004). As Adams (2002, p. 143) notes, 'ultimately, the expansion and development of women's international sport depended on the interest and generosity of men'. A sentiment supported by Leigh and Bonin (1977, p. 83) who write:

> Prior to 1936, the IOC and the IAAF had been interested in gaining control of women's athletics only to control them and to slow them down, not to promote

them. By 1936, however, the situation was different. Now that women's sports in general had proven a success and now that women's achievements could be used for ideological and nationalistic purposes, the male federations were eager to include and to promote them.

In a foreshadowing of the current tensions in the global women's sport scene, we must recognize that Milliat's and the FSFI's desire to gain entry into mainstream international sport did not radically re-envision patriarchy or male-dominated sport but rather further entrenched it as the standard by which elite international sport was to be judged. While the Women's Olympics concerned the IAAF and the IOC, it did not genuinely threaten to destabilize the importance of either organization or of the Olympics; in fact, 'the persistent lobbying of [Milliat and] the FSFI attests to perceptions about the growing popularity and indeed the centrality of the Games within international sport' (Wamsley and Schultz 2000, p. 115). Furthermore, as the FSFI disappeared into the folds of the IAAF, we see 'a resisting, challenging, but subordinate group's interests . . . absorbed, re-shaped, and re-cast in a manner which sustains the more powerful or dominant group' (Wamsley and Schultz 2000, p. 116). Many of the themes highlighted above continue to punctuate the current global sport landscape for women as well as the contemporary women and sport movement.

The disappearance of the Women's Olympic Games and the decline of the FSFI represented, on one hand, the formal (albeit still contentious) acceptance of women into the burgeoning 'prolympic system/industry' (Donnelly 1996) as well as, on the other hand, the loss of power and self-determination among women's sports advocacy groups (Wamsley and Schultz 2000). Global events such as the depression and world wars helped to dampen (but not extinguish!) women's gains in sport participation and leadership, and it was not until the emergence of second-wave feminism in the mid-twentieth century that we see renewed vigorous activity in advocacy for women's sport.

Developments within the UN buoyed some of the activity in women's sport, and mention of the *Convention on the Elimination of All Forms of Discrimination against Women* (CEDAW) is warranted, given its importance to the women's movement, broadly, and to women and sport specifically. Although the UN General Assembly noted in 1963 that despite the progress made in achieving equal rights for women, 'in various fields there still remains, in fact if not in law, considerable discrimination against women' (as cited in UNWomen.org, n.d., p. 7), CEDAW (as a legally binding document) was not developed or adopted by the Assembly until 1979. That said, it is important to note that CEDAW was ratified in 1981, therefore entering into force faster than any previous human rights convention (Short History of CEDAW Convention, n.d.). The Convention was the first international tool to define discrimination against women and the various articles with the document brought together, in legally binding form, internationally accepted principles on the rights of women. Given the focus of our book on sport, it must be noted here is that the convention explicitly speaks against the discrimination of women in sport:

> Parties shall take all appropriate measures to eliminate discrimination against women in order to ensure to them equal rights with men in the field of education and in particular to ensure, on a basis of equality of men and women: The same Opportunities to participate actively in sports and physical education. (CEDAW, Part III, Article 10(g)).
>
> Parties shall take all appropriate measures to eliminate discrimination against women in other areas of economic and social life in order to ensure, on a basis of equality of men and women, the same rights, in particular: The right to participate in recreational activities, sports and all aspects of cultural life. (Part III, Article 13 (c)) Retrieved from http://www.un.org/womenwatch/daw/cedaw/text/econvention.htm

In recognizing the wide-scale political opportunity structures – the soil in which the global women's movement has grown – the convention's mention of the rights of women to sport, both within and outside the institution of education, weighs significantly.

Within different countries around the world, women sport leaders (and their male allies) pushed for more participation and leadership opportunities in every level of sport – for example, in the United States, the push for and passing of the landmark legislation of Title IX in 1972 that bans sex discrimination in educational institutions whether in academics or in athletics and the establishment of the Women's Sport Foundation (WSF-US) in 1974 as a leading research and advocacy organization. In Canada, in this same period of time, we see the first-ever National Conference on Women and Sport (1974) out of which emerged the creation of Sport Canada's Women's Program (1974) and, eventually, the establishment of the Canadian Association for the Advancement of Women and Sport (CAAWS) in 1981 (see Comeau and Church 2010). In the United Kingdom and continental Europe, similar organizations bloomed – in the United Kingdom, the Women's Sports Foundation (WSF-UK) was established in 1984 and the Working Group for European Women and Sport (EWS) network was established in 1989 (a full standing body of the European Sports Conference by 1993). Again, at the risk of neglecting the important actions, rich histories and unique circumstances surrounding women sport leaders and organizations within different countries around the world (e.g. see Pelak 2005), let us emphasize here that women (chiefly White, Western/Eurocentric, able-bodied) were mobilizing to gain more from a system that continued to profoundly privilege men; they were not rejecting the system outright. Women did gain territory, yet not evenly or in all areas of sport. As Kidd (1996, p. 144) writes: 'girls and women gradually won new opportunities to participate, but with second-wave feminism's rejection of 'separate spheres', those women who aspired to positions of leadership lost ground. Many of the once-separate women's programs . . . were brought under male leadership, and men got most of the jobs created by the expansion in female participation'. The continued underrepresentation of women in positions of leadership in international sport governing bodies remains a central problem in the women and sport movement as will be addressed in the last section of this chapter.

Worldwide, in 1949, the founding of the International Association of Physical Education and Sport for Women and Girls (IAPESGW) founded in 1949 represented the first-established (i.e. constitutionalized) international (and initially all-female membership) organization dedicated to the promotion of physical education and sport for girls and women. According to Hargreaves (1999), although the IAPESGW had a global dimension to it, in accordance with the vision of the IAPESGW's founding mother Dorothy Ainsworth, the group 'held a distinctly middle-class, elitist and very white Western educational and cultural hegemonic stance' (p. 462). Hargreaves (1999, p. 463) adds:

> There was no authentic representation of women from different social groups and cultural backgrounds: IAPESGW members from both the developed and the developing worlds were from elite class and educational backgrounds, the strong links with Empire remained dominant, and the association remained proudly "non-political," avoiding issues of power and difference.

Western cultural and physical education discourse was privileged as universal within the IAPESGW and, by 1992, dissatisfaction with IAPESGW's narrow focus motivated a few members to separate from and establish the Women's International Sports Coalition (WISC) that eventually became part of, in 1993, WomenSport International (WSI) (Hargreaves 2001).

The vision for the WISC and eventually for WSI was far more global than that for IAPESGW and far more interventionist (Brackenridge 1995). Launched in 1994, at the International Conference on 'Women and Sport: the Challenge of Change' in Brighton, the WSI boasted a more global membership as well as a stronger research-based advocacy role in other major international (sport and otherwise) organizations (e.g. the IOC, the United Nations). A notable WSI accomplishment has been the development and publication of the *Women 2000 and Beyond: Women, Gender Equality and Sport* report for the UN in support of the Beijing Declaration and Platform for Action (United Nations 2007) – an extension of the group's representation at the 1995 Fourth World Conference on Women. While WSI has focused on a number of physical activity and health initiatives, concern has been raised that much of its work is directed at elite, competitive international sport or, in other words, institutionalized, highly competitive and commodified Westernized forms of sport (Hargreaves 1999). Despite a declaration of sensitivity for the experiences of women from other cultures, critics such as Hargreaves (1999) point out that: 'the types of sport and the forms of competition are not in question' (p. 465). She adds:

> The emphasis given to certain activities rather than others is to do with relationships and discourses of power. Women from the developed world are in dominant positions in the WSI and theirs are the most powerful and authoritative voices [that] have done little to challenge the global imperatives [that] are reducing the richness of indigenous games and cultures. (p. 465).

Neither the IAPESGW nor the WSI has been oblivious to their (social, cultural, political and geographic) privilege and the urge to 'go global' (not to be confused with whether they have been *able* to effectively 'go global') has underpinned their efforts including the first-ever international conference on women and sport, entitled *Women, Sport and the Challenge of Change* held in Brighton, England, in 1994 (organized by the British Sports Council and supported by the IOC). Drawing on his exhaustive archival work, Matthews comments that 'there were genuine attempts by WSI but . . . [seemingly] . . . not the right connections and networks in other areas of the world that wanted to advance women and sport. This affected their reach. They were going to other countries but there was no one (. . . in positions of power) who could affect change quickly enough' (personal communication, 6 November 2012). That said, nearly 300 delegates from over 80 countries attended the conference, the specific aim of which was to challenge the continued marginalization of females from all levels of sporting and physical activity and address 'the issue of how to accelerate the process of change that would redress the imbalances women face in their participation and involvement in sport' (http://www.iwg-gti.org/conference-legacies/brighton-1994/). The conference was very important in bringing together many different women's groups (sport groups and otherwise), each of whom were attempting to advance women's participation and leadership in sport in different ways (Hargreaves 2001). As Pike and Matthews (2012) note, the Brighton Conference brought together these groups to help assume a new collective.

The Brighton Conference had three major outcomes: the decision to hold a second conference in 1998; the creation of the International Working Group on Women and Sport (IWG) to monitor progress in international women's sport; and the *Brighton Declaration on Women and Sport*. The *Brighton Declaration* (including the *1994–1998 International Strategy on Women and Sport*), adopted by over 320 organizations throughout the world and still influencing major sporting and non-sporting organizations as well as national governments to this day, affirms equity and equality for women in society and sport with its 'overriding aim . . . to develop a sporting culture that enables and values the full involvement of women in every aspect of sport' (*Brighton Declaration*, 1994). The declaration, and the action items based on the declaration's principles and identified in the *1994–1998 International Strategy on Women and Sport*, became a powerful tool for organizations in their struggles for women's rights in sport (Kluka 2008). Lobbied by the IWG and other groups, groups buoyed by the Declaration, to set targets for increased participation opportunities for female athletes in the Olympics and increased female membership on national Olympic committees and international federations, the IOC responded by: establishing its own Women and Sport Commission in 1995; adding more women's events to the IOC programme; amending the Olympic Charter to include the promotion of women's sport, adding more women to the IOC including, most notably, the appointment of Anita deFrantz to the position of IOC Vice President in 1997 (Matthews et al. 2012; White 1997). The conference and its outputs got women's issues onto the international sport agenda and did go a long way in influencing sport leaders occupying powerful positions in sport.

As noted above, additional conferences have been held since the Brighton Conference. Subsequent world conferences on women and sport have occurred in Namibia, Canada, Japan and Australia and, in 2014, the world conference returns to Europe (South America is the only continent not to stage a world conference yet). In Table 3.1, a brief summary of the themes and outcomes of each conference is provided, the information of which has been drawn from the IWG website (iwg-gti.org) and Matthews with Pike and White (2012).

The table highlights only the major outputs of each world conference but it must be noted that each conference marked significant advancements for women and sport. Each conference facilitated the gathering together of women's sport leaders and witnessed new initiatives, joint efforts and increased networking between local, national and international groups. We must not minimize the importance of conferences for women's collective political mobilization and, in fact, should recognize the ways in which 'the conference' has become a specific type of movement activity, a type of tool for protest. As Ferree and Mueller (2007, pp. 594–5) note:

> Conferences are a resource for building networks around the globe among contemporary women's movements. As events, not merely sites where something else happens, conferences punctuate and focus organizing that has become less episodic and more regularized, giving a concrete form to an otherwise dispersed network. Although conferences are events in the same way that a strike, a demonstration or an urban insurrection is, they have been less readily recognized as important by social movement researchers, perhaps because women have relied on them as a mobilizing tool disproportionately than men.

Despite remarkable gains in some areas, many of the issues raised at the Brighton Conference are still being debated today, issues such as the under-representation of women in leadership and decision-making roles and in NOCs and IFs; the uneven provision of facilities, services and programmes for women's sport around the world; lack of access to sport and physical activity (including

Table 3.1 IWG women and sport world conferences 1994–2014

Date	Location	Conference title/Theme	Major outcomes
1994	Brighton, England	Women, Sport and the Challenge of Change	The *Brighton Declaration on Women and Sport* 1994–1998 International Strategy on Women and Sport Creation of International Working Group on Women and Sport (IWG)
1998	Windhoek, Namibia	Reaching Out for Change	*Windhoek Call to Action* (focused on translating the principles of gender equity raised in the Brighton Declaration into practice and connecting with the global women's movement in particular with respect to health, education and employment)
2002	Montreal, Canada	Investing in Change	*Montreal Tool Kit* (a reference manual containing resources and tools to help individuals and groups advance their efforts around gender equality in sport)
2006	Kumamoto, Japan	Participating in Change	The *Kumamoto Commitment to Collaboration*
2010	Sydney, Australia	Play, Think, Change	The *Sydney Scoreboard* (an online tracking tool designed to increase women's representation on sport governing bodies globally by highlighting progress; http:// www.sydneyscoreboard.com/)
2014	Helsinki, Finland	Lead the Change, Be the Change	TBD

Source: Adapted from International Working Group on Women and Sport (http://www.iwg-gti.org/[accessed 19 December 2012]).

physical education) opportunities for girls and women in both developed and developing countries; the continued sexualization and trivialization of female athletes in the media; as well as the need for greater education and training (Donnelly and Donnelly 2013; Hartmann-Tews and Pfister 2003; Pfister 2010). The IAPESGW, WSI and IWG, as well as numerous regional and national organizations and groups (Matthews, personal communication, 6 November 2012), continue their respective efforts in challenging these issues, and the 2014 World Conference will constitute the next collective step forward in this struggle. However, even as the Brighton Declaration nears its twentieth anniversary, tensions continue to run within the women and sport movement, and four such tensions will be explored in the final section of this chapter.

Unresolved tensions between the global women's movement and sport

Such tremendous accomplishments make it difficult to criticize the work of the individuals and different organizations (the WSI, IWG, etc.), the Brighton Conference or the Declaration itself. However, we must recognize the limitations of these milestones particularly since these continue to impact international women's sport movement to this day. With regard to the sociocultural conditions that have constrained or facilitated the women and sport movement, we must recognize the pervasiveness of patriarchy both within and outside of the institution of sport. Simply put, the structural and cultural conditions within which sport has been and is located continue to advantage men (Hargreaves 1994). It is safe to say that while some women currently enjoy more and better opportunities for participation and leadership in sport than in previous generations, as highlighted at the beginning of this chapter, not all women do so and sport remains an area of social life dominated 'by men' and 'for men' (Donnelly and Donnelly 2013; Hargreaves 2001; Lenskyj 2012; Sabo and Veliz 2012). Sport remains a contested terrain for women and whether the qualitative experience of sport for women has improved compared with earlier generations remains a more tenuous question depending upon women's social, political and geographic location. Kidd (1996, p. 144) writes: '. . . girls and women struggle to develop identities of healthy womanhood in a cultural practice largely controlled by males and steeped in discourses of masculinity. In the absence of the sort of vigorous feminist debate about alternatives . . . there is little to challenge the naturalization of the male model. That so many women succeed does not discount the enormous contradictions they experience'. While some attest to the increased rates of participation among women in sport and greater number of women in leadership and coaching roles as signs of the democratization of sport, others question how truly transformative these changes are and can be given that the current hegemonic model of sport has been neither refashioned nor re-envisioned and remains decidedly a model of sport that privileges men, domination and risk (Donnelly 1993).

The Brighton Conference did afford women working for female sport in countries around the world the opportunity to connect, network and share, and the Declaration did become a focal point around which people could rally. Yet, as the Declaration is not a legal document (rather a position statement), we must question its teeth. Yes, the IOC has responded favourably to the concerted action coming out of the women and sport movement (aided by pressure from the global women's movement and different nations) and as represented by the Declaration yet, beyond the Olympics, it is still the case that many around the world are still unaware of the Declaration. Furthermore, given its lack of legality and enforceability, it may be the case that some groups and countries have signed the declaration with little to no intention of carrying out any action to legitimately address gender discrimination in sport. As Hargreaves (1999, p. 466) notes: 'It is impossible to judge how far-reaching the effects of the Brighton Conference have been because endorsing it in order to be politically correct does not mean, necessarily, that the will is there, or the resources are available, to implement practical changes in line with philosophy' (see also Kluka 2008).

Another unresolved tension concerns the identified targets (for lack of a better way of putting it) for change within the movement. All the major initiatives that have emerged from the work of the international women's sports organizations are directed at international sport leaders and governing bodies, such as the IOC, rather than to individuals or groups at the grassroots level – people at the receiving end of policy who 'if given the chance, might have a great deal to say about them' (Hargreaves 1999, p. 468). Yes, the IOC is (and has been) hugely influential in international sport but the connection between it and the struggles and desires of women at the grassroots level is not always clear. We must also recognize that genuine and sustained change often occurs incrementally over time (cf., Della Porta and Diani 2006) and that such change in sport requires intervention (almost simultaneously) at both the highest (e.g. IOC) and lowest (e.g. grassroots) levels (see also Travers 2008). That said, even though change has occurred in the IOC – both in terms of women's participation in sport and women in leadership positions on the committee – the IOC remains a hugely privileged and self-perpetuating, undemocratic body, and its members, male and female, remain part of an elite club. The women who are now part of the IOC machinery as participants and leaders, although exceptional and transformative in their own right, are not necessarily representative of the majority and, perhaps more importantly, are being absorbed into the existing male-privileged and male-privileging elite sport, rather than genuinely threatening those discourses and structures of power (Hargreaves 2000). Therefore, when contemplating initiatives like the Sydney Scoreboard – the online tool designed to track and highlight women's representation on decision-making sport bodies around the world that was the legacy item of the fifth World Conference on Women and Sport – we need to ask the question: do we really want to democratize sport governing bodies along gender lines if the institution of sport within which these groups are located remains patriarchal? Furthermore, we must question the type and impact of change being promoted by the contemporary global women's movement – how transformative is it and can it be, given that it is not completely rejecting hegemonic sport (see also Chapter 4).

Similar criticism is directed towards the leadership/memberships of the international women's sport movements themselves. The IWG, the group that monitors change and 'progress' in women's sport (of which IAPESGW and WSI are members), is a free-floating (i.e. not bound to any specific government or larger, more established NGO such as the UN) self-selected group comprised of individuals already embedded within and active in existing sport governance systems and/or possessing strong links with state apparatuses: in other words, elite women with elite connections (Hargreaves 2001). The ties to government, on one hand, have offered the group a certain degree of legitimacy as well as access to state funds and support but, on the other hand, it has also limited the group's autonomy and weakened its potential radicalism (Hargreaves 2001). Some are sharply critical of this – Hargreaves (1999, p. 467) writes, '. . . the reality is that [the IWG] is an undemocratic body, not an organization, it has no base, no specific mission except to monitor development, and it smacks somewhat of an "elite girls" network'. But, such severe criticism runs the risk of overlooking some of the extremely positive social change in sport stimulated by the efforts of powerful women utilizing their power (Matthews, personal communication, 6 November 2012).

The challenges (and opportunities) of emergent and interactive collective identity are central to the study of the women and sport movement (cf., Pelak 2002) – how does the movement make sense of the questions: 'who are we' and 'who do we represent'? Hargreaves argues that, while women are engaged in collective political action 'as a strategy to expand sporting opportunities for girls and women across the globe' (Pelak 2006, p. 374), the reach and scope of this international movement is limited because its membership has consisted of predominantly White, Western, middle-class women joined by 'neo-colonial elites' (Hargreaves 2001, p. 215). Despite the movement's supposed self-awareness of its privilege, its stated recognition of the global and perceived sensitivity to experiences, beliefs and desires of non-white, non-Western, it remains – so far – relatively rooted in Western ideologies of sport and homogenized womanhood (Hayhurst 2011; Heywood 2007). Clearly, better understandings are required of the politics of collective identity in the movement – which, in turn, presupposes a better understanding of the political opportunity structures that frames the contexts in which identity emerges – and post-colonial feminism can assist us in this endeavour. Post-colonial feminism can assist us in unpacking the re/production and privileging of white, Western, upper-middle-class womanhood in sport and, just as importantly, helps us to resist those beliefs and strategies that try to 'save' non-white, non-Western (subaltern) women athletes from their 'marginalization' by 'speaking for' them and acting on 'their behalf' (Mohanty 1985; Spivak 1988). As Pike and Matthews (2012) note, post-colonial feminism must inform our understanding of 'how the diverse groups and individuals who attended the Brighton Conference interpreted and applied the conference proceedings, including the principles outlined in the Brighton Declaration, to their own country's context or situation'. Furthermore, additional analysis of whether the women and sport movement has acknowledged and reinterpreted any adaptations to initial policy may coincide with post-colonial feminist arguments for more attention to be paid to non-Western groups, including the limited academic focus on Latin America. Simply put, we must question whether (and how) the global women's sport movement is really global.

In questioning the 'global-ness' of the movement, one additional site of tension arises and that is the relationship (or lack) of the women and sport movement to other global social movements. The Windhoek Conference and *Call to Action* make explicit the connections between women's sports and other areas of social life such as health, education and work, but it is unclear how deeply this has been taken up within the movement. That is, while women's sports organizations foreground women's access to sport participation and leadership opportunities, it is not clear how they engage with women's struggles in other areas, some of which are related to sport – for example, women sweatshop labourers in sport clothing and shoe industries (see Enloe 1995; see also Chapter 2 in this volume). In a deeply problematic way, we must recognize that increases in women's participation in sport also represent the continued exploitation of women workers in sport-related industries in developing countries around the world.

While sport is often under-recognized (at times, unrecognized) in the broader global women's movement (e.g. see Antrobus 2004; Kuumba 2001), one could argue that other social movements and the causes they fight against, such as labour rights, are neglected in the women and sport movement. One reason why this occurs rests with the ways in which the women and sport movement has been framed. To suggest that women's sport movement is only a woman's issue or that the anti-sweatshop movement is only a labour issue denies the structural interconnections between the systems of oppression that these social movements are attempting to confront (Ferree and Roth 1998; see also Travers 2008). Social movements are interconnected and the issues taken up by social movement organizations are multidimensional and as 'cross-cutting as the systems of domination that give rise to them' (Ferree and Roth 1996, p. 643). This chapter has attempted to better understand the dynamics of the women and sport movement on its own but, admittedly, a more nuanced examination requires us to employ an approach that takes into account multiple and intersecting forms of oppression and how they are addressed through social movements that 'interact, compete, cooperate or attempt to ignore each other' (Ferree and Roth 1996, p. 628). As noted earlier, we purposefully kept the focus of this chapter on social movements that have centred on women's sport but recognize that richer discussions of these phenomena require more in-depth examination of political action that use sportswomen/women's sport as a strategy for broader sociopolitical mobilization in areas of social life other than gender and women's social movements that use sport as a site of change in broader gender relations. In doing so, we begin to draw better attention to the (existing and emerging) coalitions of individuals and groups (and the coalition politics that circulate in between and around them) who work to frame issues and struggles inclusively (see also Chapter 2's exploration of the Play Fair campaign as a concrete example of coalition activism in action). For such coalitions, 'diversity remains and solidarity is temporary, specific and strategic: current cooperation in pursuit of a common good' (Ferree and Roth 1996, p. 643).

4

Rights Movements and Sport

This chapter investigates three social movements – anti-racist and civil rights, disability rights, and LGBT rights – that have been and are associated with sport, as well as some of the institutional structures, organizations and ideologies that frame and govern human rights issues. It primarily considers the impact of rights movements on sport and the influence of sport on rights movements. While the number of researchers exploring the connections between sport and human rights has been growing in the past 15 years (Donnelly 2008; Giulianotti 2006; Jarvie 2006; Jarvie and Thornton 2012; Kidd and Donnelly 2000), and some of these authors have tried to argue that sport is a human right, the *social movements* involved with rights and sport have not been analysed in much detail in previous writing. Here, we will explore both commonalities and differences between key social movements involved with rights, their relationship to sport and sports' relevance to them.

In keeping with our overall focus in this book, the approach taken is both transnational and intersectional. In this manner, we can explore the way in which different social movements have learnt, borrowed from and developed in both the national and the international context of other social movements. As Thörn (2007, p. 898) notes, one of the major findings of social movement research (e.g. Tarrow 1998, pp 176–95 and Della Porta and Diani 2006, pp. 186–8) has been that 'the mobilization of contemporary social movements always draws upon previously existing movement networks'. As noted in previous chapters, social movements can be seen to go through a series of phases in their development – formation and problem identification, activism in search of solutions and dealing with the aftermath of new policies and practices that emerge as a result (Winter 2003, p. 33; Blumer 1971). We therefore adopt a broadly social historical approach to rights movements and sport in this chapter.

Rights are seen as inherently political and contingent – taking institutional, legal and discursive forms. Many different struggles in varied social, economic, political and ideological contexts have been wrapped up under the phrase 'human rights'. Movements identified in other chapters in this book – concerned with workers' rights, women's rights, peace, and the environment as well as specifically those involved in human rights campaigns – all, at different times and in different places, have involved struggles over civil, political, economic, social and cultural rights. The relationship of the campaigns to sport is sometimes organic, emerging from within sport, and sometimes more superficial, developing outside of sport. It is interesting to note that the development of the concept of human rights shares some of the tensions that underpinned the history of the formation of modern sport, including the Olympic movement, in the second half of the nineteenth century (particularly that between internationalism and nationalism). Yet, no *a priori* assumption that sport can be a force for human good is supported by the historical evidence, as over the past 150 years sport has been responsible for many exclusionary practices and barriers that have in turn prompted negotiations and resistance (Donnelly 2008; Kidd and Donnelly 2000). The chapter illustrates the attempts of social scientists to develop an understanding of these movements, as well as engage with their struggles, and thus demonstrate the intersections with other social movements in sport and global society.

In the next section, we briefly outline some of the forms of human rights, and the accompanying institutions and legislation that operate at a national and international level. The focus of the social movements we look at here is around social justice, social equity and social development. Then, we discuss the historical development and connections between three rights movements – anti-racism and the civil rights movement, the disability rights movement and the LGBT rights movement – and consider different campaigns in sport associated with them. The chapter concludes with a brief discussion of future developments for rights movements and sport.

Human rights as a dominant discourse

David Harvey (2012, p. 3) suggests that, 'we live in an era when ideals of human rights have moved centre stage both politically and ethically'. Why is that? What are human rights? How did the discourse develop? One view of the formation of human rights discourse is that it is an 'invented tradition' (Hunt 2007) stemming from the print culture of the eighteenth century which enabled a new sensibility and sensitivity to suffering to be communicated to the reading public, especially through the novel. Rather than focus on the formal reasoning of philosophical texts, it is possible that the creation of an awareness of wider humanity came about through the power of the imagination that aroused sympathy for oppression (Blackburn 2011). Hence broadly speaking concerns for human rights refer to concerns about injustice, discrimination and exploitation – or consciousness of humanity (Robertson 1992) – and the desire for a better world.

Human rights, however, have a contested history because, although 'NGOS working for human rights are not new' (Freeman 2011, p. 167), as Samuel Moyn (2010, p. 20) puts it, the history of the core values of human rights is 'one of construction rather than discovery and contingency rather than necessity'. Moyn argues against the dominant, elite-focused interpretation of the ancestry of the human rights emancipatory movement and instead suggests that the discourse of human rights only became predominant in the past 30 years – since 1977 in fact – because it provided an alternative to other failed 'utopian' projects and grand narratives. Moyn poses the question whether the relationship to previous 'human universalisms' should be seen as one of continuity or as rupture. Earlier claims to the 'rights of man' were the basis for the construction of the nation-state, whereas contemporary human rights discourse tends to be the basis for a critique of state repression and corporate exploitation.

It is valuable to be reminded that there are fluid boundaries around the concept of human rights, which means that at different moments in time and in different places, the term has been understood and acted upon quite differently. Social movements are seen as central in two different approaches to the development of human rights and law: 'global constitutionalism' and 'subaltern cosmopolitanism' (Nash 2012, p. 798). The former approach suggests that there is one, 'top down', human rights movement creating international laws that protect human rights and the latter one suggests that there are multiple 'bottom up' movements 'and law for progressive human rights' (ibid). The former tends to consider legislative and political elites as leading the way for social change, while the latter focuses on the role of marginalized groups. In this chapter, while we adopt the second approach, it is useful to briefly outline some of the institutions that have been developed to provide the institutional framework for international human rights law and some of the organizations that have developed to engage with this framework (for an excellent overview of the different dimensions of human rights see Freeman 2011).

Human rights institutionalized

In 1950, the UN agreed that one day – 10 December – would be set aside to mark the adoption of the Universal Declaration of Human Rights (UDHR) 2 years previously. While this is only an advisory celebration day (meaning that UN member nations can recognize, or not, the day as they wish), it signalled the formal introduction of human rights into international discussion. In the past 30 years especially human rights law has developed along with commissions, and legislation. For example, in the United Kingdom, the European Union, Canada and Australia, as well as in the UN, various bodies exist to promote human rights – the Equality and Human Rights Commission (EHRC), the European Convention on Human Rights, the Canadian Human Rights Commission and the Australian Human Rights Commission, respectively. Altogether there are 69 national human rights institutions (NHRI) accredited to the International Coordinating Committee of National institutions for the Promotion and Protection of Human Rights (ICC).

These formal institutions have developed since the UDHR was adopted in 1948. The UDHR comprises statements concerning 30 basic human rights. It begins with the statement that 'recognition of the inherent dignity and of the equal and inalienable rights of all members of the human family is the foundation of freedom, justice and peace in the world' (United Nations 1948/2012). It then continues to declare that it is 'the common standard of achievement for all peoples and nations' (United Nations 1948/2012). In the past 64 years since then international human rights law has developed more than 60 instruments, consisting of treaties, conventions and covenants agreed by the UN, that *can be* legally binding on states and comprise the international standard of human rights: 'can be' legally binding because core documents have to be signed and ratified for them to be influential within the boundaries of the nation states that make up the UN. While there are nine core international human rights treaties, the United Kingdom, Canada and Australia have only ratified seven of them and the United States only six (Amnesty International 2012, pp. 394–5). The treaties include civil and political rights (International Covenant on Civil and Political Rights (ICCPR), adopted by the UN in 1966); economic, social and cultural rights (International Covenant on Economic, Social and Cultural Rights (ICESCR) 1966); torture (Convention against Torture and Other Cruel, Inhuman or Degrading Treatment (CAT) 1984); discrimination against women (Convention on the Elimination of All Forms of Discrimination Against Women (CEDAW in 1979, see Chapter 3); racial discrimination (International Convention on the Elimination of All Forms of Racial Discrimination (CERD) 1965); children (Convention on the Rights of the Child (CRC) 1989); and disabled people (International Convention on the Rights of Persons with Disabilities (CRPD) 2006). Conventions relating to the treatment of migrant workers and their families (International Convention on the Protection of the Rights of All Migrant Workers and Members of Their Families (CMW) 1990) and enforced disappearance (International Convention for the Protection of All Persons from Enforced Disappearance (CED) 2006) have neither been signed nor been ratified by the United States, the United Kingdom, Canada or Australia. The United States has signed but not ratified the CRC. In addition to treaties and conventions, various human rights instruments – such as principles and guidelines relating to older persons and declarations relating to indigenous peoples – exist which are also not legally binding unless specifically adopted by a national government. While currently at the UN, older people and LGBT persons do not have any core treaties covering their rights, in other parts of the world, such as the European Union, a Charter of Fundamental Rights of the European Union agreed to in 2010 does include articles on non-discrimination on the basis of sexual orientation and the rights of the elderly.

Complementary to the instruments, committees and conventions, the UN has a series of special procedures it can call upon (including the position of Special Rapporteur, representative or independent expert) to monitor and attempt to enforce the promotion of human rights around the world. There are 31 country-specific (e.g. Somalia, Sudan and Haiti) and eight theme-specific special procedures (covering, for example, adequate housing, violence against women and education). The Human Rights Council is an intergovernmental body of 47 nation states and the UN High Commissioner for Human Rights has their office in Geneva, Switzerland.

Human rights organized

In addition to these formal human rights institutions, bodies and positions, and possibly comprising the more public face of human rights as part of a global, transnational, *social movement*, are international non-governmental organizations (INGOs) that monitor, promote and seek to protect human rights, the most well known of which are Amnesty International (AI), and Human (formerly Helsinki) Rights Watch (HRW). Human rights organizations such as AI and HRW arguably led the internationalization of social movements (Tilly 2004, p. 115). They monitored human rights abuses across the world, published regular human rights ratings, reported on these abuses and intervened to call for sanctions from major states and international authorities on human rights abuses. They provided 'templates, certification, connections and advise to claimants' (Tilly 2004, p. 115). According to Tilly (2004, p. 115), movements of 'self-styled indigenous peoples across the world benefitted substantially from identification of themselves as participants in a worldwide cause'. Nonetheless, as Therborn (2011, p. 2) suggests, while human rights began to emerge as a serious issue in the 1960s, mainly thanks to the formation of groups such as AI, they only reached the 'geopolitical mainstream' in the 1970s:

> The Western powers had them inserted in the Helsinki Accord of 1975, recognizing the post-Second World War borders of Europe, crucial to Poles and most other East Europeans, communist or anti-communist. In the Americas, human rights also became a key issue in the second half of the 1970s. In Latin America they became a defence in defeat, after all attempts at progressive social change (outside Cuba) had been crushed by military dictatorships. In the USA there was, for once, a positive resonance during the Carter administration. The completely unforeseen unlocking of Cold War diplomacy and US recognition of human rights in the Americas made human rights irremovable from the international political agenda, accepted in violation by the Reagan and the two Bush administrations.

Different movements, campaigns and coalitions therefore constitute the field of human rights. We agree with Stammers (2009, p. 160) that it is important to acknowledge the pre-institutional, non-legal forms that existed prior to human rights law and institutions as well as the role that social movement praxis plays in shaping intellectual developments around human rights.

The different categories of rights tend to collect around civil and political rights, to do with equality of involvement in the civil life of a nation including the right to vote in elections, and economic, social and cultural rights, relating to unequal treatment based upon discrimination that prevents the full engagement of groups in society. Echoing Moyn above, sport scholar Susan Brownell (2012, p. 315) notes: 'human rights are not pre-given moral truths, they are constructions'. The formal apparatus of human rights and the social movements that espouse and promote human rights transnationally are constantly engaged in this work of construction in what is referred to as 'global civil society' (cf., Giulianotti and Brownell 2012, p. 200). What makes human rights complex is that they are both transnational and *intersectional* – that is the different minorities and groups involved in separate struggles over rights draw inspiration from the activities of other groups acting inside and outside the boundaries of their nation states. The human rights movement, therefore, has no single identity or opponent as such, although in common with other social movements the broad goal would be to transform the core values, orientations and structures of a society – what Touraine refers to as its 'historicity' – in favour of a more just, non-discriminatory and equitable social condition. As Fraser (1997, pp. 69–98) argues, social movements are 'subaltern counter-public spheres', where oppositional interpretations of identities, interests and needs are debated, discussed and formulated.

Making sense of rights movements and sport

As noted earlier, the number of researchers exploring the connections between sport and human rights has grown in the past 15 years. Despite expressing some critical reservations about the connection between sport and human rights, including the worst excesses of naïve evangelicalism associated with belief in the inherent goodness of sport, Giulianotti (2006, p. 75) states sport 'provides perhaps the most culturally popular medium through which senses of moral obligation towards absolute strangers might be communicated through imagined belonging'. Kidd and Donnelly (2000) have argued that democracy and liberation central to human rights will not be achieved without the realization of human rights in sport and physical education. The growth and development of *social movements* connecting the struggle for rights with sport is discussed next.

The politics of 'race' and sport: The American civil rights movement and the anti-apartheid movement

The focus in the following section is specifically on the anti-racist and civil rights movement in North America and the anti-apartheid movement, indicative of the 'anti-discrimination' and 'anti-racism' struggles identified by Harvey and Houle (1994, pp. 348–9).

The American civil rights movement

Between 1950 and 1980, the aim of the Civil Rights Movement (CRM) in the United States was equality before the law. Equality meant the assertion of the rights of minorities – in this case African-Americans – to equal treatment and justice and claims for the empowerment of them as a socially excluded group. The two main foci of the struggle were desegregation (an end to the form of apartheid or separate development) that had continued after the abolition of slavery in the nineteenth century in the southern states and enfranchisement (securing equal voting rights for African-Americans). The civil rights movement in the United States coincided with struggles for self-determination and rights in countries around the world that had achieved independence from colonial rule, yet were looking to align neither with the American-dominated capitalist world nor with the the Soviet-led Communist bloc. The so-called 'Third World' became an ideology of 'counterhegemonic political movements' that developed in the mid-1950s (Gitersos 2011). During the 1950s and for most of the 1960s, the campaign involved civil resistance and social criticism through non-violent forms of activism, including such actions as boycotts, demonstrations and marches. Later in the 1960s, civil unrest and armed rebellion occurred. As the movement attempted to develop positive perceptions of self and pride in group identity – to move consciousness from a group in itself to a group for itself – it also produced such slogans as 'black is beautiful'.

In the 1950s and 1960s, the National Association for the Advancement of Coloured People (NAACP), Southern Christian Leadership Conference (SCLC), the Student Non-violent Coordinating Committee (SNCC) and Congress of Racial Equality (CORE) were the main organizations confronting so-called 'Jim Crow' laws at the local and state levels that barred African-Americans from classrooms, public conveniences, theatres, trains, buses as well as from juries and legislatures. In 1954, following a litigation strategy adopted by the NAACP, the US Supreme Court struck down the 'separate but equal' doctrine that formed the basis for state-sanctioned discrimination. This drew national and international attention to African-Americans' situation and was enhanced by the development of the Cold War (Dudziak 2011). Arguably, American government officials, including such Presidents as Eisenhower and Kennedy, became more supportive of civil rights reforms than they might have been otherwise because of the centrality of race relation problems to international perceptions of the United States. Many leaders from within the African-American community rose to prominence during the Civil Rights era including Martin Luther King, Jr., Rosa Parks, Stokely Carmichael and Malcolm X. Civil rights activism included localized actions such as the refusal to accept segregated buses in Montgomery, Alabama by Rosa Parks, the subsequent black boycott of the bus companies in Montgomery when she was imprisoned, and sit-ins in segregated lunch counters, as well as more nationally significant events such as the 200,000-person march on Washington in 1963 and the Selma to Montgomery march in 1965. Such actions did lead eventually to legislative change, such as the Voting Rights Act of 1965 and the Civil Rights Acts of 1964 and 1968 (Polenberg 1980, pp. 181–93).

The Lowndes County Freedom Organization (LCFO) was founded in Lowndes, Alabama, as a political party designed to help blacks resist oppression. Organized by the young civil rights leader, Stokely Carmichael of the SNCC, Lowndes residents launched an intensive effort to register blacks to vote in the County, using registration drives, demonstrations and political education classes. The plan was to get enough black people to register to vote to enable them to gain control of local government and thus redirect services towards them. The LCFO adopted the emblem of a black panther in contrast to the white rooster of the white-dominated Alabama Democratic Party, and this symbol was taken up as the name of another political party based in California – the Black Panther Party – formed in 1966 by Huey Newton and Bobby Seale. A different kind of politics began in the late 1960s, which endorsed uprisings underpinned by belief in theories of black nationalism and 'black power' espoused by Elijah Muhammad, Malcolm X and other pan-African leaders who took the view that reforms were not sufficient to alter the lives of African-Americans. Civil rights reforms were seen as insufficient as blacks still suffered from forms of oppression. The assassinations of Malcolm X and Martin Luther King plus in-fighting within the organizations led to a decline in protest activity after the 1960s (Van Deburg 1992). The aims of the civil rights movement turned to defending gains and strengthening enforcement mechanisms.

Consideration of the relationship between the CRM to sport demonstrates, following Hartmann (1996, p. 549), what can be considered as 'the ambiguities, paradoxes and contradictions' of the relationships between culture, political power and social change. We follow Hartmann (2003, 1996) in looking at the 1968 African American Olympic protest movement underpinned by the 'Olympic Project for Human Rights' (OPHR). The dominant image of this protest took place at the 1968 Mexico City Olympic Games. Political gestures during the Olympic Games and the use of the events to promote political ideologies had been part of them since their inception (Triesman 1984; Horne and Whannel 2012, pp. 109–45). What was distinctive about 1968 was that athletes utilized a political gesture in opposition to the status quo in order to raise an issue without the support of the nation that they were representing.

On 16 October Tommie Smith won the 200-metre race in a world-record time of 19.83 seconds, with Australia's Peter Norman coming second and the US's John Carlos in third place. The two US athletes received their medals shoeless, Smith wore a black scarf and Carlos had his tracksuit top unzipped. All the three athletes wore Olympic Project for Human Rights (OPHR) badges. Both US athletes intended on bringing black gloves to the event, but Carlos forgot his. It was Peter Norman who suggested Carlos wear Smith's left-handed glove, this being the reason behind him raising his left hand, as opposed to his right, differing from the traditional Black Power salute. When the US National Anthem 'The Star-Spangled Banner' played, Smith and Carlos delivered the salute with heads bowed, a gesture that became front-page news around the world. That such a relatively small gesture could create such a response paved the way to the Olympics becoming a major platform for the playing out of political theatre.

Smith and Carlos were members of a small group of elite athletes that sociologist Harry Edwards was hoping would help to develop a boycott of the 1968 Olympic Games, under the title of the OPHR (for more discussion see Hartmann 2003, pp. 29–103 especially; Waller et al. 2012; Zirin 2012). Those associated with the initiative at various times included basketball player Lew Alcindor (who later changed his name to Kareem Abdul Jabaar), Martin Luther King, Jr., Stokely Carmichael and Muhammad Ali (Edwards 1969). The OPHR was formed in the autumn of 1967 after a Black Power conference held in Newark, New Jersey, in the summer had urged that black athletes should boycott the 1968 Olympic Games. The idea that black Americans might boycott sports events, especially the Olympics, in order to draw attention to racial inequalities in the United States was not a new one; Hartmann (1996, pp. 563–4, n.2) lists several precursors earlier in the 1960s. As Hartmann suggests, however, what made the OPHR initiative distinctive was that it developed out of a student protest at San Jose State University and while it did not have any concrete demands initially attached to it, it was to draw attention to 'racial injustice' (Hartmann 1996, p. 552). In December 1967, a list of demands were made as follows: the removal of Avery Brundage from his office as President of the IOC; the exclusion of nations that were based on apartheid (South Africa and Southern Rhodesia) from all international sports events; the addition of black coaches and administrators to the United States Olympic Committee (USOC); the complete desegregation of the New York Athletic Club (NYAC), which held two of the most prestigious indoor track and field meetings; and the restoration of Muhammad Ali's titles and the right to box in the United States (Hartmann 1996, p. 553).

The fact that most of these demands were not met, at least in the case of the exclusion of apartheid regimes from international sport, not as a direct result of the threatened boycott, might be seen as a sign of failure. OPHR, however, seems to have mostly achieved smaller scale protests, and there were several of these in the build up to the 1968 Olympics. The February 1968 indoor meeting at NYAC was boycotted. Protests and meetings took place at 35 university campuses. The problem was that not enough of the 30–40 prospective African-American Olympians involved in the OPHR had a clear idea about what the statement about the situation of black Americans would entail. During the

Olympics, and before Smith and Carlos took to the winners' rostrum, Jimmy Hines won the 100 metres and refused to shake hands with Brundage during the medal ceremony. However, this and other small actions, including wearing black socks and armbands, 'were conveniently overlooked' (Hartmann 1996, p. 554).

Sport was considered by some of the civil rights movement and black activists as a place where they could develop a new and more forceful activism. Protest in sport was attractive because it was popular among the black population, had offered some blacks an avenue of opportunity and representation, was a place where expressions of discontent and the need for change were possible and was often portrayed in the media as an arena where discrimination did not feature (Hartmann 1996, pp. 560–1). However, Hartmann (1996, p. 559) suggests that the immediate response that Smith and Carlos received – expelled from the Olympic Village by USOC, permanently expelled from Olympic competition and sent back home to the United States – was later compounded by the controversy in the United States that their actions generated. For their critics, the problem was that they had defiled sport, a cultural form that was perceived as inherently all about racial justice and civil rights. This made it difficult for 'outsiders to racial injustice and discontent even to begin to understand, much less sympathize with, the protesters' collectivist grievances and concerns' (Hartmann 1996, p. 559). Moreover, the 1968 protest movement was controversial because it exposed 'the ways in which sport culture and liberal democratic ideology usually served (and serve) to legitimate a very particular, very interested and very individualistic vision of racial justice and civil rights' (Hartmann 1996, p. 561).

Hartmann is uncertain if his reading – that no tangible social progress resulted from the actions of Smith and Carlos or the OPHR – is a completely accurate one. Yet as he notes the 'salute' did keep issues surrounding the injustice of race on the agenda for many subsequent generations of activists, it did take place at a time when traditional forms of protest were becoming increasingly controlled, and through its transformation into an iconic image of popular culture, indicated a way in which black political struggle could remain part of social consciousness and contestation (Hartmann 1996, p. 563).

The anti-apartheid movement

Achieving human rights in sport includes both social democracy of sports participation characterized by access and opportunities for all persons, and the freedom within sport cultures for persons to participate in diverse ways. At the same time, Kidd and Donnelly (2000) argue human rights and sport are linked because of the opportunity that sport affords to advocate for the realization of universal rights, a political and strategic logic clearly evident in the best-known example of rights advocacy through sport, the boycott of South African sports federations and national teams as a protest against the racist practices and policies that restricted sports participation for the non-White majority under the 'Apartheid' regime.

Apartheid – literally meaning 'apartness' in South African language Afrikaans – was the formalized version of a system of racial segregation and discrimination enforced by successive white South African governments between 1948 and 1991 (Omond 1985). Apartheid was in fact the consolidation of a system of discrimination and segregation that had existed in South Africa for most of the twentieth century. It created separate townships, work legislation, education regulations and sport systems for the minority white population and majority black population. As the system was being formalized during the 1950s protest movements against apartheid grew, both inside and outside South Africa, along with the arrest and banning of its critics. In 1960 a demonstration in Sharpeville against new pass laws restricting the movement of black South Africans ended with police shooting 69 people dead. A state of emergency was called with two main black organizations, the African National Congress (ANC) and Pan-Africanist Congress (PAC) banned and thousands of activists detained without trial. With the ANC and PAC moving underground the era of peaceful, non-violent, protest ended. It was shortly after this that Nelson Mandela, the leader of the ANC, was imprisoned for life. In the late 1960s and 1970s, a Black Consciousness movement developed in South Africa. This movement contributed to the Soweto uprising in June 1976 in protest against the compulsory use of the language of Afrikaans in black African schools. However, in September 1977, one of the leaders, Steve Biko, died while being detained by the police and all organizations associated with the Black Consciousness movement were banned (Omond 1985, p. 17). The South African apartheid regime was to last for another 14 years, but in that time sport-related boycotts and protests began to influence global public opinion.

In 1962, the South African Non-racial Olympic Committee (SAN-ROC) was launched with the aim of replacing the whites-only National Olympic Committee. As a later chairman of SAN-ROC, Sam Ramsamy (1984, p. 44) noted: 'South Africa's first participation in the Olympics was in London in 1908. Since then, it has participated in all the Games up to 1960. The South African National Olympic Committee was exclusively white right through to its final expulsion in May 1970. Blacks were never given the opportunities not the facilities to train for Olympic participation'. Black South Africans had protested their exclusion since the 1940s, but lobbying of the IOC for the exclusion of South Africa only began seriously in 1959. With no African member of the IOC, however, South Africa was allowed to compete in Rome in 1960, despite attempts to persuade the IOC president Avery Brundage to reconsider (Maraniss 2008, pp. 62–5). Both the anti-apartheid movement (AAM) and civil rights movement shared the non-violent strategy of 'boycott' as an aspect of their movement. Internationally the AAM developed boycotts of food, products, economy, academic exchanges and eventually sport as part of the aim of bringing about change. Slogans such as 'No normal sport in an abnormal society' and 'No equal sport in an unequal society' were developed to focus public attention on the situation in apartheid South Africa.

In the late 1960s and early 1970s when cricket and rugby union – two team sports holding great popularity and significance for white male South African identity – were subject to protest, campaigns and boycotts, such as the 'Stop the 70 Tour' campaign against a tour of the United Kingdom by the South African rugby team and a subsequent tour by the SA cricket team was cancelled, it was recognized that sports isolation could have a significant effect on the position of South Africa in the international community. The AAM involved activists worldwide and was bolstered by the response to the call to undertake a 'third party' boycott of New Zealand, as that country had allowed a rugby tour of South Africa to go ahead in 1976. This lead to 19 African countries withdrawing from the 1976 Montreal Olympics in protest at the inclusion of New Zealand. South Africa was also expelled from international athletics, swimming and association football (Ramsamy 1984, p. 50). Concerned that an African boycott would ruin the 1978 Commonwealth Games scheduled for Edmonton Canadian Prime Minister Pierre Trudeau initiated the writing of a statement on apartheid in sport. *The Commonwealth Statement on Apartheid in Sport*, widely known as the 'Gleneagles Agreement', institutionalized the Commonwealth's response to apartheid in June 1977, declaring that it was 'the urgent duty of each of their governments vigorously to combat the evil of apartheid by withholding any form of support for, and by taking every practical step to discourage contact or competition by their nationals with sporting organisations, teams or sportsmen from South Africa or from any other country where sports are organized on the basis of race, colour or ethnic origin' (Ramsamy 1982, p. 69). In December 1977, the General Assembly of the United Nations also adopted a declaration to isolate South Africa from international sport (Ramsamy 1982, p. 62).

Kidd and Donnelly (2000, p. 138) argue that the ensuing isolation of pro-Apartheid sports federations constituted 'powerful symbolic condemnation' that contributed to the fall of the regime. In turn, the end of apartheid offered an opportunity to mobilize sport as a tool for development, and therefore was a significant precursor to the emergence of Sport for Development and Peace (SDP) as a significant sector, insofar as it became reasonable and intelligible to argue that marginalized people (such as Black South Africans) possessed an inalienable right to participate in sport and physical activity (Kidd 2008, p. 374; on SDP see Darnell 2012). It is also important to note, however, that boycotts alone cannot transform societies (Booth 2004). On their own they can perhaps bring about limited reforms, since the pressures they exert are relatively insignificant in comparison with the concessions demanded.

Hartmann (2003) does not specifically compare the OPHR with the AAM strategy of boycott. Anti-racism certainly provides another thread of continuity in these two campaigns and suggests a contrary argument to Moyn's 'discontinuity thesis' about the history of human rights (Moyn 2010). Blackburn (2011, p. 135) argues that nineteenth-century campaigns for the abolition of slavery and the twentieth-century movements to end white rule in Africa and Jim Crow laws in the United States were aligned: 'the 'human rights' idea was taken up in different ways by the South Africa Freedom Charter, Kwame Nkrumah, Martin Luther King Jr., the Student Non-violent Coordinating Committee and the 1968 Olympic Project for Human Rights'. The family resemblance was their anti-racist approach to anti-colonialism and anti-imperialism. He continues, 'the struggle against apartheid South Africa was an icon of the anti-imperialist movement and surely had an absolute claim to the banner of human rights' (Blackburn 2011, p. 135).

Social movements learn from the prior and contemporary experience of other social movements. From the 1950s to the 1990s, the AAM realized the importance of the media to mobilize national and international opinion, grassroots activists and transnational bodies and corporations. Unlike the CRM, the AAM developed as 'informational capitalism' was coming to the fore (Castells 1996) and the struggle over the control of information, symbols and knowledge was becoming increasingly important. As Keck and Sikkink (1998, p. 16) suggest this requires 'the ability to quickly and credibly generate politically usable information and move it to where it has the most impact'. As well as involving movements from the Global South as well as from the North, a principal focus of the AAM as a NSM was therefore its emphasis on information politics (Thörn 2007). This was very much a feature of transnational as well as national campaigns aiming to put an end to racism in sport that began in the 1990s, such as 'Football Against Racism in Europe' (FARE), 'Let's Kick Racism Out of Football' and 'Kick it Out' in the United Kingdom.

Disability rights

The disability rights movement 'is informed not only by the experience of disabled people (sic), but by the civil rights movement, movements of African-American and other minority groups, the women's rights movement and by the current movement of gay and lesbian rights' (B. Robertson 1998, quoted in Winter 2003, p. 57). The relationship between the disability rights movement and different rights movements is brought out very sharply in this quotation. As we will also see with the LGBT rights movement, social movements learn from the experiences of and thus develop in the context of other movements. Disabled people's collective action thus fits very well with Touraine's conception of NSMs, that Oliver (1990, p. 113) described as 'culturally innovative in that they are part of the underlying struggles for genuine participatory democracy, social equality and justice, which have arisen out of the crisis of industrial culture'. Winter (2003, p. 33) discusses the rise of the Disability Rights Movement (DRM) in the United States as a solution to a problem: the 'oppressive marginalization of persons with disabilities'. The aims of the DRM were to empower people with disabilities to take control of their lives and to influence social policies and practices. The overall aim was to replace oppression with empowerment and marginalization with full inclusion in society (Fleischer and Zames 2011). These are goals very similar to those of the CRM.

The DRM – as with other social movements – can be understood to pass through a series of phases. Winter suggests there are three main ones: first comes the 'definition of the problem' – in this case the personal and institutional oppression faced by people with disabilities. This led to the critique of the 'medical model of disability' that was seen to be a main part of the problem confronting disabled people. As Siebers 2008 (p. 3) explains, the medical model 'defines disability as an individual defect lodged in the person, a defect that must be cured or eliminated if the person is to achieve full capacity as a human being'. The critique of this model, and the alternative 'social model' of disability, involves seeing disability 'not as an individual defect but as the product of social injustice, one that requires not the cure or elimination of the defective person but significant changes in the social and built environment' (Siebers 2008, p. 3). The difference in perspective leads to being able to distinguish between impairment and disability, and between stigmatization and marginalization, when considering the position of disabled people in society.

The next phase in the life of a social movement is 'the solution' which is partly ideological and involved, in this case, the development of the 'social model of disability', but also leads to legislative and organizational changes. In the United States, for example, the history of efforts to bring about legislative solutions began in the 1950s with paralyzed military veterans and people with disabilities seeking greater accessibility. Such issues for people with disabilities became one of civil rights and not just help. In 1965, a national commission in the United States set out to study 'the problems involved in making all Federal buildings accessible to disabled citizens' (Winter 2003, p. 36). The DRM actively sought to develop and protect 'the integration and full inclusion of individuals with disabilities into the mainstream of American society' as expressed in federal law ('The Rehabilitation Act 1973' quoted in Winter 2003, p. 34). The beginning of disability activism in the United States is often located with students with quadriplegia at the University of California-Berkeley in the 1960s. Inspired by the civil rights movement, Ed Roberts and other disabled students began to campaign to live in 'regular' accommodation (rather than the infirmary where Roberts had been expected to live while studying). They argued for accessible housing, classrooms, public transport and pedestrian routes and founded the first Center for Independent Living (CIL) in 1972.

The third phase in the course of a social movement can be conceived as 'the aftermath'. This features the recognition that there is a need to maintain the gains made by legislative and other reforms, possibly by strengthening the means of ensuring meaningful compliance. The slogan 'Nothing about us, without us' began to be used in conjunction with disability activism to emphasize the idea that no policy should be decided by any representative without the full and direct participation of members of the group(s) affected by that policy (Charlton 2000). This phase of the social movement sees the further raising of consciousness of and about people with disabilities and a related number of increasing demands. To illustrate this, we briefly account for the development of the disability rights movement in the United Kingdom.

In the United Kingdom, the first campaigning organizations controlled by people with disabilities dated from the late nineteenth century – the British Deaf Association, 1890 and the National League for the Blind 1899. As Davis (1993, p. 287) notes, however, while these and many other organizations that developed in the United Kingdom over the course of the first 60 years of the twentieth century demonstrated, people with disabilities could run their own organizations, there was little 'cohesion between them'. Some sought charity, others challenged it, 'some wanted integration, others supported segregation; some were working for greater control by disabled people over their own lives, others were calling for more professional providers and other "experts"' (Davis 1993, p. 287). During this period, social injustice was seen as a problem for the individual disabled person (medical model) not the society in which it took place (social model).

The formation of the Union of the Physically Impaired Against Segregation (UPIAS) in the United Kingdom in 1972 came about partly as a result of a letter by Paul Hunt published in *The Guardian* newspaper, calling for a radical new disability organization to be formed. The UPIAS then published a document laying out the 'Fundamental Principles of Disability', espousing the social model of disability, which had been drafted by Vic Finkelstein. UPIAS formalized a critique of the medical model of disability, along with a rejection of a reliance on (well meaning) 'experts' to solve disabled people's problems for them. UPIAS adopted a definition of disability that clearly located it as a result of the social conditions which people with disabilities encounter and not their own personal impairments: 'the disadvantage or restriction of ability caused by a contemporary social organisation which takes little or no account of people who have physical impairment and thus excludes them from participation in the mainstream of social activities. Physical disability is therefore a particular form of social oppression' (cited in Davis 1993, p. 289).

The early 1970s were 'pivotal' for the DRM (Davis 1993, p. 288) and soon after many other solidarity groups connecting disabled people with different struggles were established in the United Kingdom (e.g. GEMMA, disabled lesbians; Sisters Against Disablement, disabled women; and Disabled People Against Apartheid, in solidarity with black people in South Africa). UPIAS encouraged its members to have 'pride' in themselves, but also 'offered an incentive for the growing number of organisations to come together' in order to struggle for social change (Davis 1993, p. 289). The British Council of Organisations of Disabled People (BCODP), formed in 1981 from representatives of 16 groups controlled by disabled people, was the end result (and UPIAS was wound up in 1990). In December 1981, three representatives of BCODP attended the First World Congress of the Disabled Peoples' International (DPI) in Singapore (Davis 1993, p. 285). Within ten years, membership of BCODP had risen to over 80 different groups and the DPI had increased its scope to 70 national assemblies run by disabled people around the world (Davis 1993, p. 285).

How activists in different social movements in different societies translate their visions and goals into plausible rights claims varies. Some social movements do pursue changes to laws; some do not. The mobilization of law in the case of disabled rights social movement actors in the United States (and the United Kingdom) is not a distinctive strategy of all social movements but the product of a consensus that developed that legal alterations were needed to enhance the lives of disabled people (Vanhala 2011). Strategic litigation as a mobilization device works for some, but not all social groups, and at different times in their development (Vanhala 2011, p. 6). Social movement politics is thus bound up with social movement identity politics. Equally activist identities are bound up with different social movements as the following illustrates. Vic Finkelstein, co-founder of UPIAS, had been deported to the United Kingdom from his native South Africa for his support of the anti-apartheid movement in the 1960s. He had been in a wheelchair since 1954 when he broke his neck attempting to pole-vault. Following treatment and rehabilitation at the Stoke Mandeville hospital in Buckinghamshire in the United Kingdom, Finkelstein returned to South Africa and became a member of the Congress of Democrats, an organization for white people in the anti-apartheid Congress Alliance which provided covert support to banned groups. On coming to Britain as a refugee, he continued to have contact with the ANC but also began to meet politically active disabled people. As well as being prominent in setting up the BCODP and becoming its first chair, he was one of the British delegates to the First World Congress of the DPI in 1981.

Finkelstein's life thus linked two of the leading human rights movements of the past 50 years, but tragically this was a result of his accident in sport. What other connections are there between sport and disability rights activists? What has been the relationship between disability rights activism and major sports events for people with disabilities? Provision for disability sport, both for the physically disabled and for the learning disabled, has been limited in all nations until relatively recently. Sport for the physically disabled was first developed after World War I and more fully after World War II, especially in the context of attempts to improve the lives of those with spinal injuries. Here we will briefly discuss the development of the Special Olympics and the Paralympic Games.

The idea of sport as a means for improving the health, self-esteem and general well-being of those with learning disabilities was not taken up until the founding of the 'Special Olympics' movement in the United States in the 1960s (Barton 2009; http://www.specialolympics.org, [accessed 4 October 2012]). The purpose of the Special Olympics movement was 'to provide sporting opportunities for the learning disabled regardless of ability or age with an emphasis on participation rather than excellence' (Barton et al. 2011, p. 12). Eunice Kennedy Shriver, from the influential American Kennedy family and former director of the Kennedy Foundation, established summer camps (which she called 'Camp Shriver') for people with learning disabilities in 1962. The staging of the first international (World) Special Olympics took place in Chicago in 1968 when Shriver pledged that the Special Olympics would offer people with intellectual disabilities everywhere 'the chance to play, the chance to compete and the chance to grow' (http://www.specialolympics.org/eunice_kennedy_shriver_biography.aspx, [accessed 4 October 2012]).

In 1971, the United States Olympic Committee (USOC) gave the Special Olympics organization official approval to use the name 'Olympics' in the United States, and in 1988 the IOC also endorsed use of the name worldwide. Organized through clubs taking part in national and international competitions the Special Olympics is based on recognizable Olympic formats such as opening and closing ceremonies, the awarding of gold, silver and bronze medals, host cities and a four yearly cycle of the major international events. At the time of writing, for example, the next Special Olympics World Winter Games will be held in PyeongChang, South Korea, from 29 January 2013 to 6 February 2013, and the next Special Olympics World Summer Games will be held in Los Angeles, California, in July 2015 (http://www.specialolympics.org, [accessed 4 October 2012]).

In 2004, the Special Olympics received support through legislation for the first time in the United States, when the 'Special Olympics Sport and Empowerment Act' was ratified. This gave $US15 million every year for the next 5 years to Special Olympics programmes. During a visit to the Special Olympics World Winter Games in Boise, Idaho, in 2009, US Vice President Joe Biden stated that special needs advocacy was 'a civil rights movement'. In 1986, the UN launched 'The International Year of the Special Olympics' and the Special Olympics has continued to develop beyond the United States. In the United Kingdom, for example, Special Olympics Great Britain was formally established in 1978 and was first represented by athletes in the 1979 International Special Olympics. Following Eunice Shriver's death in 2009, her son Tim Shriver has since become CEO and chairman of the Special Olympics board. As Special Olympics International, the Special Olympics currently has a presence in over 200 countries (http://www.specialolympics.org, [accessed 4 October 2012]). It is interesting to contrast this 'movement' with the key developments and evolution of the Paralympic Games.

Unlike the Special Olympics for the learning disabled, the Paralympic Games, which includes some events for the learning impaired, has become a component part of the Olympic Games mega-event spectacle. Howe (2008, pp. 15–37) describes three stages in the development of sport for the disabled that lead to this situation. As we have noted, sport provision was initially designed to aid in the *rehabilitation* of war wounded service personnel, and thus reintroduction into productive (working) life (Anderson 2003). This certainly was the main impetus behind Dr Ludwig Guttmann's, a German Jewish neurologist, establishment of a National Spinal Injuries Unit at the Ministry of Pensions Hospital in Stoke Mandeville in the United Kingdom in 1943. The second phase in the development of sport for the disabled developed from this in terms of the recognition that *participation* in sport could be beneficial to disabled people in wider terms than simply their employability could be. Athletes in different impairment groups – those with spinal cord injuries, the visually impaired, the hearing impaired, cerebral palsy and amputees – became organized through the International Organization of Sport for the Disabled (IOSD). The IOSD introduced a systematic classification system to create equal conditions for athletes to compete with these different impairments.

The third phase in the development of sport and the disabled involves the development of *high-performance achievement* sport, organized through the International Paralympic Committee (IPC), which was first established in September 1989. It was from this time on that Howe (2008, p. 16) suggests we can talk about a 'Paralympic Movement' as the forming of the IPC brought together a number of different organizations that had previously represented sport for the various impairment groups. The story of this development in sport for disabled people can be found in several sources (see for example Bailey 2008; Brittain 2008, 2010 and 2012; and Howe 2008). The term 'paralympic' is now understood to refer to the fact that sports events for disabled people take place alongside (or 'para') the Olympic Games. Initially it was considered that the word combined 'paraplegic' and Olympic, but this was not accurate as people with disabilities other than paraplegia participated in the Paralympic Games. The history of international sports events for the disabled can be charted back to the day in July 1948 when the Stoke Mandeville Games began at the same time as the London Olympic Games of that year were commencing 35 miles away. Use of the name 'Mandeville' by the local organizers for one of the two mascots for the London Olympic and Paralympic Games of 2012 tried to reinforce this 64-year inheritance (Brittain 2012). However, the first generally recognized Paralympic Games was held in Rome in 1960. It was here for the first time that the Paralympic events used some of the same locations as the Olympic Games. Formal recognition and use of the term by the IOC, however, did not occur until the Seoul Olympics in 1988. The roots of 'paralympism' as a concept underpinning the development of sport for the disabled are thus embedded in the history of both the rehabilitative and the participatory models, but truly became focused on *high-performance* sport after 1988. As Howe (2008, p. 19) remarks, 'Guttmann's lasting legacy is the fact that physical activity and sport are widely acknowledged to be central to contemporary rehabilitation for traumatic and congenital impairments'.

In 2012, the Paralympic Games Opening and Closing Ceremonies were spectacular, and drew attention to the diversity of human kind and even featured performances referring to the Universal Declaration of Human Rights. But what is the connection between this and other major international sports events for disabled athletes and the disabled majority? Some journalists suggest that the 2012 Paralympic effect has had a positive impact and the number of enquiries from people with disabilities in the United Kingdom to get involved in sport has grown (Walker and Holman 2012). Others suggest that there is no significant impact on the lives of 'ordinary' disabled people (Brindle 2012; Muir 2012). At the time of writing, it is still too early to tell if a positive impact will be sustained or if there is the sports infrastructure in place to support an increase in demand from people with disabilities. What is clear is that the disability rights movement has been wary of and somewhat distanced from the sport for disabled 'movements' during the past 50 plus years. Why is that? We want to suggest three reasons.

First, disability sport relies upon medical classification and evaluation on the basis of impairment in order to create the different classes of sport, whether it is participatory or competitive. As we have seen, the disability rights movement developed a major critique of the medical model of disability, and thus it may not have wanted to engage fully with practices that rely so much on such forms of medical scrutiny and classification. Second, another aspect of the politics of the disability rights movement has been to develop organizations that avoid paternalistic relationships between the able-bodied and the disabled. Yet the main organizations for sport for the disabled, including the SO, the IPC and the IOSD, can be seen as expert-led – rather than collective and self-organized bodies – that in some ways treat athletes as 'charity cases' (Howe 2008, p. 36). This links to the third reason why the disability rights movement and the main international sports for disabled movements have not shared common ground. The practice of high-performance sport is not an inclusive activity. As Howe (2008, p. 34) puts it, both the Olympic and Paralympic Games 'exclude the (dis) abled or, to put it another way, "those who can't"'. Sport, particularly high-performance sport, is fundamentally underpinned by the 'ideology of ability'. This entails a view that ability is the marker of being truly human (Siebers

2008, see Chapter 9). Siebers (2008, p. 178) argues instead that 'human-rights discourse will never break free from the ideology of ability until it includes disability as a defining characteristic of human beings'.

LGBT rights

Private, consensual, same-sex relationships are illegal in over 70 countries, with punishment ranging from imprisonment to death. The struggle for rights for people with different sexual orientations is ongoing (Baird 2004). Even the umbrella term used to describe these rights has frequently altered to try and better capture the focus of the movement. This section will use the relatively short and well-known acronym, LGBT, standing for Lesbian, Gay, Bisexual and Transsexual persons, while recognizing that longer alternatives exist that embrace more of the diversity of sexual orientations and gender identities (see Symons 2010, pp. 260–3 and p. 264 fn.1 for a discussion of sex, gender and sexuality terminology).

As we noted earlier, acknowledgement of LGBT rights is a part of the European Union (EU) Fundamental (Human) Rights Charter; but attempts are still being made to get them accepted at the UN and among many of the governments that form part of the Commonwealth. Dr Navanethem ('Navi') Pillay, UN High Commissioner for Human Rights, wrote in 2012 that 'the case for extending the same rights for lesbian, gay, bisexual and transgender (LGBT) persons as those enjoyed by everyone else is neither radical nor complicated' (in UN HRC 2012, p. 7). Yet the UN does not have a core treaty or convention on sexual orientation. Dr Pillay (UN HRC 2012, p. 7) argues that the case for extending rights to LGBT persons rests on the two pillars of international human rights law: equality and non-discrimination. Homophobic attitudes plus lack of legal protection from discrimination create conditions oppressive to LGBT persons. In 2011 the UN Human Rights Council (HRC) adopted a resolution expressing grave concern at violence and discrimination meted out to individuals based on their sexual orientation and gender identity. Although not legally binding on UN member states, the publication *Born Free and Equal. Sexual Orientation and Gender Identity in International Human Rights Law* (UN HRC 2012) set out legal obligations that states have towards LGBT people. These obligations were based on five main issues of concern that the UN HRC uncovered after it conducted a universal periodic review of the records of all UN states. The obligations identified by the UN HRC (2012, p. 13) were protection from homophobia and transphobic violence; prevention of the torture and cruel treatment of LGBT persons; repeal of laws criminalizing homosexuality; prohibition of discrimination on the basis of sexual orientation and gender identity; and safeguarding of freedom of expression for LGBT people.

The UN HRC review followed shortly after the publication of two documents concerning LGBT rights in the 2000s: the 'Declaration of Montreal' that was made during the International Conference on LGBT Human Rights of the first World Outgames in Montreal in 2006 (http://www.declarationofmontreal. org/declaration/[accessed 8 October 2012]); and the Yogyakarta Principles on the Application of International Human Rights Law in Relation to Sexual Orientation and Gender Identity that were agreed after a meeting of international human rights law experts in the same year (http://www.yogyakartaprinciples.org [accessed 8 October 2012]). Yet as Joke Swiebel, one of the main drafters of the Declaration of Montreal, argues deeper engagement with LGBT organizations at the UN has 'been blocked by the cultural and religious values of some of the organization's main actors' (Swiebel 2009, p. 20). She attributes the relative success in getting sexual orientation and the rights of LGBT persons 'on the agenda' at the EU, but not at the UN, to a number of factors relating to the strategies adopted and the institutions involved.

The organisers of the International Conference on LGBT Human Rights of the 1st World Outgames sought to fill this gap by drafting the 'Declaration of Montreal' (Swiebel 2009, p. 28) that summarized the main demands of the international LGBT movement at the time, but also 'tried to illustrate that, by defining LGBT issues as human rights issues, the very concept of human rights had to change; that concept should no longer be allowed to reinforce the traditional, male-dominated, heteronormative vision of the world' (Swiebel 2009, p. 28). This was done by aligning the demands of the LGBT movement with those of the women's' movement: '"our right to control our bodies and choose how we wish to live . . . (and) . . . to challenge the rigidity of the fixed roles allocated to women and men and the dominance of heterosexual male norms and interests"' (quoted in Swiebel 2009, p. 28). The Declaration proposed the creation of a UN convention on the elimination of all forms of discrimination on the basis of sexual orientation and gender identity and has been adopted by several municipal authorities around the world, including the Montreal borough of Ville-Marie. In addition, it was adopted by one of Canada's three major political parties, the New Democratic Party (NDP), in August 2006. It is important to note, however, that the convention has no binding legal status. International developments thus have coincided with domestic cultural and policy change. In Canada, for example, the rights focus of the LGBT movement and ready acceptance of the Declaration of Montreal can part be attributed to the much earlier adoption of a Charter of Rights and Freedom in 1982, which brought about a 'rights revolution' in Canada (Smith 1999).

The politics of challenging the privileging of heterosexuality (or heteronormativity), at the core of the LGBT movement, have developed over time. Although there had been homophile organizations earlier in the twentieth century, and 'Gay is good' as a slogan was developed in the early 1960s, the

Gay Liberation Front (GLF) developed after incidents at the Stonewall Inn in Greenwich Village, New York, in June 1969 when gay and lesbians converged to protest against police tactics surrounding this 'gay' bar. In the late 1960s and early 1970s, the gay liberation movement adopted a collectivist ideology that sought to challenge the social structures of oppression rather than focus on rights alone, that was perceived as a more individualistic ideology at the time (Kollman and Waites 2009, p. 4). The GLF was short-lived but it was emulated internationally. As Kollman and Waites note 'since the emergence of gay liberation movements in Western countries in the late 1960s and early 1970s LGBT organizations have framed their demands in terms of equality and/or liberation, but human rights discourses did not become central to national and international debates over gender and sexuality until the early 1990s' (2009, p. 2).

In the early 1990s, the LGBT movements took a 'human rights' turn – although LGBT rights were absent from previous conceptions of human rights and this is 'suggestive of the absence of LGBT people from previous conceptions of the human' (Kollman and Waites 2009, p. 2). The human rights 'turn' owed much to the strengthening of transnational LGBT networks. The International Lesbian and Gay Association (ILGA), established in 1978, had remained a loose affiliation of disparate national groups until the 1990s when it created six regional groups covering all the continents. Another prominent LGBT human rights NGO, the International Gay and Lesbian Human Rights Commission, was created by United States and Russian LGBT activists. Alongside AI and HRW, these made up a more influential global network of human rights LGBT campaigners (Kollman and Waites 2009, p. 4).

Griffin (2012) outlines and identifies the key moments in the development of a 'LGBT sports equality movement', especially in the United States, since that time in the mid-1970s. For example, 6 years after the Stonewall riots, former NFL player Dave Kopay came out. As she notes, before 1975, 'the cultural social consensus was that being LGBT was sinful, sick and immoral and publicly identifying oneself as LGBT invited ridicule and discrimination' (Griffin 2012, p. 2). Sexual prejudice and heterosexism have been and remain pervasive in many areas of sport. Yet there is a different environment than three decades ago. Campaigns against homophobia have taken place and continue to increasingly do so, in sport, although the few male athletes who have come out have usually done so at or towards the end of their careers, like NFL's David Kopay, NBA's John Amaechi and Rugby Union's Gareth Thomas. NBA centre, Jason Collins, was the main exception to this when he came out in a feature article in *Sports Illustrated* in April 2013 (http://sportsillustrated.cnn.com/magazine/news/20130429/jason-collins-gay-nba-player/[last accessed 13 May 2013]). In the professional football (soccer) leagues in Europe, there have (at the time of writing) only been three male players who have publicly self-identified as gay – the late Justin Fashanu, who played for various teams in England between 1978 and 1997, Robbie Rogers, who came out after leaving Leeds United in January 2013 and Anton Hysén in Sweden (Barkham 2011, McRae 2013). Caudwell (2011) provides a valuable analysis of the way that football fans in England produce homophobia within the spaces of football stadia. She demonstrates the normalization of homophobic chanting and homophobic gesticulation, and suggests that it is dominant ideas surrounding gay men's sexual activity, penetrative sex and men's bodies, which are central to these articulations of homophobia. She notes the ways that 'The Justin Campaign' – an 'anti-homophobia in football' project established in Brighton, United Kingdom, on 2 May 2008 – has sought to make the tragic death of Justin Fashanu (in May 1998) visible and his plight as a young gay black player.

Unlike the disability rights movement and its relationship to major international sports events for disabled people, Symons (2010, p. 241) stresses the importance of other social movements emanating from civil rights, second-wave feminism and gay liberation movements of the 1960s and 1970s in Western societies for the formation of the Gay Games in 1982. For example, the founder of the Gay Games, Dr Tom Waddell, shifted politics 'from Republican to radical left in the 1960s' (Symons 2010, p. 15) informed by his experience as an Olympic decathlon athlete, the OPHR at the 1968 Mexico City Olympic Games and later his work with the Black Panther movement (Symons 2010, p. 241). The Gay Games iterations and issues have included since then the use of competitive sport by the organisers to maintain LGBT sport and normalize LGBT sexualities, as well as its financial viability based on emulating the Olympic Games through such means as the use of corporate sponsorship (Lenskyj 2005).

In its early stages, Waddell and others organizing the Gay Games mobilized dominant sport ideologies that position the body in sport as both normal and healthy to counter the pathologizing of LGBT sexualities (Caudwell 2012). Symons (2010, pp. 41–4 and pp. 70–71) captures this well in the subheadings to Chapters 3 and 4 of her book: 'we are normal' and 'we are healthy'. Both Gay Games I (1982) and Gay Games II (1986) took place in the context of the attempt to launch a Gay 'Olympic' Games and HIV/AIDS in the 1980s. But as with other major international sport events, political, economic and ideological conflicts and tensions underpin their development. Unlike the Special Olympics, the USOC would not allow Waddell to use the word 'Olympic' in the title of 'his' event and so the name Gay Games developed. The Gay Games moved away from North America for the first time in 1998 and 2002 (to Amsterdam and Sydney respectively) but issues around tolerance and acceptance and financial sustainability continued to underpin them. In 1994, Gay Games IV reached 'a watershed . . . organisers maximized the significance and resources of New York as one of the leading commercial, media, fashion and political centres of the world. The emphasis on celebrity, big and brash events and commercial success was certainly centre stage' (Symons 2010, p. 146).

Internal fissures over participation, competition, finance and using the event to promote cultural, political and social rights agendas lead to the creation of two major international sports events for LGBT people in 2006. Symons (2010, pp. 217–40) discusses in detail the split that developed in the Gay Games movement resulting from a breakdown in contract negotiations between the Federation of the Gay Games (FGG) and the organizers for what was going to the seventh Gay Games in Montreal in 2006. Montreal had won the right to host the seventh Gay Games with a mixed programme of sport, culture and human rights. The FGG wanted a more focused GG with sport at the centre and less emphasis on culture and human rights (Symons 2010, p. 12). The Montreal 2006 organizers and FGG disagreed, and the latter awarded the Gay Games VII to Chicago instead. A rival international gay and lesbian sports association – the Gay and Lesbian International Sports Association (GLISA) – was developed and the 1st World Outgames were held in Montreal just 2 weeks after Gay Games VII were held in Chicago in 2006. The Outgames attracted substantially fewer sports participants than it had originally estimated including 'lower attendance of US athletes who previously made up over 40 per cent of people at a Gay Games' (Symons 2010, p. 239).

Montreal 2006 also created a significant financial deficit for the organisers, which tarnished the reputation of the inaugural event, although the conference that preceded it made a major input into LGBT international politics as we have already seen with the Declaration of Montreal launched at the largest ever conference for LGBT human rights. As the director of the 2nd World Outgames, held in Copenhagen in 2009, Utte Elbaek said '"We want to . . . put the focus on human rights"' (Eriksen 2009, p. 24). The boards of both GLISA and FGG met in Montreal in May 2012 to try to establish a single quadrennial event, but were unable to reach agreement, so the next events in their respective competitions will take place in 2013 and 2017, and 2014 and 2018. The 3rd World Outgames will be held in Antwerp in Belgium in summer 2013 and Gay Games IX in Cleveland in 2014.

Symons (2010, p. 245) identifies various tensions at the heart of the rationale for the Gay Games. The Gay Games provides a space for LGBT persons to enjoy and achieve in sport in a welcoming and supportive environment. But this potentially goes against the goal of integrating LGBT persons into wider society, by providing a ghettoized space, leaving homophobia and homophobic practices in sport and elsewhere in society untouched. Another of the tensions involves the contrast between the mainstreaming and transformative aspects of the Gay Games sports programme. Mainstreaming or sanctioning 'proves that lesbian and gay sports are conducted in strict accordance with the norms of sport' (Pronger 2000, p. 232). However, the norms of sport are often heterosexist and 'two-sexed' that does not neatly fit 'the more fluid and diverse sexed and gendered lives of LGBTIQ peoples' (Symons 2010, p. 245); hence some people, who are transgendered, would be excluded. Rules surrounding drug taking also create problems for those members of the LGBT community who require drugs for serious medical conditions, such as transsexuals undergoing sex reassignment therapy. The distinction between the drive for professionalization and the community orientation of the Gay Games created a division within the LGBT sports movement and a 'massive smorgasbord of programme offerings to participate in, watch and be part of' (Symons 2010, p. 245). While some critics question the progressiveness of the development of the Gay Games (e.g. Davidson f/c), nonetheless as Symons (2010, p. 247) concludes, 'In a largely homophobic and heterosexist world the staging of the Gay Games, the implementation of progressive participation policies and the development of an extensive international lesbian and gay sports movement have been significant achievements'.

Conclusion

For the CRM/anti-racism, disability rights and LGBT rights movements, political developments in the 1950s and 1960s gave rise to a range of similar strategies in the struggle for rights: non-violent protests and boycotts as a strategy to shame and embarrass their oppressors, as well as mass marches and demonstrations, were part of the weaponry used in the struggles. Equally issues of mainstreaming, gaining legitimacy and transformation underpin all three social movements involved with rights and sport (Symons 2010): mainstreaming and becoming part of the existing sport system carried the cost of entering into structures that were racist, disabilist and/or homophobic. Yet, to gain legitimacy, athletes had to participate to a certain extent in mainstream sport and abide by the official regulations and only then might progressive transformation take place within sport. With respect to 'race', the overt barriers may appear to be down but the struggle against discriminatory and inequitable treatment against people of colour continues in more subtle ways. With disability, there is greater acceptance of the abilities of athletes with disabilities (the inclusion of double-amputee South African athlete Oscar Pistorius in two track events in the 2012 Summer Olympics marked a new era for athletes with disabilities) but disability sport raises issues around the use of new technology to enhance predominantly exclusive and excluding, high-performance, sport. In the case of LGBT rights, sexual orientation, gender identity and homosexuality continue to be highly regulated in many societies. The three movements thus share political tensions stemming from the choices of seeking reform or revolution, mainstreaming or transformation, and assimilation or separatism.

This chapter has considered the *rights movements* as a plurality of different campaigns, protests and demonstrations not all bearing the label 'human rights'. 'Human rights', as with 'movement', gains greatest clarity after a campaign or protest has happened, while at its core is 'the idea of protecting individuals (and perhaps groups) from *the abuse of power*' (Freeman 2011, p. 201). Equally it needs to be noted that no teleological end point is reached in this story. That is, there is no (inevitable) happy ending. The movement against the apartheid regime in South Africa remains the only major example of a successful human rights campaign involving sport, although the build-up to the Olympic and Paralympic Games in Beijing in the summer of 2008 offers a valuable example of a more recent concentration of social movement activity concerning human rights in a sports context (Brownell 2012; Kidd 2010; Rowe 2012; Worden 2008).

5

Sport and the Global Peace Movement

This chapter explores the history, characteristics, politics and implications of the global peace movement as it connects to sport and physical culture. The central argument of the chapter is that while the peace movement has connected to and informed the organization of sport at least as far back as the nineteenth century – for example, through the internationalist ethos that underpinned the revival of the modern Olympic Games – notable and significant distinctions can now be seen between the oppositional and resistive political goals that characterized the peace movement during most of the twentieth century and the current trend towards sport as a 'tool' useful for inclusive peace education. Commensurate with this shift, rather than engaging in political resistance against militarism, many of the current efforts connecting sport to peace tend to theorize, position and mobilize sport as a tool or metaphor by which to achieve peaceful relations through improved social and political understanding and/or effective post-war reconciliation (e.g. Dyck 2011; Gasser and Levinsen 2004; Höglund and Sundberg 2008; Sugden 2006, among others). As such, these approaches connect to a recent 'cultural turn' in twenty-first-century peace organizing, in which efforts have been concentrated more on building relations of peaceful understanding and less on challenging the undemocratic militarism of domestic and international relations and social life more broadly that constitute the traditional resistive principles associated with the peace movement (see Galtung 1988). Through historical examples, and contemporary comparisons, the implications of this distinction are discussed.

The chapter proceeds in three parts. In the first section, the history and features of the peace movement and various peace movement organizations (PMOs) are discussed, drawing attention to the specificities of its political ethos and the shifting goals and approaches of the global peace movement since the late nineteenth century. This is followed by an analysis of the ways in which some peace activists and PMOs have connected to and shaped sport and of how various athletes and sport organizations have come to approach and support struggles for peace. The chapter concludes with a review of critical, scholarly appraisals of sport and the peace movement and a discussion of the implications for sport and peace when the traditional ethos of the peace movement is contrasted against the current turn towards more inclusive, yet individualized, notions of peace education and a commitment to building a 'culture of peace'.

History and features of the global peace movement

Any discussion of the global peace movement must recognize its historical, political and geographical specificities. The peace movement has been marked by trends, divisions and shifts in its organization, goals, geographies, membership and strategies. Yet, despite these pluralities and divergences, some important historical trajectories and ideological similarities can be established that allow for a general conceptual basis of the global peace movement.

It is reasonable to suggest that the roots of the peace movement extend back at least to the early nineteenth century. A general longing for peace following the end of the Napoleonic wars in 1814 facilitated the simultaneous emergence of pacifist communities, or peace societies, in both Britain and the United States. These peace societies were often underpinned by religious and/ or moral commitments to non-violence and the rejection of militarism (Brock 1998). By the late 1800s, a peace movement could be seen within an emerging internationalism and a growing belief in the distinction and rights of nation states, promoted, for example, through the hosting of World's fairs designed to celebrate a global humanity (Quanz 1994). The 'pacifists' who supported this movement put forth critiques about the destructive effects of war and the general illogic of extended militarism and held as their principal concern improved international relations and understanding that would reduce conflict and promote stability and development. The Interparliamentary Union, established in 1892, and the International Peace Bureau based in Switzerland were illustrative of this era and had a direct influence on Alfred Nobel as well as the establishment of the League of Nations (Quanz 1994). This was not a socialist, idealist or utopian movement, but one that embraced a detached realism and practicality in the face of the geo-political challenges posed by the sovereign nation state (Quanz 1994). As discussed further below, this nineteenth-century peace movement contributed to Pierre de Coubertin's ambitions to create the modern Olympic Games based on nation-based character and gentlemanly understanding, and also influenced the ideological positioning of the Olympic Movement itself as an exemplar of peace promotion (Loland and Selliaas 2009; Quanz 1993; Wassong and Muller 2007).

While these features of peace promotion in the nineteenth century were influential, the peace movement proper is generally considered to be a twentieth-century phenomenon. It was after World War II that many in the scientific community began to organize in order to call for a ban of atomic weapons that had led to incredible destruction during wartime and that posed unprecedented potential for devastation on a global scale (Meyer 1999). In turn, the emergence of insurgent and resistive social movements more generally in the 1960s began to include calls for peace, notably the iconic and influential organizing within the United States against the Vietnam War. These movements called for an end to military incursions and the conscription of citizens into military service as part of activism aimed at broad social change. Eventually, the peace movement of the 1980s focused on resisting the proliferation of an international nuclear arms race and calling attention to the threat it posed to nothing less than the future of humanity (Meyer 1999). Many of the efforts of the peace movement in the 1980s focused on critiques of the political logic and rhetoric of the Cold War, and challenged the aggressive and threatening foreign policy of countries like the United States. In this sense, there have been two main political tracks in peace movements since the end of World War II: protests against the proliferation of nuclear weapons (the aspect of the movement that achieved the greatest attention and participation), and opposition to aggressive military intervention and antagonistic foreign policy (Meyer and Whittier 1994; Rose 2000).

Importantly, while some viewed the peace movement of the 1980s as situated primarily in Western Europe (Galtung 1988, p. 380), by this time the peace movement was a global phenomenon; it was active in North America in response to US participation in the Cold War arms race, as well as in regions of South America, resisting military control of the political process. It was also during this time that the global peace movement arguably reached its peak with regard to its social profile and political import, a zenith that was evident in both Europe (Meyer 1999) and the United States (Edwards and Marullo 1995). Indeed, by the end of the twentieth century, the relative invisibility of peace movements as compared to those 20 years earlier led some to conclude that social movements calling for peace had subsided (Meyer 1999; Rochon 1990). From this perspective, one of the features of the peace movement as it reached its apex in the 1980s was its extended social and political reach, but also its reduced depth of critique as it moved from, for example, calls for complete demilitarization of Europe to a specific focus on doing away with Cruise and Pershing missiles (Rochon 1990). In addition, this late twentieth-century peace movement can be characterized by its increased willingness to work with political authority, not simply to challenge it. In this sense, the peace movement, like other social movements, was itself forced to deal with the implications of its own increased political acceptance and palatability. As Rochon (1990, p. 120) argued, 'the strategy of mass mobilization limited the ability of the peace movement to preserve its critique of the political system and to maintain its focus on cultural revolution'. As discussed further below, this trajectory has implications for the current turn towards peace education and a culture of peace as opposed to resistance to military industrialism.

It is important to remember, though, that the declining visibility and even political importance of the peace movement after the Cold War did not result in the absence of active PMOs, nor did it signal a simple reversal of the movement's growth phase (Edwards and Marullo 1995). Indeed, in response to unilateral and even illegal military action by the United States and its allies post-9/11, the global peace movement has enjoyed something of a re-emergence. Some of the features of this re-emerging peace movement are familiar, whereas others are less so. Clearly, the advent of online communication increasingly features in the contemporary peace movement to the extent that current political struggles in and around military conflict can be understood as the struggle against government, military and even complicit media sources to control information (Pickerell and Webster 2006). The contemporary peace movement has also 'evolved' in that it can be seen to have learnt from previous criticisms that peace activism was unpatriotic; it has adopted new discursive strategies to build popular support, such as arguing that ending war is the best way to 'support the troops' (Coy et al. 2008). Importantly, the connectivity and breadth of groups involved in the contemporary peace movement suggests that they do fit within notions of alter-globalization as a 'movement of movements' (Pickerell and Webster 2006). In particular, there has been significant youth engagement in the contemporary peace movement – particularly in protesting against military actions in Iraq – though the public images of this movement, and to some degree its effectiveness in mobilizing support, is regularly and routinely subject to media criticisms (see Cushion 2007).

In the broadest terms then the peace movement has been, and to some degree remains, characterized primarily by its opposition to institutionalized, corporatized and state-supported militarism. As modern states increasingly embraced and normalized militarism in support of domestic security and international relations, and regularly assumed full control of this military power, social movements organized in order to question the sanctity of state-led military power and call for peaceful resolutions to conflict and security threats. Peace historian and theorist Johan Galtung (1988, p. 378) has provided a cogent and useful definition of what can be considered the central mission of this peace movement:

> The essential task of the Peace Movement in a historical perspective is to challenge monopoly control over coercion in general, and military power in particular, by the government in the modern state . . . Thus the basic argument of the Peace Movement is that the state abuses military power. (The Peace Movement) is an expression of fundamental distrust of the responsible state officials, whether military or civilian.

In addition, several other characteristics of the peace movement can be identified. First, its general commitment to resistive politics has regularly overlapped with other social movements, such as human rights, organized labour, women's rights and environmentalism. Thus, while the focus of the peace movement has been opposition to military power, it has always been indispensable, for both ideological and practical reasons, for the peace movement to connect itself to those concerned with power in other formations (Galtung 1988). Indeed, the peace movement that emerged in the latter half of the twentieth century had strong connections to anti- or counter-cultural movements of the 1960s; it was not simply a movement of anti-militarism, but an extension of anti-establishment attitudes and organizing to include calls for peace (Salomon 1986).

For example, as Rose (2000) has documented, organized labour in the United States supported anti-war measures and organizing as far back as the 1880s, given that labour understood the working classes to disproportionately bear the brunt of military policy. Similarly, the peace movement has overlapped on a transnational scale with women's rights and feminist movements since the mid-nineteenth century (Rupp and Taylor 1999) and, in the 1980s, was underpinned by, and intimately connected to, feminist organizing and the women's rights movement that critiqued traditional and aggressive masculinity while calling for legitimate participation of women in social and political life (Meyer and Whittier 1994). Finally, the peace movement has enjoyed strong relationships with organized environmentalism, particularly since the 1970s and 1980s when emerging organizations like Greenpeace brought together concerns with ecology, nuclear proliferation and global poverty as fundamental to long-term and sustainable peace (Mol 2000).

At the same time, these relationships of solidarity between peace activists and other social movements have been marked by ambivalence, and in some cases even conflict. The phenomenon of enforced military conscription came into existence in Europe in the same era as the Declaration of Human Rights (Galtung 1988). The freedoms promised in this new rights-based social contract were simultaneously understood by some to require military defence and enforcement, a logic that clearly put peace and human rights in an ambivalent relationship (Galtung 1988). Similarly, the peace movement and organized labour have had a tenuous relationship that has served to identify and solidify the often stark class distinctions between the two (Rose 2000). After World War II, the workers' movement in the United States tended to support US military expansion as necessary for creating and maintaining jobs, and viewed the peace movement as a problematically socialist enterprise (Rose 2000). Conversely, during anti-Vietnam protests of the 1960s, many peace activists came to view organized labour as connected to the 'establishment' and therefore as part of the social structures against which they were protesting (Rose 2000). There was even tension in the case of peace activism and women's movements, as feminists in the 1980s called for their place as leaders and actors in peace organizing, not just social and domestic support for the men who had led calls for peace in the early half of the twentieth century (Meyer and Whittier 1994).

Clearly then, the peace movement has connected to other social movements. Still, it is precisely its focus upon questioning the sanctity of military power specifically that has set peace activism apart from other forms of social activism. By questioning the historically sacrosanct notion that the sovereign and/or state should control military activities unilaterally – and that military service was a laudable and even necessary feature of citizenship in order to protect freedoms and ways of life within modern states – the peace movement succeeded in drawing attention to military power alongside cultural, economic and political power as a central element of social formation and stratification and one that should be subject to democratic processes (Galtung 1988). In historical context, unilateral military power has been one of the last sources of authority and dominance to be targeted by social movement processes and criticized for being undemocratic and oppressive, and it is the peace movement that subjected this form of power to scrutiny.

A further characteristic that applies across the peace movement is the understanding that its various incarnations emerged not simply due to social discontent, but also in response to shifts in the political and social environment that simultaneously demanded and allowed for its organization (Jenkins and Perrow 2003). In other words, the internal characteristics, visions and goals of the peace movement supporting and advocating for pacifism solidified within the political and policy context that made military action a fact of modern life and militarism a significant social and political issue (Meyer 1999). Rather than understood as a strict ideological adherence to pacifism, therefore, the peace movement is more accurately conceptualized as an historic and organized response to the specificities of the political climate. This was perhaps most notable in the mid-twentieth century amidst concerns over the newly identified 'military/industrial complex', the term used to describe (and to warn against) the self-supporting relationship between corporate and military interests, particularly in the United States (see Mills 1959). As US President Dwight Eisenhower famously stated in his farewell address of 1961, the '. . . conjunction of an immense military establishment and a large arms industry' was negatively shaping the country at economic, political and even spiritual levels (Fallows 2002, p. 46). As Fallows (2002) argues, Eisenhower's concern was not simply that the military/industrial complex increased the likelihood of war and military violence, but that it had cemented the US economy into a system whereby the proliferation of arms was profitable and even necessary for economic growth, a trend that continues through to the present day. In this sense, the peace movement was a response not just to war or the threat thereof, but also to the militarization of everyday life.

With these examples of coherence in mind, one of the notable divergences within the peace movement has been the various ways in which its members have attempted to 'frame' the issue of peace so as to most effectively influence policy, particularly those of states and their militaries. As Marullo et al (1996) describe, when calling for change, the peace movement has attributed war and violent conflict to several sources: the anarchic structure of international relations, the aggressive behaviour of a small number of nations, and/or the social legitimacy and acceptance of violent problem-solving. In turn, the peace movement has framed their struggle along these lines at different times, depending on the context and the strategy under employ. For example, the first of these frames – a focus on international relations – was preferred at the beginning of the twentieth century in the era of world wars, whereas by the time that the peace movement had taken to protesting the Vietnam War, the unilateral aggression of the United States was deemed the principle cause of conflict (Marullo et al. 1996). In turn, the third frame that posits violence as the result of a lack of understanding and peaceful problem-solving can be thought of us the most intelligible in the twenty-first century.

In sum, the peace movement has never operated in any social or political isolation, but has always drawn from, and been connected to, other forms of political organizing and resistance. In addition, the peace movement has tended to understand and define peace itself as not only the absence of physical violence against people but also the absence of structures of inequality, broadly defined, and a concomitant promotion of social justice. In this way, the definition of peace embraced within the peace movement has been one based on non-violence but also one that '. . . embodies the view that economic and political injustice is a form of 'structural violence' and cannot be called a state of peace' (Marullo et al. 1996, p. 13, drawing on Galtung 1969). In keeping with the theoretical framework under employ in this book, the general characteristics of the global peace movement can be identified as follows. The collective identity of the peace movement is one of pacifism and belief in and commitment to non-violent means of problem-solving particularly in the face of international conflict and threats to domestic security. The opposition of the peace movement has been directed at the sanctity and normativity of violence, and threats thereof, as a legitimate means of global politics, as well as an opposition to militarism as policy, particularly as institutionalized through national governments, international allies (such as the North Atlantic Treaty Organization, NATO) and supranational organizations. For example, the global peace movement of the 1980s formed around, and was regularly identified by, its opposition to NATO's infamous 1979 double-track decision that deployed 572 nuclear weapons across Western Europe (Salomon 1986). Even though the goals of the peace movement have varied between calls for transarmamentism (i.e. doing away with the most dangerous weapons, such as nuclear warheads) to disarmamentism, meaning a complete removal of the military (Galtung 1988), the movement has been unified by its calls to reject and resist policies of militarism and violence. In other words, as Salomon (1986) remarked, the peace movement of the 1980s was fundamentally concerned with seeking to alter security policies and challenge the accepted notion of military deterrence. Finally, the totality of the peace movement has been towards a de-militarized, and increasingly democratic geo-politics, one based on negotiation and understanding rather than the utility of the threat of war and the Cold War logic of 'mutually assured destruction'.

Like most social movements, it is difficult to assess in any absolute terms the actual influence of the peace movement on government policy and decision-making, or the success of the movement in challenging militarism and threats of war. Meyer (1999) argues that the peace movement did play a role in ending the Cold War by shifting, and ultimately constraining, the political palatability of aggressive military policy, much like social movements had succeeded in making the Vietnam War socially and politically unpopular. The sheer numbers of people participating in the peace movement and demonstrations of the 1980s made it increasingly difficult for leaders of the time, like US President Ronald Reagan and New Zealand Prime Minister David Lange, as well as organizations like NATO, to justify aggressive military policies or to offer these as part of their election platforms. Still, the extent to which the peace movement has made any direct incursion into the end of particular wars or even reductions in military policy is difficult to quantify and remains a topic of ongoing debate and analysis.

It is here though that an important shift needs to be recognized, particularly for its implications for connecting the current peace movement and PMOs to sport and physical activity. As the preceding paragraph shows, an organized and oppositional peace movement still clearly operates and has even remobilized and reinvented itself post-9/11. Yet, some of the most recently organized initiatives calling for peace, particularly those connected to sport, can be viewed as produced and constrained by an institutional, and even populist, move away from political reactions and opposition to violence and militarism and towards 'cultural responses' to the problems of war and violence (see Adams 2000; Mayor 2004; De Rivera 2004; Smith Page 2001). This shift was evident in the conceptualization of, and broad support for, the United Nations' designation of 2000 as the *International Year for the Culture of Peace* and was also seen in UNESCO's development of the *Culture of Peace News Network*, an initiative designed to offer an international repository for people to record and share local peace initiatives (Smith Page 2001). In the broadest terms, these actions were deemed necessary and appropriate steps to begin a paradigm shift from a 'culture of war' to a 'culture of peace' given that global peace efforts at the end of the twentieth century were faced with the realization that they had largely failed to convince national governments to acknowledge or even recognize the extent to which global geo-politics continued to be underpinned by a fundamental culture of war and militarism (Adams 2000).

This failure was particularly significant given the military violence in the Balkans at the time, and further solidified by the attacks of 9/11 and subsequent invasion of Iraq. As a result, a *Declaration and Programme of Action on a Culture of Peace* was adopted by the United Nations based on eight subject areas: Education, Sustainable development, Human rights, Gender equality, Democratic participation, Understanding and tolerance, Participatory communication, and International peace and security. While social progress in each of these areas as they connect to peace align with the traditional goals of the peace movement, they should also be recognized as signifying a shift in the orientation of peace-focused social action, away from opposition to powerful institutions of militarism and towards cultural solutions and bases of peace. Smith Page (2001, p. 348) describes this trend in the peace movement:

> In many ways, the culture of peace movement reflects the trend within peace research and theory towards a greater emphasis on an intrapersonal interpretation of peace. One can trace in the work of influential writers within the field of peace research a greater tendency to seeking cultural solutions for the problem of war.

Thus, while this call to adopt a culture of peace model as the basis of a new global peace movement aligns with the trends of interconnected social 'movements of movements', the current importance and agency of civil society organizations, and approaches to alter-globalization based on new subjectivities (Pleyers 2010), it also represents a significant shift in the political orientation of global peace movements towards building understanding rather than challenging power and policy. Calls to establish a culture of peace as the basis of anti-war organizing have thus created new challenges and contemporary ambivalences for the peace movement as a resistive practice. For example, Smith Page (2001) draws attention to how a culture of peace model is largely sermonic in that it focuses attention on self-evident and non-threatening rhetoric at the expense of direct action and challenge. Similarly, and perhaps most importantly, mobilizing a culture of peace model as the basis for new global movements, can be seen to run the risk of offering a poor substitute for criticisms of global capitalism that are arguably more important to the peace movement in the new millennium than ever before. Given that industrial militarism and war in the twenty-first century can be traced directly to renewed forms of national exceptionalism and the violent enforcement of neo-liberal policies on a global scale (Roberts et al. 2003), the culture of peace model has been found wanting:

> It can be argued that the culture of peace is very much an individualistic and bourgeoisified approach to peace, looking at how individuals should change their thinking and act more peaceably, and tending to downplay the importance of structural change (Smith Page 2001, p. 350).

This insight has significant implications for the current connections between sport and peace efforts, discussed below.

Nevertheless, while the culture of peace model can be criticized as one-dimensional, liberal or unrealistic, it has come to stand as the basis for much current peace activity and research. For example, De Rivera (2004, p. 546) suggests that the UN's culture of peace model may be 'somewhat simplistic', but he also suggests that the concept's limitation is not its conceptualization or politics but that it lacks a primary measure, namely 'the extent to which there is education for the peaceful resolution of conflict and training for nonviolence'.

He uses this lack as a basis to call for assessments of how and where such peace education is taking place. As the next section demonstrates, much – though certainly not all – of the current mobilization and organization of sport in the service of peace, and the articulations between peace activism and physical culture, tend to embrace this logic of peace education. Particularly given the burgeoning interest in 'sport for peace' among civil society and non-governmental organizations (NGOs) (see Darnell 2012; Wilson 2012), it is reasonable to argue that the culture of peace model is now hegemonic in structuring the relationship between sport and the peace movement. In the next section, a brief history of sport and the peace movement, from the nineteenth century through to the present day, is offered in order to illustrate this shift.

Connecting sport to the peace movement

Writing in the *International Review for the Sociology of Sport* in 1985, Sven Güldenpfennig posited that the emergence of a new peace movement presented a challenge and a controversy to the social scientific study of sport. He suggested that given recognition of the fundamental social and political changes being called for within the peace movement, support for peace was required from all sectors and institutions of society, including sport. He argued that sportspeople were clearly in support of the peace movement and that the peace movement of the time was influencing understandings of the organization and role of sport in society. The important issue, as he identified it, was whether or not those in a position to have an influence on the organization of sport itself should position sport as separate from the peace movement where it might have some indirect or 'spillover' effect, or whether sport should carve out an explicit political mandate in support of the peace movement itself. For Güldenpfennig, the former of these choices was clearly the majority practice in the sporting institutions of the day, though he argued that ultimately, sport should be concerned with both of these approaches.

In this section, the argument is made that the latter of these two understandings of sport in the service of peace and peace activism – in which sport organizations and stakeholders formulate and adopt an explicit political mandate for peace in the tradition of the peace movement – remains in a minority position, though it has changed and even undergone a form of hybridization since Güldenpfennig's writings more than 25 years ago. While there are undoubtedly contemporary anti-war peace movements and actors that connect to sport in important ways, the majority tendency is still towards the political independence of sport and concomitant belief in 'spillover', and in turn, a commitment to the promotion and mobilization of sport for peace education in a way that aligns with recent shifts towards a culture of peace.

Before discussing the current situation, it is important to acknowledge that sport has had a connection to the peace movement since the late 1800s. One of the earliest and most explicit connections of the peace movement to sport can be seen in Pierre de Coubertin's revival of the Olympic Games. Coubertin was directly influenced by his personal and professional engagements with those who were active in the peace movement of the time, notably progressive politician and educator Jules Simon (Wassong and Muller 2007). For Coubertin, the logic of connecting sport to peace was rooted in the positive pedagogical effects of physical education. From his perspective as a political conservative and aristocrat (Loland and Selliaas 2009), Coubertin believed that effective and meaningful education should include sport and the physical, and if administered properly, this kind of educational experience would lead to the production of citizens (albeit limited to white, middle-class men) who committed to peace and led peaceful lives, ideas that were reflected in the emerging peace movement (Quanz 1993; 1994). This relationship between Coubertin and peace activists of the time was co-constituting; not only did Coubertin draw on the peace movement to inform the revival of the Olympics, but his friends and colleagues from the peace movement called for recognition of the burgeoning Olympic movement as an example of the peaceful internationalism for which they were advocating (Quanz 1994).

The peace movement and emergent peace organizations of the late 1800s (such as the Red Cross and Esperanto Movement) that influenced Coubertin most directly were committed to the Enlightenment values of rationality and reason, as well as to human rights and to the sanctity of the modern nation state (Loland and Selliaas 2009). Similarly, Coubertin advocated for sport, in the form of modern Olympism, to be part of the securing of national independence and sovereignty, albeit indirectly (Quanz 1994). This meant that for Coubertin, the modern Olympic Games could contribute to peace, but Olympism as he saw it was not in and of itself, a peace movement (Quanz 1994). Rather, the influence of the peace movement on the Olympic movement can be seen in its decisions to adopt structural models of international peace organizations, to promote 'enlightened patriotism' and to support peace education for young people through sport (Loland and Selliaas 2009, p. 59).

This history suggests that while informed by the peace movement of the late nineteenth century – and while currently self-promoted as a force of and for global peace (see Hoberman 2011) – the Olympic Movement was distinct from more radical pacifist organizing around sport in the late nineteenth and early twentieth century, particularly the peaceful ideals attached to and promoted by workers' sports movements. For example, more radical social movements of the time coalesced around the Spartakiade, a socialist Workers' sports event held in Paris in 1934 that attracted 12,000 participants around the world and was dubbed the 'Anti-War and Anti-Fascist Sports Meet' (McQuarrie 2010, p. 398). Further, as we have seen in Chapter 2, the

Workers' Olympics, organized by the Socialist Workers' Sports International beginning in the 1920s, were international sporting events based on socialist and pacifist values, including the 1925 version in Germany held under the banner 'No More War' (Kidd 1996, p. 154). Indeed, these events were not only held in opposition to war, but also to the ways in which sports events like Coubertin's Olympics exacerbated nationalist fervour; in contrast, the Workers' Olympics called for sport in support of international worker solidarity. In sum, while the organized pacifism and the peace movement of the time no doubt informed Coubertin's directions, he did not embrace their agenda in its totality. Rather:

> Coubertin felt responsible for a certain pacifistic mood in ways that were more modest and more emotionally effective than rational political pacifism (Quanz 1993, 17).

Beyond Coubertin and the Olympics, the world of sport did connect to the peace movement in its resistive formations throughout the twentieth century, and often did so through the action of famous athletes. Perhaps no example of this is more renowned than that of iconic boxer Muhammad Ali who, in 1966, refused to accept his drafting into military service by the United States government to serve in the Vietnam War. His statement 'Man, I ain't got no quarrel with no Vietcong' became 'one of the most famous phrases of the decade' in the United States. (Zirin 2005, p. 64). Notably, Zirin (2005) reminds that at the time of Ali's declaration, the anti-Vietnam movement in the United States was still in a state of relative infancy. In fact, it would be another year before revolutionaries like Dr Martin Luther King, Jr. would join in the movement denouncing the war. In this way, Ali stands as an important and unique example of sport and athletes *leading* anti-war efforts and the peace movement; as Zirin (2005, p.67) concludes: 'Ali's defiance was far more than a footnote to the (anti-war) movement' (see the discussion of Ali and struggles for human rights in Chapter 4).

Since Ali's initial anti-war stance in 1966, other high-profile athletes have spoken out on social issues, including military incursions in ways that connect to peace and anti-war movements. For example, National Basketball Association player Steve Nash wore a t-shirt to the league's all-star game in 2003 which read 'No War – Shoot for Peace' and his fellow NBA-er Etan Thomas gained significant notoriety for his public speaking – often using slam poetry – between 2005 and 2007 that was highly critical of the US-led wars in Iraq and Afghanistan. Similarly, Major League Baseball Player Carlos Delgado delivered his own anti-war protests in 2004 by refusing to stand for the playing of the US National Anthem and God Bless America during baseball games. While these are somewhat individualized example of sport-related anti-war activism, they do illustrate the ways in which peace activism has found its way into the world of sport and suggest a legacy of anti-war athletes started by Ali.

Calls for peace also connected to twentieth-century sport in the organization of sports events and calls for peace through these events. For example, in the era of Olympic boycotts between Cold War rivals, during which the United States refused to attend the Moscow Games in 1980 and the Soviet Union reciprocated by refusing to participate in Los Angeles, 1984, media mogul and CNN founder Ted Turner created The Goodwill Games as a way to '. . . ease tensions during the Cold War through friendly athletic competition between nations' (goodwillgames.com). First held in 1986 in Moscow, the Goodwill Games were staged five more times before ceasing operations, with the final version of the event staged in Brisbane in 2001 (Horne and Whannel 2012). Turner promoted the event as an Olympic-style sporting contest designed to build positive relations amidst international tensions and threats of war, and some analysts have attributed the non-proliferation treaty between the United States and Soviet Union, at least in part, to the diplomatic 'thaw' that the Games created (Bastian 1987). At the same time, the Goodwill Games were also clearly a tool of public relations and media promotion (L'Etang et al. 2007), features that call into question its organic or substantive connections to the global peace movement.

Still, the culture and organization of sport continues to offer a social and political site or node around which the anti-war and peace movement has organized, demonstrated and brought attention to their claims and issues in the new millennium. Given the global scale of these peace activities, and the extent to which they can be thought to overlap with other social movements, they can indeed be considered examples of contemporary 'alter-globalization'. For example, during the international torch relay ahead of the 2008 Olympic Games in Beijing, protesters in India used the relay as an opportunity to call for a peaceful resolution to the ongoing Chinese occupation of Tibet and the exile of the Dalai Lama. As Majumdar and Mehta (2010) demonstrate, local manifestations of the movement in Delhi leveraged the image of peace symbolized by the Olympic flame – an image propagated by the IOC itself – as a platform to call for recognition of the Dalai Lama as a peace leader, to agitate for Tibetan independence, and to promote the global peace movement more generally. Their actions demonstrated the positioning of the Olympic flame – and Olympism more broadly – as a floating signifier of peace. That is, while the IOC has been roundly criticized for perpetuating hollow and apolitical commitments to peace that are based on 'amoral universalism' (see Hoberman 2011), demonstrators in Delhi showed the peace-focused discursive legacy of Olympism to be one open to their use and co-optation. In fact, the protests led the Chinese government to extend discussions with the Dalai Lama's envoys, a result, in Majumdar and Mehta's words (2010, p. 105): 'made possible wholly by the global symbolism of the Olympic flame, (and which) once again helped underscore the potential of this global peace movement, often unknowingly passed off as a simple sports competition'.

Crucially, then, this analysis demonstrates the extent to which the agency of citizens and actors – including those within alter-globalization movements – remains crucial to the ways in which sport connects to peace in the new millennium. While current forms of political and cultural power coalesce around sport in ways that support militarism and nationalist fervours (see Butterworth 2012; Kelly 2012; Scherer and Koch 2010; Schimmel 2012), sport also continues to offer an opportunity for peace activism in a range of national and cultural contexts. For example, national and international media have promoted cricket tests between India and Pakistan as a nationalist competition, potentially perpetuating the militaristic tension between the bordering nations, but research shows that there has also been enough common interest in cricket among the people of the two countries to resist these emotional trappings and spread a sense of goodwill and internationalism (Bandyopadhyay 2008). On the one hand, this kind of analysis demonstrates the seemingly interminable ambivalence between sport, war and peace (see Güldenpfennig 1985; Shields and Bredemeier 1996; Donnelly 2011). On the other hand, it demonstrates the extent to which sport offers a site at which the contemporary peace movement can organize in resistance to the militarism of everyday life.

Recent examples from Canadian ice hockey and British football further illustrate this phenomenon. While hockey in Canada has offered a cultural site for the political legitimization of Canadian military policy in recent years (Scherer and Koch 2010), it has simultaneously constituted a focus for the peace movement and peace activists. On 8 December 2010, a group calling itself 'Hockey Fans for Peace' published a statement in *New Socialist* magazine, and launched a Facebook page, calling for recognition of the public opposition to Canadian military action in Afghanistan. They also called directly on the National Hockey League (NHL) and hockey journalists and broadcasters to end 'the practice of using hockey games and broadcasts to promote the view that full support for the war is the only acceptable position for any genuine hockey fan'. Much of their attention was focused on bombastic Canadian hockey broadcaster Don Cherry who routinely uses his television programme 'Coaches Corner' on the Canadian Broadcasting Corporation as a pulpit to recognize Canadian servicemen and women. Hockey Fans for Peace co-founder Kimball Cariou subsequently wrote that 'the psychological aim of this strategy is to sow divisions among Canadians, particularly among the solid majority who want an early return home for the troops in Afghanistan' (Cariou 2011). As such, hockey in Canada became a site for peace activists to draw attention to military power and call for reform.

Further, in 2011, when a NHL franchise returned to the city of Winnipeg – and adopted the city's traditional nickname of 'Jets' – the club unveiled military-themed logos and uniforms at a Canadian Forces Base. This also became a source and site of protest for anti-war activists in Canada, who drew connections between the choices made by the club and the policies of foreign military action taken in recent years by Canada's Conservative government. Writing on the Canadian alternative news website rabble.ca (26 July 2011), union activist Tyler Shipley drew attention, and called for resistance, to sport as a site of militarization of Canadian life:

> the team's new owner made no secret of the fact that the logo was designed in consultation with the Department of National Defence. In fact, Mark Chipman's comments in the unveiling of the new logo had more to do with the air force than the hockey team. He noted in the press conference that he only felt comfortable with the "Jets" name when he determined that he could re-brand the team around the RCAF.

Such protests against the militarism of the Jets – and of sport more broadly – drew support from the broader activist community as well. John K. Samson of the Winnipeg-based rock band, The Weakerthans, declared his opposition to the Jets military theme in a magazine interview (prairiedog 2012):

> I think the logo and the name are atrocious. I think it's just a terrible, terrible mistake. And I'll continue to say that. I can't understand why they caved to the pressure of a bullying minority in the city. Or even maybe a bullying majority who wanted to call it the Jets and then tie themselves to this awful war machine to have as a logo. I just think it's a terrible idea.

Similar protests have occurred in the United Kingdom, where sports like football (soccer) have lent institutional, financial and discursive support to the military's participation in the War on Terror in ways that have contributed to the 'hero-ification of British militarism' (Kelly 2012, p. 10). For example, the Football League's official charity partner in 2009–10 was *Help for Heroes* (an organization discussed below), and all English and Scottish Premier League clubs have worn shirts embroidered with specially designed Earl Haig poppies during Remembrance Day weekend matches (Kelly 2012). In response, supporters of Glasgow Celtic FC protested this increasing connection between professional football (soccer) and state-led militarism by distributing leaflets at matches that described civilian deaths in Iraq and Afghanistan amidst participation by the British military (Kelly 2012). These supporter groups have also refused to enter the stadium during Remembrance Day services and, in 2010, unveiled a banner during a match reading 'Your deeds would shame all the devils in hell: Ireland, Iraq, Afghanistan. No bloodstained poppy on our hoops' (Kelly 2012, p. 11).

In the cases of Don Cherry and the Winnipeg Jets in Canada, and Celtic FC in the United Kingdom, sport – and in particular the iconic national sports of Canadian hockey and British football – has offered cultural hubs at and through which the peace movement, connected to other social activist causes, could protest and resist state-led militarism. These activists protested in a manner clearly reminiscent of the twentieth-century peace movement. When considered alongside the Olympic-focused peace protests in Delhi, these activities suggest that amidst alter-globalization, sport continues to offer an important cultural repository for the contemporary peace movement to draw attention to its causes, crystallize and disseminate its anti-war messages, and agitate for the democratization of military policy. These opportunities for resistance are important to recognize given that sport still connects to, and even increasingly features in, the securing of state-sanctioned militarism in the twenty-first century. In addition to the British example of football and the War on Terror, the incredible popularity of sports like American football as overseen by the National Football League continues to provide opportunities not only to celebrate, but also simultaneously to legitimize and de-politicize, the US military-led 'War on Terror' (Schimmel 2012) and the deification of fallen war heroes like Pat Tillman in ways that secure the nobility of war and violence (Butterworth 2012; King 2008).

It is also against this backdrop that peace movements and anti-war protesters in sport regularly face significant backlash, criticism or dismissal of their message. For example, Celtic FC officials stated that the fans who led anti-war protests had 'embarrassed' and 'tarnished' the club and Scottish journalist James Traynor called for these fans to be silenced (Kelly 2012, p. 11). In a more extreme fashion, Sunderland football player James McClean received death threats via twitter in response to his decision during the 2012 season not to wear the club shirt that featured a poppy (Fifield 2012). McLean's refusal to wear the poppy – a statement against support for state-sponsored militarism and military action – led to him being booed on the pitch and also led Cody Lachey, a former British soldier, to tweet '. . . he deserves to be shot dead + body dragged past the cenotaph!! (Fifield 2012)' Similarly, in the case of the Winnipeg Jets, hockey journalists routinely dismissed and/or denigrated anti-war protests on the grounds that they were politically biased, misinformed or problematically mixing sport with politics. Winnipeg Sun columnist Kevin Engstrom accused Shipley of 'pathetic pandering' while Engstrom's colleague Tom Broderick encouraged readers to depoliticize the issue, writing: 'This is a hockey jersey. It's not parliamentary procedure and it's not constitutional wrangling . . . So don't sweat it. Just enjoy the hockey'. Such responses from journalists call attention to the resistive dimensions of the peace movement, even in their contemporary forms. Whereas positioning sport for peaceful education and tolerance (discussed further below) rarely, if ever, produces a cultural or political backlash, anti-war activism such as that focused on hockey in Canada or football in the United States questions the very sanctity and normativity of everyday life as it is manifest through both sport and militarism. Such protests are always likely to produce a hostile response or counterattack.

Sport and peace education

The examples listed above of anti-war activism coalesced around sport have been accompanied by an increasingly institutionalized relationship between sport and contemporary peace efforts. As described above, the burgeoning support for 'a culture of peace model' is now evident in its connections to sport, particularly in the recent organizing of various 'sport for peace' initiatives. This shift is discussed next.

Within contemporary efforts connecting sport to peace, there has been a significant and recurring focus on issues of reconciliation and social cohesion in places of violent conflict or in post-war settings. For example, using post-Apartheid South Africa as a case study, Höglund and Sundberg (2008) recently identified four processes of peace and reconciliation through sport: symbolic acts, fair representations through sport policies, resistance to stereotypes and individual development. In each of these processes, the focus is on building inclusion – at an individual or collective level – as opposed to resistance to militarism and violence.

This approach echoes efforts that have drawn on sport as a form of peace education from a social psychological perspective. This perspective has tended to recognize the ambivalence between sport, peace and war – namely that sport can exacerbate violence and aggression as much as support peace and anti-violence – and to use this ambivalence as a platform to call for reforms to sport. By this logic, sport should be constructed in such a way as to support peaceful co-existence based on unifying values that support a positive social psychology (Shields and Bredemeier 1996; Schwebel 1996). This logic also extends to the communication of sport itself, with recent calls to recognize the media construction and dissemination of sport as popular 'discursive opportunities' for the promotion of peace and understanding (Rivenburgh 2009). It is not the importance or even the effectiveness of these approaches at issue here, but rather (a) the extent to which the logic of sport in support of reconciliation and understanding diverges from the resistive principles of the peace movement, and (b) whether this has become the preferred, or even hegemonic, political approach to connecting peace and sport.

Indeed, it is reasonable to argue that the preeminent sport and peace organizations in the new millennium fit into this category of promoting a culture of peace, rather than political opposition to war and militarism. There are several organizations and initiatives consistent with this general mandate, including *Athletes United for Peace*, *Peace Players International*, *Football for Peace*, *Soccer for Peace*, the *Soccer for Peace Foundation* and *Fight for Peace*, among others. While it is beyond the scope of this chapter to analyse each of these organizations, they all align with the general mandate of using sport to foster peaceful relations rather than opposing military action. One of the highest profile organizations in this field is *Peace and Sport*, a non-governmental organization formed in 2007 by Olympic Medallist Joel Bouzou. Based in Monaco, and operating under the patronage of Prince Albert II, *Peace and Sport* works to mobilize sport towards the building of sustainable peace throughout the world. To do so, 'it promotes the practice of structured sport and sporting values to educate young generations and help foster social stability, reconciliation and dialogue between communities' (Peace and Sport 2011). The organization defines sustainable peace as not just the absence of war and conflict, but also a process and result that is taught and learnt. According to *Peace and Sport*, sport offers a metaphor and set of guidelines for building sustainable peace because 'it is a tool for dialogue, brotherhood and respect that transcends political, social, racial and religious differences that are often at the heart of conflicts in this world'.

Peace and Sport is a high-profile example of the cultural turn in the peace movement and peace theorizing, away from direct and critical activism against military policy and the state, and towards a more inclusive, less politicized vision and version of peace activism. Indeed, the organization celebrates its position in Monaco as illustrative of its general political neutrality in geo-political terms. The extent to which sport has been taken up by and within these kinds of peace organizations and this approach to peace building is notable given that sport has regularly been recognized for its ability and reputation to exacerbate global and international conflict (Donnelly 2011). To some degree then, it is likely that this coupling of sport to the cultural turn in peace education and a culture of peace discourse is part of an attempt to reform sport in ways that make it more amenable to peace promotion, such as that called for in the social psychology literature and discussed by Güldenpfennig (1985) in response to the peace movement of the 1980s.

Another prominent example of the logic of peace education and efforts to reform sport is the recent activity around the Olympic Truce. Based on the ancient Greek tradition of *Ekecheiria* that called for warring city states to suspend violence so that athletes could travel to and compete in Olympic competition, the modern Olympic Truce has called for a cessation of war and violent conflict, even if only temporarily, during the Olympic fortnight (Burleson 2012). Supported by a 1993 non-binding UN resolution calling for its recognition and observation, the Olympic Truce has been credited, for example, with a delay in the implementation of Operation Desert Fox in Iraq by the US Armed Forces during the 1998 Nagano Olympics, an effect that has led some to conclude that while the Olympic Truce cannot enforce peace, it may increase the chances of peace becoming the preferred option or choice of individuals and governments (Briggs et al., cited in Burleson 2012). Notably, Burleson (2012, p. 805) connects the logic and recent momentum enjoyed by the Olympic Truce to the cultural turn in peace activism as promoted and solidified by UNESCO and the UN's 1999 Culture of Peace Resolution which served to set the current agenda for peace education.

A further example of this trend in peace promotion that connects to sport is *Help for Heroes*, a registered charity in the United Kingdom that raises money in support of injured service men and women. According to its website, *Help for Heroes*: '. . . provides direct, practical support to wounded, injured and sick Service personnel, veterans, and their families. . . through grants to individuals and other Service charities, capital build projects and support for life at our four Recovery Centres across the UK'.

Its connections to sport can be seen not only through the support it receives from sporting organizations like the Football League in the United Kingdom, but also in the money *Help for Heroes* channels to partners like the Combined Service Disabled Ski Team to provide equipment and training for former soldiers to take up skiing. Notably, and in keeping with the cultural turn in peace activism, *Help for Heroes* is explicit about its neutrality when approaching the political dimensions of war: 'We don't care about the rights and wrongs of war but we believe that if young men and women are prepared to volunteer to serve our country on our behalf, and are hurt while doing so, they deserve our support'. In this sense, *Help for Heroes* illustrates a strategic commitment to transcend the political resistance to war traditionally exemplified by the peace movement, and to move towards an inclusive practice of peace activism, one that can solicit and secure the support of people and communities across the political spectrum regardless of their views on military policy and its effects.

It is possible to read this cultural turn in sport and peace activism as illustrative of contemporary alter-globalization in that rather than rejecting globalization outright, organizations like *Peace and Sport, Help for Heroes* and advocates of the Olympic Truce seek reforms and changes to globalization and its effects (see Harvey et al. 2009; Wilson 2012) and do so by creating and drawing upon global networks of various actors interested in organizing sport towards peace and building new subjectivities in and through the sporting experience (see Pleyers 2010). To this end, *Peace and Sport* draws on the opportunities and tools afforded by globalization, to work towards peace building, conflict resolution and tolerance and understanding. It thus operates, to a degree, as a social movement. In Wilson's (2012, pp. 94–5) recent theoretical appraisal of sport and social movements interested in peace (broadly defined), he suggests that it is still reasonable to recognize social movements and their success by their ability to mobilize resources, secure political acceptance and influence, and effectively frame issues, usually through the work of 'social movement entrepreneurs'. By this logic, *Peace and Sport* constitutes a social movement, exemplified by Bouzou's capacity to draw attention to the role that sport can play in peace building, and the success of the organization in mobilizing resources amidst a broader desire for sport to play a broader social role (see Coalter 2007; Darnell 2012).

The cultural turn in the relationship between sport and peace is also reflected in the strong influence of 'global civil society' actors and institutions that now support the relationship between sport and peace (Giulianotti 2011a and 2011b). As Giulianotti (2011b, p. 211) describes it, the term 'global civil society' recognizes and illustrates the global dimensions of actor networks that work towards improved conditions for humanity. Such actors can be from different types of organizations and often interact with each other in complex ways. In this sense, the social complexity and political challenges of mobilizing sport in support of the peace movement appear, in the new millennium, to be somewhat mitigated by a common commitment to the cultural turn that makes such work less politically polarizing. In this sense, amidst the transnational challenges of trying to organize sport as a meaningful and effective form of peace building, an apparent consensus has been reached to do so through peace education and inclusive practices, rather than through resistance to state-led militarism characteristic of the twentieth-century peace movement. As stated throughout this chapter, this cultural model of mobilizing sport for peace-building and rehabilitation based on notions of inclusivity that largely transcend resistive politics is qualitatively different from the NSMs focused on peace in the twentieth century and likely signals a shift in the political orientation of contemporary peace activism connected to and through sport.

This shift requires, then, an updated understanding of the politics of the peace movement as they connect to sport. The cultural turn in peace seems to embrace a sense of deliberative democracy – which strives to include as many people as possible – rather than agonistic democracy which is concerned with constructing a space of and for disagreement (see Macgilchrist and Böhmig 2012). Following Coy et al's (2008) argument that contemporary peace organizing is informed by both past discourses and contemporary political events, in current connections between the peace movement and sport, and despite ongoing and seemingly interminable violent incursions in places like Iraq and Afghanistan, the discourse of peace education has proved attractive in the face of the failed legacy of opposition and resistance to military power. Further, if social organizing and protest cycles in the peace movement are connected to broader political processes and the structures and spaces of opportunities to organize (see Meyer 1993 and 1999), then the trend towards sport focused peace education is illustrative of current opportunities, both stable and dynamic. That is, current organizing and theorizing about peace results in civil society leadership and a goal of building consensus, not making enemies, socially or politically. This logic clearly informs decisions currently made by many sport organizations that are committed to peace-building, peace education and conflict resolution but not to critiques of military power that could put such organizations in an explicitly politicized oppositional position.

At the least, though, it is reasonable to conclude that it is now more popular, acceptable and palatable to promote peaceful inclusion through sport than to call for a commitment to anti-war principles in the tradition of the global peace movement. As Cunningham and Regan (2011) have argued, it is less politically palatable for athletes to speak out about war than it is for them to lend their names to causes that do less to challenge the dominant logic of the global neo-liberal era. If this is the case, then it is important to note that the historical legacies of iconic anti-war athletes like Muhammad Ali have been co-opted into the mainstream of global culture and capital (Zirin 2005) in ways that make it difficult to recall the extent to which these sporting figures used their popularity and profile to challenge the undemocratic militarism of everyday life. This is similar to the cultural incorporation of human rights struggles into the dominant sporting culture as described by Hartmann (2003) (and discussed in Chapter 4). Against the cultural turn in peace-building, it appears that the peace movement may have been co-opted into the dominant culture and organization of sport, as well as vice versa.

6

Sport and the Environmental Movement

In 2012, in celebration of the fiftieth anniversary of its first publication, a new edition of Rachel Carson's *Silent Spring* was released. *Silent Spring* remains arguably the most influential book of the twentieth century to focus on issues of environmental degradation; it remains highly relevant today, underlines Canadian writer Margaret Atwood in her commentary (Atwood 2012), at a time when biodiversity, climate change and pollution are of central importance to citizens of the world. Indeed, concerns with the environment and sustainability are now at the core of all fields of human activity. In this chapter, dedicated to sport and the environmental movement, we argue that sport is no different than other domains of social and political life and, although it was late to pay attention to this issue, sport is now directly confronted and challenged by the issues raised by the environmental movement.

The chapter is divided into four sections. In the first section, we outline the history of the environmental movement through its different evolutionary stages. In the second section, we discuss how the question of the environment became a central issue for the Olympic Games and use this as a case study to analyse the increasing importance of environmental issues in sport. In the third section, we consider and contrast three actors that have been particularly active on the issue of sport and the environment both locally and globally: Greenpeace, Surfers against Sewage and the Global Anti-Golf Movement (GAGM). Before concluding this chapter, we discuss further the institutionalization of environmentalism in sport, and precisely how it has infiltrated the discourses and strategies of the sports industry.

A brief history of environmental movements

Nisbet (1983, p. 101) writes that 'it is entirely possible that when the history of the twentieth century is finally written, the single most important social movement of the period will be judged to be environmentalism'. Touraine (1983) saw the environmental movement as the driving force behind a shift in historicity, enabling a departure from modernity towards a 'new' post-industrial society. The environmental movement comprises '. . . networks of informal interactions that may include, as well as individuals and groups who have no organizational affiliation, organizations of varying degrees of formality (including even political parties, especially Green parties) that are engaged in collective action motivated by shared identity or concern about environmental issues' (Rootes 2007, p. 1428). The key point here, and one that spans the entire study of social movements, is that the environmental movement has never existed as a singular protest or campaign undertaken by a specific group or association. Rather, the environmental movement is best conceived as the result of links created *between* those groups, associations and collective actions that form around concerns for the environment. As described below, the main issues that first drove the environmental movement were the devastating consequences of industrialization and the near complete disregard for the finitude of natural resources. Coupled with the critique of the New Left, these new concerns sparked the creation of organizations such as Friends of the Earth and Greenpeace, radical groups explicitly denouncing the harm done to the environment by capitalistic extraction and exploitation.

From this perspective, the identity of the environmental movement is relatively clear, although also hard to pinpoint because it embraces various local initiatives, rarely cited outside of particular *milieux*, as well as large, overarching international campaigns that touch the lives of millions of people. However, demonstrated within Rootes' definition of the environmental movement, these various groups share a common identity based around the defence of environmental issues. The opposition, or that against which the environmental movement has fought, is the deterioration of the environment, be that on a local scale or an international basis. The totality of the movement has been to steer contemporary society towards environmentally friendly practices and, more broadly, towards a general respect for the fragility of nature, ecosystems and the environment, all necessary conditions for the existence of life on this planet. Four major phases in the evolution of environmental movements can be identified as follows: (1) conservationism and preservationism; (2) environmentalism; (3) ecologism/grassroots environmentalism; and (4) global/transnational movements (Ford 2011; Rootes 2008, p. 33; Silveira 2001). Each of these phases is discussed in more detail below.

Conservationism and preservationism

In *American Sportsmen and the Origins of Conservation*, Reiger (1975 [2000]) illustrated how hunting came to be the first major activity responsible for drawing attention to environmental and ecological issues pertaining to land use in North America (Rome 2003; Rootes 2008). Game hunters were the first groups to issue public warnings relating to the destruction of natural habitats. Of course, this was a largely self-interested concern as hunters strove to keep the land pristine so that game remained available for hunting. Nevertheless, hunters and outdoor people made a conscious effort to preserve land in its original condition and later some of these parcels of land became protected public parks (Rootes 2008). The first major academic study of the conservation movement was Hayes' *Conservation and the Gospel of Efficiency: The Progressive Conservation Movement 1890–1920*. In this work, Hayes argued that the driving force among conservationists in the United States 'was a commitment to scientific management of resources by experts' (Rome 2003). In the United Kingdom, David Evans (1996) described the specific context in which the conservation movement evolved in *A History of Nature Conservation in Britain*. The rapid development of industrialization in England left scars on the countryside and on nature in general; industrial growth was viewed in terms of profitability with almost total disregard for the possible impacts on nature and its conservation (Evans 1996). In this sense, the conservation movement progressed from an early disregard to environmental degradation linked to industrialization to a larger encompassing movement embracing such causes as the protection of natural predators and bird species.

In France, a conservation movement also emerged in the late 1800s with the involvement of several different parties. First, according to Lapoix (1976), the 'sociétés savantes' helped shape the context behind the movement by publishing scientific accounts detailing the impact of human development on nature. Second, specialized associations, mostly linked to local contexts, also played an important role, as they were able to establish a link between abstract scientific concepts and actual practice. This was the case for *La ligue française de protection des oiseaux* and les *Amis de la forêt de Fontainebleau*, who, at the turn of the nineteenth century, established ties with governmental authorities via different forms of legal backing (Lapoix 1976). The aim of these institutes was, quite simply, to fight for the conservation of the natural resources in place. In the case of *La ligue française de protection des oiseaux*, efforts were made to have certain species of birds recognized by governmental authorities in order to protect them against over-hunting and complete decimation. Beyond their respective roles, these associations had a mandate based around the circulation of information to the general population; they struggled over the recognition, by competent authorities, of the causes they defended (Lapoix 1976).

In sum, conservationists in the United States, United Kingdom and France campaigned for land, water and forests to be conserved in pristine shape. For the so-called preservationists, actions and goals went further: these groups reasserted the importance of maintaining a spiritual relationship between humans and nature (Rootes 2008). Wilderness was seen as an escape from the chaos of the city and the growing pains of mass industrialization. Roderick Nash's *Wilderness and the American Mind* (1967 [2001]) outlines how, for some writers and artists, the countryside came to be a romantic place replete with national pride (Rome 2003). The work of celebrated photographer Ansel Adams in capturing images of national parks, particularly Yosemite in Northern California, United States, in the twentieth century can be understood as part of this development, as well as the earlier writing of Henry David Thoreau in *Walden; or, Life in the Woods* first published in 1854.

Contrary to conservationists, preservationists wanted the land to remain intact and free from human intervention. Rootes (2008) cites, as an example, the will of US authorities to dam the Hetch Hetchy Valley's river that meanders through Yosemite Park. The project was proposed in the first decade of the twentieth century and environmental hazards related to the damming of a river were not well understood. The growing opposition of preservationist groups, such as the Sierra Club, led to a massive struggle against the dam in order to preserve and protect wildlife. Even though their efforts ultimately failed (the dam was erected in 1923), the notion that environmental groups could mobilize to effect the outcome of large and environmentally unfriendly projects was increasingly evident. As noted by Rootes (2008), the conservationist and preservationist agendas were largely responses to particular issues, in the sense that they tended to become involved when specific situations required an intervention. Still, at this time, a broad definition or view of the relationship of humans with nature had yet to be developed within the movement, and thus a wider vision for the movement based on broader social change was rarely articulated and circulated.

Environmentalism and the formation of the environmental movement

If the conservationist and preservationist movements were the main proponents of environmental awareness at the turn of the nineteenth century and in the first decades of the twentieth century, much changed after World War II. Indeed, the public's consciousness about environmental issues was to be altered forever by the advent of new technologies such as the Atomic bomb. Increasingly, the public did not uniformly accept the so-called technological progress, especially if it came at a steep environmental price (Rome 2003). As mentioned above, Rachel Carson's influential book *Silent Spring* (1962/2012) can be cited as one of the first sources to galvanize the American public's perception about environmental issues:

> Emphasizing the problems associated with industrial society, Carson argued that science and technology had been effectively removed from any larger policy framework and insulated from public input and opinion. Carson's controversial thesis not only made *Silent Spring* an epoch event in the history of environmentalism, but also helped to launch a new decade of rebellion and protest in which the concept of "nature" was broadly construed to include quality-of-life issues (Silveira 2001, p. 504).

Silent Spring (Carson 1962/2002) was first published in three serialized excerpts in the *New Yorker* magazine in June 1962. The book itself was published in September of that year and the outcry that followed led to the banning of the use of DDT as an insecticide and stimulated changes in the laws affecting the environment in North America and around the world. For Rootes (2008), the growth in participation in higher education also contributed to the increase in public awareness about environmental issues at the time.

It is also important to understand the opening of new political spaces made possible by the efforts of the New Left and the student protests for the development of the environmental movement (Rootes 2008, p. 613). As a broad movement, the New Left regrouped activists, groups, intellectuals, members of political parties and others who viewed a decline in traditional Marxism and were interested in rekindling the spirit of the Left. At the forefront of the New Left voices was C. Wright Mills, an American sociologist who believed in abolition of the old leftist traditions. In his well-known *Letter to the New Left* (1963), he argued that the historical agency of the left, traditionally represented by the working class, had to be reoriented, as the grip it had on political powers susceptible to implement real, effective change had diminished to a point where its powers were obsolete. The long-established dichotomy dividing the owners of the means of production and the proletariat could no longer be applied to a rapidly evolving society, where the traditional lines of power structure were constantly blurred. This social climate also gave birth to the work of Alain Touraine. His understanding of the decline of the Old Left led him to formulate his first ideas about the existence of 'new' social movements, that is, movements created outside of the traditional workers movement and focused on a single issue. His studies of the French anti-nuclear movement were particularly important since they marked the transition towards the newfound importance of the New Left and its ramifications in the several different areas of society.

In this sense, the 1960s were the first time when students came to realize the power they could exert on social issues. While students of the social sciences and humanities focused on broader social and political issues and the denunciation of capitalist society, as the protests in Berkeley, California and Paris showed, it was arguably students in the natural sciences that had a more profound influence on the environmental movement (Rootes 2008). As the study of nature entails a deep and profound understanding of its functioning, at a macro or micro level, students of natural sciences understood the grave consequences behind the exploitation of nature and non-renewable resources.

Issues of mass pollution, woeful environmental management by major companies and general disregard of environmental issues by governments and corporations fuelled a growing counterculture. For Gottlieb (cited in Rootes 2008, p. 614) 'the counterculture, along with the New Left, served as a transition to a new environmental politics in which the question of Nature could no longer be separated from the question of society itself'. Given the focus of conservationists and preservationists on specific environmental issues, and combined with the advent of the New Left and general social uprising of the 1960s and 1970s, the environmental movement developed a more inclusive framework in which environmental issues were to be tied to social issues.

Earth Day 1970, attended by more than 20 million Americans, can be seen as one of the outcomes of the environmental critique that developed in the 1960's (Rootes 2008, p. 614). As Jehlicka (1994, p. 114) suggests in a periodization of environmentalism from 1960, 'Two main peaks can be identified: one at the beginning of the 1970s and another at the end of the 1980s'. Moreover, Earth Day marked the transition to a more mainstream environmentalism in which the general public could participate. The mainstreaming of environmental issues also contributed to its institutionalization. The creation of the Environmental Protection Agency (EPA) by US President Richard Nixon, which received no opposition in Congress, had a profound impact on the management of environmental issues in the United States:

> With the establishment of the EPA and the passage of a variety of environmental laws and policies in the 1970s, environmental issues themselves became "mainstream." Primarily comprised of attorneys, engineers, and economists, the EPA developed a complex regulatory structure that categorizes and addresses environmental issues by pollutant and medium (Silveira 2001, p. 508).

While Earth Day 1970 and the EPA are both related to the American context, Rootes (2008) points out that many other Western countries were impacted by this new wave of environmentalism mainly through the increasingly clear demonstration of the ways in which environmental awareness could be mobilized through a nationwide day of action. Further, it showed how environmental issues could be institutionalized within a powerful (and right wing) government structure that was not necessarily inclined towards forms of change that inhibited business growth and contradicted capitalism.

In turn, it was sustainability, as a key environmental concept, that started to gather momentum with the publication, in 1987, of *Our Common Future*, a report focusing, for the first time, on the importance of sustainability in environmental issues and management. Issued by the United Nations World Commission on Environment and Development (WCED) and chaired by Gro Harlem Brundtland, the report notably argued that sustainable development should '". . . meet the needs of the present without compromising the ability of the future generations to meet their own needs"' (Hollins 2011). The concept of sustainable development was launched by the WCED as a 'global objective' to guide policies orientated to balance 'economic and social systems and ecological conditions'. It is often represented by reference to the 'triple bottom line' of economy, environment and society.

For sustainability to be a realistic concept, the report specified that in practice, it should not inhibit economic growth. According to the report, sustainable ventures, linked to sport or other domains, could incorporate a framework based on sustainable development without compromising the quality of the product and the possible revenues to be generated. Sustainability was to be applied within the triple P triangle: Profitability, People, Planet (Seghezzo 2009) and this 'triangle'/model is now incorporated in sport and business more broadly (Seghezzo 2009). Indeed, in public policy making, the notion of sustainability can now rarely be overlooked, as a balance with ecological considerations must at least appear to be struck in order for most public policies to go forward. Even with the adverse conditions created by the financial crisis of 2008, capitalist growth (read: profitability before quality of life) remains the predominant system by which government, through neo-liberal thinking, operates. This, to a degree, reaffirms the importance of sustainable development as the main channel through which the grand meta-narrative that is capitalism remains beholden to environmental concerns.

Ecologism and grassroots environmental groups

Based on the assertion that the Earth contains finite resources and that pollution and the general misuse of nature could bring about grave consequences, the environmental movement developed in ways that the conservationists and preservationists had not achieved. Embracing the principles of ecological democracy while advocating for citizen participation as critical in environmental decision-making, grassroots environmentalism developed, in part, because of the reaction to the global rise of neo-liberalism and the grave environmental consequences it had on natural resources and the environment in general (Silveira 2001). With Margaret Thatcher taking over 10 Downing Street and Ronald Reagan, the White House, the tone was set for a full decade of conservative policy measures culminating, at the end of the 1980s, with the so-called 'Washington consensus'. As noted earlier in the book this encompassed a series of initiatives advocating the '. . . heightened privatization of public services, increased support for free trade, and the liberalization/deregulation of national and international markets, as well as drastic fiscal austerity with regard to government spending' (Harvey et al. 2009, p. 400). In this climate of austerity and of general disregard for environmental causes by government officials, grassroots groups emerged from a diverse set of ideologies and social backgrounds:

> These new citizen-based groups reflect the evolution of environmentalism from a narrow, wilderness-centered philosophy to a richer, more inclusive ideology encompassing . . . a spectrum of ideologies, including: deep ecology, social ecology, bio-regionalism, feminist ecology, spiritual ecology, native ecology, and Not in My

Backyard (NIMBY) groups. Moreover, grassroots environmentalism cuts across ethnic, racial, and class barriers to introduce a diversity previously absent from the environmental movement (Silveira 2001, p. 512).

Of these diverse points of views, one of the most radical was 'deep ecology'. For the proponents of this ideology/method of action, every creature, every plant and every organic substance is part of a wider overarching natural system (Rootes 2008). All environmental degradation that humans perpetrate thus has an impact on this single system and disrupts the fragile balance that took thousands of years to achieve. One of the more popular deep ecology groups, *Earth First!*, reiterates, in their organizational mission statement, that it first existed in response to the:

> ...lethargic, compromising, and increasingly corporate environmental community. Earth First! takes a decidedly different tack towards environmental issues. We believe in using all the tools in the tool box, ranging from grassroots organizing and involvement in the legal process to civil disobedience and monkey wrenching (Earth First! 2012).

Earth First! can thus be considered a radical environmental group. Their motto is based on a no compromise approach. Confrontation, civil disobedience and group actions are all part of Earth First!'s arsenal against destructive environmental practices. Their worldview is radically different from that of the government, agencies and other, more moderate environmental groups. The co-founder of Earth First!, Dave Foreman, was a high ranked member of the Wilderness Society, a well-respected environmental lobbying organization (Lange 1990, p. 478). He left, disillusioned, after a failed attempt to implement change through a lobbying stance. Along with friends Mike Roselle and Howie Wolke:

> . . . they hit the Mexican border running on beer and tequila and an agenda: preserve natural diversity by any means, legal or not, and reclaim lost ground – close logging roads, tear down dams, reintroduce grizzlies and wolves and elks. They united as a "disorganization" with no official members and no directors, and they called themselves "Earth First!" (Kane, cited in Lange 1990, p. 479).

Splinter groups were eventually formed by individuals leaving mainstream environmental groups to form their own variation(s) in accordance, usually, with a more radical ideology and the will to pose immediate action (Silveira 2001). One of the most famous examples remains David Browers' Friends of the Earth (FOE), an organization he created after the Sierra Club fired him for being too 'radical' while entertaining a disagreement about the construction of nuclear power plants in the United States. Bower made it clear that in contrast with the organization he chose to quit, FOE would have an international scope. In addition, '. . . instead of delegating publications, as secondary to the organization, they would be central, instead of being highly bureaucratized, establishing multiple oversights on individuals' activities, it would be decentralized and more anarchic; finally, it would take an unabashed stance against nuclear power and nuclearism more generally' (Wapner 1995).

FOE is now established worldwide, with an annual budget of over $US 15 million, mostly derived from its multiple charitable foundations (Wapner 1995). Its presence worldwide is due to the flexibility provided by its 'central' authority. National chapters are tied to FOE only by name and general orientation. The concrete actions, campaigns, fundraising and spending are solely the responsibility of the chapters without the intervention of a central authority.

A further important illustration of grassroots environmentalism was the development of 'Not In My Back Yard' or NIMBY groups. The motivation to create NIMBY groups stemmed from local environmental concerns: the creation of a golf course, for example, or, as has been the case in Québec or in the United States, the digging of wells for shale gas exploitations (McEvoy and Foisy 2011). The close relationship between a local population and an environmental issue affecting their daily lives has often been enough to fuel the formation of NIMBY movements. Fundamentally, these groups want to address the unequal distribution of pollution and the benefits of environmental protection by situating environmental issues within the broader context of civil society, and connecting them to social justice, civil rights and the democratic process (Silveira 2001).

Global/transnational reach

The next step, or, in Tarrow's (2003) vocabulary, the 'scale shift', in the environmental movement has been to that of 'transnationalism' or the emergence of transnational environmental movements establishing global cooperation based on similar goals and aspirations. The UN Conference on the Environment and Development (UNCED) held in Rio de Janeiro in 1992 is usually referred to as a 'watershed' moment for such transnational or global environmental movements (Ford 2011). For the first time, actors from around the globe representing NGOs, pressure groups, institutionalized organizations and social movements were at the same table, working towards establishing a comprehensive framework to guide post-Cold War decision makers towards a more environmentally friendly future. As Dalby (1996, p. 594) noted:

> In the case of the Earth, quite how the post-Cold War order might be written was one of the themes for discussion, but with matters of development and environment clearly on the agenda of possible new "writings." It is precisely the conflation of the discursive themes of geopolitics, development, environment and the possibilities of a new departure in global politics that make this event particularly interesting . . . .

Also, as Ford (2011, p. 33) states:

> transnational environmental movements are movements that are creating links and acting transnationally because they perceive the root causes of environmental degradation to be tied up with the forces of globalization, such as the increasing globalization of capital and with it the globalization of governance structure.

Reflecting the debate between Tilly and Touraine in the study of social movements, Ford (2011) refers to Tarrow (1994) to define the nature of transnational movements while McDonald (2006) is clearly inspired by the work of Touraine for his work on global movements. Whichever term is used, the strong link between the local and the global is of prime importance when thinking about global/transnational environmental movements. Indeed, 'rooted' action and the relation with the local environment, places or 'milieux de vie' are essential to achieve some form of connectedness between what is often seen, for the regular citizen, as large and abstract global environmental campaigns. Hence movements such as the *Transition Initiative* clearly attempt to articulate the local with the global.

By acting as a buffer or translator between global environmental concerns and concrete local gestures, the *Transition Initiative* offers the chance for people to take part in actions having an impact on both local communities and global campaigns. Small-scale initiatives are put together, and then coordinated by the *Transition Initiative* that is able to articulate the smaller local visions with coherent change at the macro level. As Griffiths (2009) notes:

> Many people feel that individual action on climate change is too trivial to be effective but that they are unable to influence anything at a national, governmental level. They find themselves paralyzed between the apparent futility of the small-scale and impotence in the large-scale. The Transition Initiative works right in the middle, at the scale of the community, where actions are significant, visible, and effective.

At the same time, in 2012, a parallel conference to the first Rio environmental summit was organized that included alternative organizations and movements excluded from official talks and gatherings. Rather than build on the previous 20 years, however, the 2012 Rio Conference left environmentalists generally disappointed as the environmental challenges highlighted at the 1992 conference remain present in people's lives. As Monbiot (2012) noted:

> The efforts of governments are concentrated not on defending the living Earth from destruction, but on defending the machine that is destroying it. Whenever consumer capitalism becomes snarled up by its own contradictions, governments scramble to mend the machine, to ensure – though it consumes the conditions that sustain our lives – that it runs faster than ever before.

In this section, we have briefly outlined the evolution of the environment movement. In the following one we will analyse how this movement has had an increasing connection with the Olympic Games and sport.

The Olympic games, sport and environmental sustainability

As shown in the previous section, while the roots of the environment reach as far as the 1890s, it was not until one century later that environmental issues started to become a concern for the Olympic 'movement'. Although the issue was raised periodically in the previous three decades, it was arguably deployed for the first time in conjunction with the 1964 Tokyo Olympics. (Holden et al. 2008; Hollins 2013). Still, there is a consensus among analysts (Cantelon and Letters 2000; Chappelet 2008; Holden et al. 2008; Hollins 2013; Karamichas 2013) that it was with both the 1992 Albertville Games and the 1994 Lillehammer Games that the environment and issues of sustainability forced their way onto the agenda of the IOC. Since then, a long series of landmarks followed that punctuated the increasingly important intermingling of the environmental issue with the Olympics, or in other words the increasing institutionalization of the environment within the Olympic 'movement'. Drawing extensively from Holden et al. (2008) and Hollins (2013), in the following pages we offer an overview of these events. Although other detailed inventories of references to the environment in the Olympic official literature are to be found, such as in Leopkey and Parent (2012), for the purpose of this chapter, we have adapted and updated the table first published by Holden at al. (2008) which serves as a road map through this recent history (see Table 6.1).

Although the organizing committee of the Lillehammer Games announced in 1991 that the 1994 Games were to be the first 'green Games', it was the environmental disaster of the 1992 Albertville Winter Olympic Games that is widely seen as the first important landmark in environmental awareness and non-sustainable development regarding the organization of sports mega-events. The 1992 Games were spread out over 1657 square kilometres of competition sites located within 13 different alpine communities (Cantelon and Letters 2000, p. 299). Each of these communities had to contend with the construction of several Olympic sites, according to strict International Federation regulations. The bobsleigh track in La Plagne, the ski jump facilities in Courchevel, the XC skiing and biathlon courses in Les Saisies and the downhill run in Val d'Isère were all the target of environmentalists protesting against the total disrespect for the fragile local fauna (Cantelon and Letters 2000). The environmental degradation at Albertville was significant to the extent that it forced the IOC to deal with the environment. As Cantelon and Letters (2000, p. 301) noted:

> it should be stressed that the combination of the obvious environmental impact of the Albertville Games and the IOC denial of any serious environmental problem demonstrated a critical disjunction between the transnational ideology of Olympism and the pragmatic nature of IOC transnational operations.

Protests by environmental groups during the games, negative media coverage and the bad environment record of the Games meant that the lack of attention

Table 6.1 Landmarks in environmental sustainability and the Olympic games

Year	Event
1964	Citizens of Tokyo voice concerns about pollution and water quality
1974	Denver citizens turn down the Games for environmental reasons
1987	Release of the Brundtland Report
1991	Lillehammer decides to formally pursue a 'green games'
1992	Albertville Games criticized for causing massive environmental damage; International Olympic Committee (IOC) signs the Earth Pledge
1994	Lillehammer hosts the first 'green games'; the environment is adopted as the IOC third 'pillar' (along with sport and culture); United Nations Environment Program (UNEP)/IOC sign an agreement on sport and the environment
1995	Cities bidding to host an Olympics are officially evaluated on their environmental plans for the first time; UNEP/IOC host the first World Conference on Sport and the Environment
1996	Creation of the Sport and Environment Commission; the Olympic Charter is modified to refer to the environment
1997	UNEP/IOC host the second World Conference on Sport and the Environment
1999	Creation of Olympic Agenda 21
2000	Sydney sets a new global Olympic standard by hosting the 'green games'; Greenpeace releases its 'Greenpeace Olympic Environmental Guidelines'
2001	IOC begins the process of setting economic, social and environmental indicators
2003	Vancouver is selected as host city of the 2010 sustainability Games
2005	London Organizing Committee of the 2012 Olympic Games (LOCOG) wins the rights to the 2012 'one planet Olympics'; Beijing Organizing Committee of the 2008 Olympic Games signs agreement with UNEP for the 'greenest ever' Games and completes its initial Olympic Games Global Impact Study (OGGI) report
2006	Torino hosts the 2006 Winter Games in an urban setting for better use of city centres and a recycling of sports infrastructure, and purchases carbon credits; UNEP signs an agreement to make the 2008 Beijing Games 'the greenest ever'; London 2012's sustainability policy is approved and LOCOG submits the OGGI study structure; VANOC completes its initial OGGI report

Table 6.1 Continued

Year	Event
2007	UNEP names IOC and President Jacques Rogge 'Champions of the Earth 2007', citing Torino as a shining example. UNEP publishes 'An Environmental Review' of the Beijing Olympic Olympics 2008
2009	UNEP publishes report entitled 'Independent Environment Assessment' of the Beijing Olympic Games
2010	UNEP publishes 'SOCHI 2004, Report of the UNEP 2nd Expert Mission', as a result of its review of the construction of a combined road/railway, following protests from non-governmental organizations. The report calls for action to better protect the environment.
2012	London, the 'first sustainable Olympic games'?

Source: Adapted from (Holden et al. 2008, p. 888).

paid by the IOC to the environmental impact of the Games could not be repeated after Albertville. In a first gesture to offset the crisis and restore its image, the IOC signed 'The Earth Pledge' the same year (Holden et al. 2008).

This set the stage for new environmental policies for the organization and preparation of the Games. The Lillehammer organizing committee sensed that environmental concerns were to be put forward in the bid process in order to address a subject seldom touched on by the IOC and previous host cities and formally pursued 'green Games'. One of the main reasons behind this innovation was the fact that Norway's Prime Minister, Gro Harlem Brundtland, was the former President of the World Commission on Environment and Development whose landmark report introduced the notion of sustainability in 1987. As Cantelon and Letters (2000, p. 303) remark, 'Lillehammer must have been music to the collective ears of the IOC. Here was a bid city that was taking environmental issues seriously and in later years, the IOC would affectionately refer to the Norwegian Games as an "environmental-political showcase"'.

The 1994 Games in Lillehammer thus had an important effect on the IOC's capacity to capitalize on the organizing of 'greener games' and, for that matter, on integrating the environment as a key principle for the consideration of future host cities. In fact, Jean-Loup Chappelet (2008) argues that the Winter Olympic Games, and the Lillehammer games in particular, are more responsible for the establishment of sustainable development policies within the IOC than the Summer Olympic Games (Chappelet 2008). In 1994, a Cooperative Agreement between the IOC and the UN Environment Program (UNEP) was established. Since that landmark year, a host of sport and environment initiatives unfolded in the Olympic 'movement' (and in other sport mega events for that matter). Among the ones listed in Table 6.1, of particular note are the creation in 1996 of a Sport and Environment Commission, the modification in 1996 of the Olympic Charter to refer to the environment, the adoption of Olympic Agenda 21 and the appointment, for each Olympic Games, of a qualified environmental advisor (Hayes and Karamichas 2012, p. 9).

Another response to Albertville can be seen in David Chernushenko's book *Greening our Games* (1994). As Wilson (2012, p. xx) suggests of this text: 'one of its key contributions was, quite simply, raising awareness about sport related environmental problems – problems that received little or no attention in the years leading up to the book's publication and *problems that remain centrally relevant to this day*'. As a sports manager, Chernushenko was concerned with the negative impacts that sporting events were having on the environment and with how the creation of greener, more sustainable events, would, in return, prove to be a sound investment for the future of the planet and sport. The organization of major sporting events is not, by any means, an eco-friendly endeavour, but with some calculated efforts, Chernushenko argued that improvements could be made while retaining economic profitability. Echoing the definition of sustainability in The Brundtland Report, Chernushenko (1994) wrote that 'Sport is sustainable when it meets the needs of today's sporting community while contributing to the improvement of future sport opportunities for all and the improvement of the integrity of the natural and social environment on which it depends'. Through his consulting firm 'Green and Gold', he was able, for a host of events, to implement the general guidelines proposed in *Greening our Games*.

The managerial vision employed by Chernushenko, although applauded by many, was critically analysed by scholars, in particular, Helen Lenskyj, who accused him of being entrenched in corporate environmentalism by focusing on greening for-profit environmental practices that remain beholden to a capitalist paradigm (Wilson 2012). Lenskyj (1998) argued that Chernushenko's political position in environmental terms is one of 'light green'. His focus is to help organizers of sports events achieve financial stability and growth while simply showing some consideration for the environment. Conversely, a 'dark green' political position on the environment, explained Lenskyj (1998, p. 342), is one in which 'the natural environment is seen as having intrinsic worth and existing political and economic systems are to be challenged when they pose a threat'.

Importantly, the issues raised by Chernushenko, and critiqued by Lenskyj, have come to find their way into the policies of international sport organizations. For example, in a document entitled *Green Goal*, FIFA clearly states the importance of incorporating a sustainable framework in the organization of the 2006 World Cup in Germany:

> Sustainable effects of the World Cup were at the centre of planning by the German Football Association and its Organizing Committee for the 2006 FIFA World Cup from the very beginning. A few months after the final in Berlin we notice

that Germany and German football profit from the sustainability of the World
Cup as a result of newly-created jobs, the construction of spectacular stadiums
and rekindled enthusiasm for honorary posts. (FIFA 2004).

Although this might be seen to exaggerate the achievements and legacy of
the Football World Cup and the Olympic Games, the document states how
sustainability is to be incorporated into the construction of the stadiums and
other venues. The document does not acknowledge, however, that sustainable
development might be achieved by avoiding such constructions in the first
place, and if possible using what is already built. Equally as Blühdorn (2009)
argues, sustainability policies are still developed within a 'growth' paradigm,
limiting their effectiveness and reducing their ability or likelihood to question
the negative effects on the environment of economic growth itself.

While the first links between sport and the environment were mainly tied to
such large-scale sports mega-events, World Cups, Olympic Games, and World
Championships continue to have serious environmental consequences. As
such, the key characteristics of contemporary sports mega-events make them
an easy target for a variety of environmentalist concerns. However, as Hayes
and Karamichas (2012, p. 10) note: '[they] provide a platform for economic
growth oriented approaches to environmental protection and amelioration
[and facilitate] the creation and growth of new markets'. Thus, sports
mega-events represent a difficult conundrum: the ideal solution for hosting
completely eco-friendly sports mega-events would simply be to stop staging
them; this would align with the 'dark green' position. But as they are deeply
entrenched in society's collective consciousness, and they generate immense
profit for some corporations, sports mega-events will likely continue to exist
and environmental activism will continue in order to minimize the (inevitable)
strain they put on the environment.

Environmental movements and sport

While the previous section discussed the progressive preoccupation of the
Olympic movement with the environment in general and with the issues of
sustainability and legacy in particular since the disaster of the Albertville Games,
in this section we consider and contrast three examples of organizations and
movements that have been particularly active on the issue of sport and the
environment both locally and globally: Greenpeace, Surfers against Sewage
and the Anti-golf Movement. These examples provide various angles through
which the environmental movement can be seen to have influenced sport.

Ranging from Cousteau's crusade against nuclear bomb testing to the Detox
movement, Greenpeace deals and has dealt with a host of issues during its long
and dramatic history. As one of the world's most important international non-
governmental organization (INGO), it also delves, through multiple avenues,

into the world of sport. The goal of this short section is to go a bit further into the relationship of Greenpeace with sports and to explain some of the ties fuelling this important relationship.

Perhaps the most widely known and oft-cited role of Greenpeace within sport was its actions regarding the environmental impact of the Olympic games (Lenskyj 1998). Starting in 1992, Greenpeace played an important role in what was to be Sydney's winning bid for the 2000 Games. Greenpeace arranged a proposition around an eco-friendly construction of the athletes' village and was selected by the SOCOG to deliver green guidelines to be implemented for the construction of this infrastructure (Greenpeace 2000). A set of environmental guidelines was also developed by Greenpeace and other environmental groups for the bid committee and SOCOG. And yet, to many, the Sydney Games did not meet its promises of environmentally protective practices and outcomes. Sometimes referred to as the 'Greenwash Games', the Sydney Games were, in a sense, the culmination of the light green position advocated by Chernushenko and other environmentally conscious organizers. In fact, Greenpeace itself, and other organizations, were critical about the impact of the Games; the IOC was to be blamed for the environmental mishaps that occurred during the Games:

> Greenpeace's analysis of the Sydney Games highlighted the absence of involvement at a detailed level by the IOC and its failure to intervene to ensure that the Games' Environmental Guidelines were not breached. The IOC must increase its capacity to advise, direct and pressure bidding and host cities to ensure that their environmental commitments are met. (Greenpeace 2000, p. 2)

Somewhat ironically, Greenpeace ended up criticizing its own involvement in the organizing and bidding of the Games since, as stated earlier, they were directly involved with SOCOG by way of multiple projects. Lenskyj (1998) describes how Greenpeace activists actually cleaned barrels of toxic waste from a site situated near the Olympics stadium, thus pointing to an environmental mismanagement by SOCOG. The response from SOCOG to this was to criticize Greenpeace for being 'unpatriotic' and for interfering with the Games. An assessment of Greenpeace's involvement in the 2000 Games is complicated. On the one hand, Greenpeace states in official documents that they positively impacted the Games by pushing SOCOG to adopt strict environmental guidelines. On the other hand, they were criticized for undertaking actions that actually impacted the image and legacy of the 2000 Games.

Following this complex relationship with the Sydney games, Greenpeace has continued to be associated with the Olympic Games. In a report entitled *China After the Olympics: Lessons from Beijing*, Greenpeace focused on the positive and negative environmental issues related to the Beijing Games. While it praised BOCOG's environmental initiatives outlined in the bid documents and the fact that it ended up respecting some of them, Greenpeace also noted that the Beijing

Games could have ensured a better short-term and long-term 'environmental Olympic legacy' for the city (Greenpeace 2008, p. 3). Greenpeace clearly stated that, in environmental terms, Beijing surpassed Athens's 2004 performance and that for a city with enormous pollution problems due to exponential growth, the environmental legacy was not to be dismissed.

Given their profile, it is understandable that Greenpeace has had an involvement in sports mega-events. But Greenpeace has also undertaken other initiatives linked to sport over the years. Recently, for example, Greenpeace published a report criticizing outdoor clothing companies for their use of perfluorinated compounds (PFC), a toxic substance harmful to the environment and to health (Greenpeace 2012). Ironically, almost all the companies targeted in Greenpeace research have a clear environmental policy clearly stating how 'green' they are and how they oversee the manufacturing process. The report created quite a stir in the outdoor industry. ISPO's news site stated that 'Greenpeace had once again attacked outdoor brands for using toxic or even carcinogenic substances in their products'. (ISPO 2012). In a related manner, in Canada, Greenpeace has denounced the over-hunting of grizzly bears in British Columbia. If we were to summarize Greenpeace's involvement in the domain of sport, it could be divided into two main areas. First, there is a wider, more encompassing vision, relating to Greenpeace's participation in the Olympic Games and other sport mega-events. Second, there is a more localized approach, focusing on particular issues, such as outdoor clothing or wild life.

A second illustration of the relationship between sport and the environmental movement can be found in the campaigns of the UK pressure group Surfers Against Sewage (SAS). Initially concerned with the quality of the water at surfing locations in the United Kingdom, the organization now has a broader remit, focusing on a host of environmental issues linked to the practice of surfing (and wind-surfing). SAS is a registered charitable organization, meaning it officially receives donations, which are then funnelled into diverse programmes reflecting the organization's goals and priorities.

SAS was established in 1990 by a group of British surfers concerned with the gradual degradation of their local surfing spots. At that time, sewage and other waste were dumped directly into the sea, resulting in poor water quality, especially in densely populated areas. Some of SAS's first actions were the creation of a national campaign to improve water quality in the United Kingdom and this first 'campaign led water companies to invest approximately £5 billion in sewerage infrastructures, thus making a dramatic improvement in the cleanliness of our oceans and rivers' (SAS 2012). As the organization evolved, so did the outreach and goals of the campaigns. Now, SAS is involved in broader environmental campaigns tackling issues such as beach cleanliness, marine litter, climate change, offshore development, toxic chemicals and shipping lanes.

For Ward (1996), SAS remains one of the first civil-society organizations, in Britain at least, to intelligently utilize the 'new politics of pollution' approach. By using unconventional methods of awareness, such as inflatable pieces of faeces with the SAS logo to raise consciousness about the presence of coli forms in water. In this sense, SAS succeeded in their actions through irreverence and humour, and by employing tactics inspired by other well-known environmental campaign groups such as Greenpeace. Their actions helped define the beach as not only a place fit for leisure and sporting activities, but also a battleground where serious issues affecting the health of thousands of people could be brought out and exposed in a humorous way.

Wheaton (2007) argues that SAS started during a period when NSMs were in their infancy. As discussed in earlier chapters, NSMs were often attached to a single cause while being removed from the old workers party political formations; women's rights, LGBT rights, anti-racism, as well as the environment were of great importance during that era. SAS fits the NSM description well, in that they were involved in diverse environmental causes, but were also confined to a particular national setting. As noted the original focus of SAS was the beach. However, as the issue evolved, so did the methods of outreach, and with efficient technologies of communication, SAS was able to establish worldwide ties to other beach communities, thus extending local concerns to a global audience: '. . . environmentalism's inherent trans-nationalism leads to questions about the need for new (cosmopolitan) global conceptions of democracy and citizenship such as the ideas of 'ecological' or 'environmental citizenship' (Wheaton 2007, p. 297). This perspective highlighted by the work of Wheaton is now of prime importance because of the steady decline of NSMs and the evolution of a few overarching global social movements, including the global environmental movement (Wieviorka 2004). It is precisely this shift from the local to the global that is of interest when looking at an example like SAS. Environmental organizations are now prone to establish worldwide ties but will often try to localize the impact, meaning that in an effort to grasp the public's attention, they will link the cause to a local environmental concern. Such is the approach taken by SAS: 'UK survey research has indicated that people are more likely to show environmental awareness when they conceive of issues in concrete and local ways' (Wheaton 2007, p. 290).

The two organizations discussed so far have aimed to raise awareness about different environmental issues. They are tied to a sporting practice, which, in return, serves as a launch pad to highlight diverse environmental issues. What they are not though is anti-capitalist. In this way, the Global Anti-Golf Movement, our third example, is different. Struggles against golf development in the 1990s led groups such the Asian Tourism Network (ANTENNA) based in Thailand, the Asia-Pacific People's Environmental Network (APPEN) in Malaysia and the Global Network for Anti-Golf Course Action (GNAGA) to join together on a worldwide day of action entitled 'World No-Golf Day' in

April 1993 (Wheeler and Nauright 2006, p. 434). That date also saw the launch, by those three organizations, of the Global Anti-Golf Movement (GAGM). The GAGM website explains the rationale behind its development:

> At the heart of the golf industry is a multi-billion-dollar industry involving transnational corporations, including agribusiness, construction firms, consultancies, golf equipment manufacturers, airlines, hotel chains, real estate companies, advertising and public relations firms as well as financial institutions. . . . The bulk of the foreign exchange earned from golf courses and golf tourism does not stay in the local economy. The benefits which do remain, are reaped by a few business people and their patrons. (Anti-Golf Movement 2010).

The unofficial leader of GAGM is Gen Moriata, also known as the 'golf killer'; he claimed responsibility for the cancellation of the construction of more than a hundred golf courses in Japan after 1988 (Horne 1998). The tactics employed to thwart golf course construction were diverse: '. . . electing an anti-golf mayor; raising local awareness about the impact of golf course construction on local people's lives; or adopting a standing tree trust'. (Horne 1998, p. 178).

Looking at the history of organized opposition against the construction of golf courses leads us back to the 1990s when people from North America to Asia first began assembling to challenge golf-related development and its adverse consequences on the environment. Local communities were frequently overcome by the interests of the very same developers seeking to turn local fauna into green alleys of lush, well-trimmed, grass. While shutting down opposition is common in developed countries (see: Andriotis 2008; Briassoulis 2010; Kalant 2004), Wheeler and Nauright (2006, p. 434) rightly point out to the even more unequal distribution of power regarding local communities in developing countries:

> These problems are more pronounced in developing countries where there are few laws or regulations requiring full disclosure of information. After losing their battle against developers, local residents often lose their land next. They end up either working as laborers on the course or moving to big cities, as there are no other employment opportunities available. These types of changes can wreak havoc on rural communities while also exacerbating urban problems of slums, pollution and congestion.

Briassoulis's (2010) analysis of the anti-golf movement concentrates on the discourses used by a local population against the construction of a golf course. The site studied at Crete's Cavo Sidero peninsula appeared to be an important part of how the population reacted to the construction of the golf course. The value given to the place, as a qualitative and tangible good, had a profound impact on the people's reaction:

> Opposition does not arise in a vacuum; it concerns specific proposals for golf development in often ecologically and culturally valuable locations. Specialist

and nonspecialist signees alike did not react to abstract images but to an elitist, exclusionary image of golf and golf tourism *in conjunction with* the negative environmental, social and economic impacts of golf development *at the particular location*. (Briassoulis 2010, p. 308)

Interestingly, Andriotis (2008) also points to local resistance to the same Cavo Sidero golf resort development, but contrasts the often positive aims of the resort developers with the stark local reality they leave behind. The local population, while mostly aware of the general impact of such a project, is often ignorant of the environmental damages that can arise from such an endeavour. It is thus hard to evaluate the amount of resistance competent enough to be linked to the wider anti-golf movement, for those issues are often new to the population.

One population that famously resisted a golf course expansion is the Mohawk population of Kahnawake, in Oka, near Montreal, in Canada. In what would become a watershed example of resistance against the construction of golf courses as well as of native-government relations (Kalant 2004), the crisis, dubbed the 'Oka crisis', pitted members of a native community against golf developers. The proposed expansion of the golf course would have encroached on a traditional Mohawk cemetery, and the mayor of the city of Oka awarded a permit to the developers without a formal consultation process with the Mohawks, the population of Oka and competent environmental authorities (Kalant 2004). This resulted in a heated standoff between members of the Mohawk community and the provincial police, leading to violent altercations and important political repercussions. The proposed expansion was never developed, and the federal government finally bought the land making it off limits to potential developers.

The evolution of the GAGM clearly transcends the local-global dialectic, as the issues fought over are essentially localized in different areas all over the world but are highlighted by the work of the people behind GAGM and different organizations. Local resistance regularly occurs in response to the construction of a golf course. Although most people taking part in these forms of resistance are not official members of a worldwide anti-golf movement, they are undertaking an important task, namely to put forward some form of resistance. The challenge for GAGM is now one of coordination: finding local resistance and elevating them to a worldwide standard so they are heard and seen on an international platform.

Sport and corporate environmentalism

In the second section of this chapter, we outlined the relationships between the environmental movement and the Olympics, and the landmarks listed in Table 6.1 illustrate how environmental issues have been institutionalized in the

Olympic movement as a result of the actions of environmentalist organizations such as Greenpeace. In this final section, we attend to another facet of the institutionalization of the environment movement, corporate environmentalism. We argue that issues of environmental degradation, protection and sustainability have reached such prominence that they have now infiltrated the sport culture industry and new corporations can market themselves as being part of, or inspired by, environmentalism.

One example of this is *Deeper* (2011) a snowboarder movie featuring the adventures of professional snowboarder and self-described environmentalist, Jeremy Jones. It portrays the life of snowboarders taking on the challenge of riding some pristine and untouched mountains. The narrative sounds very similar to any other ski or snowboard movie, but it differs in one important respect. The protagonists vow never to use any form of motorized transportation (for example, a snowmobile, helicopter, float plane, chairlift, or snow cat) to access the peaks and mountains. They set out on foot from a set location, proceed to camp in the wilderness while ascending and descending peaks under their own power (a practice called 'skinning' in reference to the skins employed underneath the skis or splitboard used to ascend the mountains). Ironically, the movie never reveals how the riders get to the actual spot where they can walk to the mountains, and virtually all ski, snowboard and surf movies with a strong environmental theme avoid this question. Teton Gravity Research (TGR), the company behind the movie, stated that the movie was 100 per cent carbon neutral, again using an environmentalist discourse. Of note is that *Deeper* and its sequels *Further* and *Higher* are all, in some way, illustrative of Jones' commitment to the environment, further shown through an organization created in 2007, *Protect our Winters* (POW).

POW presents itself as dedicated to climate change issues while fusing these to the practice of alpine winter sports (like snowboarding). POW is a non-profit foundation funded by donations from both corporate sponsors and individuals. They claim to address the climate change issue by taking it to the forums of authorities that they believe retain the power to make effective changes. For example in a video posted on their website entitled 'Jeremy goes to Washington', Jones dons a suit, along with hiking boots and a toque, to lobby politicians in Washington DC. As he states:

> When I started Protect our Winters, like, the last thing I wanted to do is get into the political side of things. But it became really apparent to me that in order to really move the needle in climate change, it needs to be won on Capitol Hill (POW 2012).

Sherpas Cinemas' ski movie *ALL I CAN* (2011) is another illustration of the institutionalization of environmental values into corporate sport, in this case freestyle skiing. Promoted as an environmentally concerned ski movie, *All I CAN* combines the traditional elements of the genre, that is, technical prowess executed by professional skiers, with a strong emphasis on the ever-changing environmental conditions regulating the practice of skiing. Hence the studio claims:

> The film strives to unite global mountain culture and bind us together as the leaders of a revolution. We must be inspired to do all we can for the environment, and must learn how to take that first tiny step in the right direction (Sherpas Cinema 2011).

Clearly Sherpas Cinema, while not associated themselves with any particular environmental group, utilize discourses influenced by the environmental movement to promote the film.

As we saw in the first part of this chapter, the evolution of the environmental movement has been marked by many trajectories, leading to the creation of different political tendencies. The biggest success arguably, however, has been the mainstreaming of environmental issues into public consciousness. Skiers in this movie effectively see themselves as agents of global change. J. P. Auclair, a famous French-Canadian skier, is shown skiing a run where he dodges cars, slides on handrails and jumps over driveways, all that in an urban context, far away from the mountains. This segment appears to try to raise awareness about global warming and the gradual disappearance of ski areas due to a systematic depletion of snow. In addition, some of the athletes featured openly target environmental change as the most important social and political issue of the day: 'Every generation in history has had their own big problem to deal with, and this is ours' (ALL I CAN 2011). The pre-eminence of the topic among the skiers in the film suggests an acute form of involvement towards environmental causes; an involvement made possible by a blend of environmentalist preoccupation meshed with sports.

Dubbed the 'Cold Revolution' by Alpine winter sport pundit Auden Schendler (2011), environmental awareness in winter sports has influenced the entire winter sports equipment and apparel manufacturing industry:

> The explosion of consciousness and advocacy on climate change is . . . increasingly backed by savvy, and booming, outdoor businesses, like Black Diamond and The North Face. . . . The North Face, through its support of groups like Protect Our Winters and All.I.Can, has quietly become the leader in climate advocacy in the apparel industry. The vibe they've helped create is palpable.

Another illustration of this development of 'green consciousness' or what some might argue is industrial greenwash, is the alliance between the Surfrider Foundation and POW:

> The Surfrider Foundation, the leading name in beach and coastal protection, has teamed up with Protect Our Winters, the top non-profit from the world of snow sports to offer a combined membership that will allow boardsports enthusiasts to protect where they play (Surfrider.org 2011).

Another surfing-related company, Green Foam Blanks, exemplifies the will to put into practice environmentally friendly production methods in order to reduce the amount of toxic waste produced in the manufacture of boards. Along with other surfboard companies such as Lost Enterprises, Green Foam Blanks aim to produce a cleaner, greener product. 'Surfing would seem to be the ultimate environmentally friendly industry, what with its nature-boy image and surfers' passion for keeping the ocean and beaches clean and green' (Woody 2009).

Conclusion

As awareness of the environment has changed over the years, so has the environmental movement and so too has its relationship with sport. Is there a single, definitive, environmental movement within sport? The answer for now is uncertain. With Greenpeace activism associated with the Olympic Games, we can see an example of a major actor within the global environment movement challenging sports mega events to become more environmentally friendly. However, with the examples of SAS and the GAGM, we witnessed two movements that are environmentally sport specific. Yet with the various landmarks in the evolution of the relationship between the Olympics and the environment, as well as the development of a so-called environmentally friendly sports culture industry, we have noted the extent of the institutionalization of the environmental issue in sport.

In Tourainian terms, it is possible to identify a unity of sport, environment and social movements in a global identity, that is, an identity clearly oriented towards the defence of environmental causes as they are related to sport in one way or another. The totality of these organizations, groups, foundations and spokespersons is aimed at ensuring the long-term habitability of the planet. This suggests that the environment is bound to occupy yet a more central role in political debates, including within sport, especially with regard to the staging of sports mega-events, as actors associated with the environmental movement keep challenging sport around that issue.

Conclusion

This book aimed to do three things: to explore how and why sport has been and is connected with social movements; to describe some of the key episodes in this relationship; and to thus contribute to a better understanding of the connection between sport and the political (field). The book has therefore offered a broadly developmental account of social movements and their relation to sport and sport as a site where (today) global social movements operate. Globalization creates different conditions and opportunity structures, which lead social movements to adapt their policies, practices and politics (Hobsbawm 2011). We have noted how global or transnational social movements have developed partly in response to changing national opportunities to promote their cause and partly as a response to the development of transnational governance and the growth of international agencies such as the United Nations. The book has therefore offered insight into the 'pre-history' of these global social movements, as much as their contemporary form, by considering the development of selected social movements that have most influenced sport.

It will be evident to readers that there are several limitations to it. We have predominantly used library and archive sources close to hand – which have been predominantly Western, advanced capitalist, English and French language resources – rather than undertaken extensive fieldwork. In the future, we suggest that research will need to explore the process of social movement formation around sport even more empirically, ethnographically and globally (Burawoy et al. 2000). In particular such research would seek to identify the recruitment patterns, networks and organizational structures of global social movements. We recognize that scholarship on social movements has tended to neglect sex and gender despite the fact that political protest is and has been profoundly gendered. This dimension would be axiomatic in future research. Future research would also examine the political implications of the tensions that arise as a result of the shifts we have identified in previous chapters from engaging in resistive struggles to attempts to engage with institutions, especially at the global level. Such research will enable us to understand better how global social movements operate in relation to sport, and also identify the global forces, connections and imaginations that underpin contemporary global social movements. We conclude the book with some suggestions for where more detailed research needs to be undertaken.

As stated in the introduction, we have sought to address what we consider to be key questions: How are social movements and alter-globalization influencing the current sport order as well as the wider world order? How do the different forms of political actions spurred by social movements differ from previous forms in their reach and goals for change? Are there existing sports forms or sports organizations whose goals are consistent with global social movements? And what actual or potential influence have these organizations had on the global social order of sport?

In doing this we have often noted the ways that major sports competitions, and sports mega-events such as the Olympic and Paralympic Games and the FIFA Men's Football World Cup Finals especially, have acted as key sites for the activities of social movements related to sport. Mega-events offer an opportunity to both organisers and movements to attempt to 'seize the platform' as a vehicle for communicating their ideals and values, challenging regimes and bringing powerful corporations and organizations to account (Price 2008). This relationship between social movements, social protest and sports mega-events is not new. In the 1960s, as we have seen in Chapter 4, questions were raised by the anti-apartheid movement about the regime in South Africa that led to the country's expulsion from the IOC until 1992, and the same sanctions were applied to Rhodesia until the end of white minority rule. Yet these expulsions were exceptional. More recently, in 2012 before the London Summer Olympic and Paralympic Games, questions were raised about the inclusion of Syria at the event in the light of the massacres of civilians that had taken place there and also the conditions for workers in factories supplying Adidas, one of the main producers of sports apparel and equipment. As we noted in Chapter 2, also prior to the 2012 Olympics, several organizations combined once again as 'Play Fair' and developed a campaign around the London Olympic and Paralympic Games (Timms 2012). The Olympic 'platform', built at huge expense by large investments from others, remains an attractive 'fora to advance political and commercial messages' (Price 2008, p. 86) through legal channels of sponsorship or less mainstream ones such as ambush or guerrilla marketing and hijacking or 'piggybacking' by social movements (Price 2008, p. 87). The default setting with the IOC, however, is that involvement in the Olympic 'movement' can serve as an agent of change. Hence as Rowe (2012) remarks, mega-events such as the Olympics provide claims for 'global civil legitimacy' to be made by hosts and wannabe hosts alike.

The IOC and local mega-event organizers claim to uphold human rights. The current version of the *Olympic Charter* for example states: 'The practice of sport is a human right. Every individual must have the possibility of practising sport, without discrimination of any kind and in the Olympic spirit, which requires mutual understanding with a spirit of friendship, solidarity and fair play' (IOC 2011, p. 10 available at http://www.olympic.org/Documents/olympic_charter_en.pdf [accessed 9 October 2012]). Campaigners seek to discredit what they consider to be the hypocrisy of the organisers and/or host nations. The opening and closing ceremonies that are viewed by vast global audiences do allow space for implicit if not overt political statements to be made. Hence the 2000 Sydney Olympics Closing ceremony is considered to be one of the 'gayest' featuring as it did several iconic gay singers and dancers (Scupham-Bilton, n.d.). In London in 2012, the opening ceremony of the Summer Olympics featured suffragettes and the opening and closing ceremonies of the Paralympic Games (with undeniably smaller global television audiences) featured an extended celebration of the UN Declaration of Human Rights, human diversity and disabled persons in particular.

Yet in struggles over the mega-event platform critics point out how there are often huge gaps between the rhetoric of promoters and the unfolding reality of the event itself. To illustrate this consider the 'High-Level Panel on Sport and the UN Declaration of Human Rights' that took place on 27 February 2012 at the 19th Session of the United Nations Human Rights Council held in Geneva, Switzerland (for details see: http://www.un.org/wcm/webdav/site/ sport/shared/sport/pdfs/HRC_19th-session_High-level-panel-on-sport.pdf [accessed 9 October 2012]). The aim of the meeting was to discuss the ways in which 'sport and major sporting events, in particular the Olympic and Paralympic Games, can be used to promote awareness and understanding of the UDHR and the application of its principles. Similar to other declarations in recent years, great emphasis was placed on the value of sport as a vehicle for peace and human development. The UN High Commissioner for Human Rights, Dr Navi Pillay, opened proceedings by stating that sport and human rights shared many fundamental values and objectives, and that part of the Olympic Charter chimed perfectly with the UDHR. She felt however that there had been 'little interaction between the human rights movement mechanisms and the world of sports'. She urged the host organizers of the next four Olympic and Paralympic Games – to be held in London in the United Kingdom (2012), Sochi in Russia (2014), Rio de Janeiro in Brazil (2016) and PyeongChang in the Republic of Korea (2018) – to pay special attention to the promotion of human rights. Dr Pillay's comments were followed by observations from representatives of countries hosting the next three Olympic and Paralympic Games, including a United Kingdom Minister of State for the Foreign and Commonwealth Office, Keith Mills, Deputy Chair of the London Organizing Committee of the Olympic and Paralympics Games (LOCOG), Carlos Nuzman, President of Rio 2016, and Vladimir Lukin, Human Rights Ombudsman and President of the Russian Paralympics Committee. In various ways each speaker affirmed the relationship between the Olympics and human rights: the UK government minister stated that when people tuned in to watch the London 2012 Olympics, there would be a wider agenda visible including human rights; Keith Mills suggested that sport could be a valuable means by which to promote peace and human rights; Carlos Nuzman stated that the Rio 2016 Games was in line with the focus of the Rio de Janeiro Master Plan which was to prioritize projects catering for young people and that between 2009 and 2011, 8,000 households had been successfully resettled without 'judicial authorization'; and while overcoming racism in sports remained an issue for the international community, Vladimir Lukin warned against increasing attempts to politicize the Olympic Games.

Following these statements a discussion developed that enabled interested parties to contribute. These included representatives from other nations and a representative of Amnesty International (AI). The latter raised the issue of the 1984 toxic gas leak from the Union Carbide pesticide factory in Bhopal, India, which killed between 7,000 and 10,000 people immediately and another 15,000 in the next 20 years. Since 2001 Dow Chemicals became the parent company of the Bhopal factory, but had consistently denied any responsibility. In 2010, Dow became a worldwide sponsor of the IOC through its 'TOP' programme. In 2011, it agreed to sponsor the fabric wrap around the stadium built for the 2012 London Olympics. This prompted calls from the Indian Olympic Association and other bodies for the IOC to terminate the relationship with Dow and LOCOG to drop the sponsorship of the stadium materials.

Taking these two statements – those about Dow and Rio – we can see the potential for gaps to open up between the rhetoric and the reality of the Olympic movement at such 'High-Level' meetings. While the Dow sponsorship issue remains of ongoing concern to critics of the way the Union Carbide disaster in Bhopal has been handled, no major criticisms emerged during the 2012 Olympics. There were no reports of challenges to the comments from the President of Rio 2016 made in February 2012. Yet in the period since Rio was awarded the hosting of the 2016 Summer Olympic and Paralympic Games, there have been several cases of forced evictions and the displacement of local communities identified (and also in other cities in Brazil scheduled to host the 2014 FIFA Men's Football World Cup Finals). Development corporations continue to focus on economic and infrastructural development through the Games that are largely exploitative and unsustainable (Darnell 2012). Research by activists and groups working to identify human rights abuses related to forced evictions and displacements within Brazil would appear to challenge the complacent statement of Mr Nuzman (see Horne and Whannel 2012, pp. 138–42; Millington and Darnell, in press). As Chapter 4 illustrated, human rights discourse has a contested history, and so this potential for contradictions to emerge around statements about human rights and sport should not be surprising.

As we also noted in Chapter 5, the peace movement has historically been concerned with the broader social, political and economic forces at work that produce and sustain violence and conflict, namely renewed notions of national exceptionalism and the violent enforcement of global neo-liberalism. Since the 1980s, however, the increased breadth of the movement led to a decrease in the depth of its critique; in the current case of organizing sport for peace, the increased acceptance of sport as an approach to peace building and conflict resolution leads to a more politically palatable and less challenging approach to anti-war politics. Yet in a recent critique of the Olympic Movement as a supposed force for peace and understanding around the world, Hoberman (2011) forcefully argued that the IOC has routinely promoted a version of peace that is ostensibly apolitical, neutral and universal. While the attraction of this political identity for a supra-national organization like the IOC – one that wishes to maintain a neutral basis for interacting with nations around the world – is clear, the IOC's vision and version of a sport-based peace movement is based on what Hoberman (2011, p. 21) calls 'amoral universalism, the traditional Olympic dogma that all human tribes must take part in the Games, no matter how repressive or inhumane their governments may be'. Not only has such amoral universalism resulted in dubious friendships and relationships between the IOC and a raft of political despots and human rights abusers, but also it necessarily prevents the IOC from criticizing powerful institutions and governments around issues of violence and conflict, or participating in anti-war criticism or peace activism. As a result, the IOC's credibility as a force for peace, or as part of the peace movement, is severely compromised given that, in Hoberman's (2011, p. 25) words, 'No international bodies that induct (as members) such morally compromised people in such numbers can be taken seriously as a peace lobby or as a humanitarian enterprise similar to a well-managed NGO'.

We have in this book started to examine the tensions that arise as a result of the long-term tendency for social movements to move politically and strategically from resistive struggles towards more active engagement and involvement with powerful institutions, including governments and NGOs at national, regional and global levels. We noted in Chapter 5 for example how this shift has materialized in the relationship between sport and the peace movement. While there are few other sport organizations that can be directly compared to the IOC, given its size, scope and resources, it is reasonable to argue that the position taken by the IOC aligns with the cultural turn in the peace movement towards peace education and inclusive understanding and away from resistive politics. As such, sport-focused peace initiatives of the kind proffered by the IOC are open to at least two significant criticisms. The first is the resultant lack of attention paid to structural and political causes of violence, war and conflict – issues fundamental to twentieth-century peace theory and activism (Galtung 1969) – as a focus on the fundamental structures and causes of military violence is replaced with an emphasis on encouraging individuals to account for their own positioning amidst social stratification and marginalization. From this perspective, organizations like the IOC can promote peace and understanding in and through Olympic sport and global Olympism without being beholden to any responsibility for the processes of capitalist exploitation and industrialized militarism that exacerbate violence.

A second criticism of recent sport-focused peace initiatives connects with Donnelly's (2011) reminder that we should recognize the ambivalent relationship between sport and violence. Sport has regularly and historically demonstrated proclivities for exacerbating war as much as promoting peace and understanding, and yet much of the currently dominant model of peace building through sport promotes an essentializing and universalizing version of sport as fundamentally positive or pro-social. At issue is the need to recognize the necessity of peace-focused reforms *within* sport more so than peace *because* of sport, and to use sport as an opportunity to resist war and militarism, neither of which are regularly promoted within the cultural turn towards peace education. Indeed, the uncritical promotion of sport for peace, based on a notion of its essential characteristics, runs the risk of exacerbating violence and conflict by failing to deal with such issues.

It is here that the issue of resistive politics becomes most important. If and when sport for peace programmes, discourses and activism are championed, but done so in ways that are unaccompanied by political activity based on resistive anti-war, anti-militarism principals, a result is the downloading of the chore of peace building onto the people who suffer most from war. That is, if sport becomes a tool for peace education that primarily focuses on 'educating' young people towards cultural understanding, then it potentially and perhaps unwittingly serves to ask people to solve problems of violence not of their own making. The general acceptance of conflict resolution practices related to sport offers credence, at least to an extent, that such practices do little to produce change because even as young people 'learn' to respect one another through sport, violence and militarism continues to offer those in positions of power a legitimate political outlet to assert their dominance over others. While it is popular and politically palatable to position and promote sport in the service of peace education and understanding – both international and personal – this arguably does very little to attend to the roots of the problem.

The need to promote and implement peace initiatives and youth development in places of violent conflict like Afghanistan (through, for example, sport-focused NGOs like 'Skateistan') is not simply the result of the limitations or wrongdoing or lack of cross-cultural understanding on the part of the Afghan people, but a product of neo-liberal globalization, state exceptionalism, pre-emptive military action and violent neo-colonial policies. Yet, by promoting sport for peace as a cultural phenomenon, these relationships and structures are arguably obscured, particularly as they are replaced or overshadowed by a focus on affect, particularly pleas for compassion, care and support for the comparatively less fortunate Afghan people (see Thorpe and Rinehart 2012).

Similarly, International Relations scholars increasingly recognize that internationally created norms of proper behaviour may propel states to redefine their interests and change behaviour (Kollman and Waites 2009, p. 9). The awarding of the hosting of the Olympic Games to regimes with dubious human rights records, for example, might enable demonstrations about this situation to be developed. Perhaps this does enable a slow, evolutionary, path to social reform through moral suasion to take place? Brownell (2012) questions if the campaigns around the Olympic Games hosted in Beijing in 2008 by human and workers' rights critics (discussed in Chapter 2) were mainly gestural politics, without any real chance of being effective? For her the IOC is not such a powerful organization and cannot bring about lasting change. For other writers, such as Hoberman as we have seen, it remains a corrupt organization that pretends to be able to achieve changes it is actually incapable of securing. The politics of moral suasion is complicated, and it can take many years to determine if an impact has been made.

At the same time, we have been careful not to adopt a teleological under-standing of social movements and sport, nor have we championed one or other of the social movements analysed in this book. We recognized from the outset that there could be no guarantee of positive or progressive outcomes in the struggles they engage in. Indeed as Teeple (2005, p. 19) notes with regard to the struggle over human rights, the individual 'freedoms' that human rights protect often also support the corporate autonomy necessary for international exploitation of marginalized groups within capitalist relations. This suggests that the system of universal human rights may serve as part of a 'global enabling framework' for mobile transnational capitalism. Sport is far from exempt from such relations. Similarly Hartmann (2003, pp. 268–70) describes how the post-protest racial regime in American sport recuperated the image of the 'black power' salute made in 1968 by Smith and Carlos, and yet arguably athletes and activists in sport have no more progressive template. Over time socially radical images, objects and practices associated with the 1960s have been appropriated and transformed into commodities available to mass and mainstream markets. Capitalist consumer culture dilutes and subverts the original meaning and intentions of the protesters and critics. Critical experiences and grievances and the radical intent that prompted the 1968 Olympic, and other, demonstrations tend to become portrayed in terms of a focus on the individual courage of the athletes, and abstracted commitments to 'equality', 'dignity' and 'justice' is often all that results. Muhammad Ali is especially portrayed in this way.

Enabling mass participation in globally popular sports through various programmes (e.g. Slum Soccer) may also fail to challenge, and in fact may further facilitate, the continuously unequal flows of global capital that contribute to the 'underdevelopment' of the Global South. As Kidd (2008, p. 376) rightly points out, the need to focus on, and advocate for, sport as a human right stems in large part from diminished social welfare policies and structural inequalities characteristic of contemporary neo-liberal and neo-conservative political regimes. Similarly, Gruneau (in press) contends that sport for development and peace initiatives align more with the expansion of a rights-based culture, than with political struggles or resistance against the politics of unequal development. Attempts to address issues of human rights in and through sport have problematically tended towards the privileging of high-performance sporting systems that exclude mass participation to the benefits of elite athletes and performance maximization (Donnelly 2008). Utilizing sport to advance a rights or social justice agenda is not easily done. Advocacy and engagement, through the work of those claiming to be public intellectuals seeking impact through public sociology (Donnelly et al. 2011), is evident in some writing about social justice and sport. This enthusiasm to engage may miss a vital point. Sport has contradictory aims and can promote diverse responses.

Nonetheless, we have seen that in the past 10–15 years, social movements have developed that are global in outlook yet operate at both local and global levels. These global social movements propose, celebrate and attempt to strengthen 'global consciousness', including sometimes offering alternative models of sport. These global social movements attempt to go beyond the successes and limits of earlier social movements, develop more than resistant activism and globalize issues through developing new networks of actors. As Pleyers (2010) notes alter-globalization has developed both according to subjectivity and reason. The former has involved experiments in lived experience, creating new autonomies of subjectivity. The latter has seen new forms of social and political organizing – with more egalitarian, environmentally responsible and ethical consequences for all global citizens. Changing the sporting political imaginary is, as we have shown in this book, quite complex. On the one hand, institutionalization and legislation can create 'neutral spaces' in which urgent social issues can be effectively depoliticized. On the other hand, alternative ways of organizing sport and organizing sports practice in relation to the environment have been and continue to be developed. We hope that this book encourages others to investigate the role that social movements play and have played in shaping, contesting and developing sport.

Throughout this book, important issues and themes from the social movements literature have been discussed in relation to sport, such as the formation of collective identity, the role of sport in facilitating social action and the relative success or failures of sport-focused social movements. At the same time, the analysis of these topics and themes remains necessarily incomplete and is therefore worthy of ongoing scholarly attention. We thus conclude with a list of themes identified in earlier chapters and an agenda for future research into sport and social movements.

First, the analysis in the book illustrates that, to a significant extent, sport offers a site or theatre for social actors to engage in particular struggles and to draw attention to issues of social justice. Notably, this effect and opportunity can be seen both through positive and through negative aspects of the organization, culture and experience of sport itself. For example, the relationship between sport and the environmental movement shows that particular sports, such as surfing and snowboarding, constitute both a site at which to celebrate and experience the natural environment but also a node which forces sports people to confront the degradation and exploitation of the environment. Thus, sport can be a site of struggle because of the progressive action that it promotes but also in response to the injustices that it exacerbates or the inequalities in which sport is implicated. Ongoing attention should be paid to the ways in which sport-focused social movement actors and organizations negotiate this tension and the techniques they use in order to connect meanings to sport as part of the promotion and renewal of social movements locally and globally.

Second, the extent to which the values of sport, oft-contested, connect to or diverge from social movement organizations is worthy of ongoing analysis. While sport and sport culture possess no inherent values, particularly across geographies and eras, the question remains as to how and why social movement organizations embrace, adopt and even adapt and update the values of sport in pursuit of their reforms and movement goals. For example, peace movement values of pacifism and global brother- and sisterhood are likely at odds with the hyper-competitiveness, jingoism and celebration of violence found in many dominant sporting forms. And yet, the possibility to celebrate sport as a common form of humanity likely remains attractive or useful to some social movement actors. The ways in which social movement organizations reconcile such tensions requires further understanding.

Third, the ways in which sport becomes part of the formation of collective identity among social movement actors and organizations remains largely under-analysed and undetermined. Given that a sense of united interests and actions is central to the theoretical and empirical understanding of what constitutes a social movement and how movements are formed, the ways in which collective identity may (or may not) form in and around sport is of central importance. Further, given the role of sport – particularly communal dimensions of the sporting experience like fandom – in constructing collective identities, synergies may exists between fans and activists, synergies that remain less than fully understood within the study of sport and social movements.

Fourth, understanding the ways in which sport becomes an event, and by extension an opportunity, through which to advance a social movement agenda requires further investigation. This understanding of events can refer both to temporal and to staged events (such as a football fixture or the Olympic Games) that may provide a practical opportunity or backdrop for social movement organization, but should also take into account sport as a cultural phenomenon, one with social and economic significance, that may facilitate opportunities for, and recognition of, social movement efforts.

Fifth, given that the dominant sporting model remains one that is corporate led, and in addition sometimes coupled with or supported by state interest and power, the ways in which social movement organizations that connect to sport negotiate corporate influence and the interests of the state remains an important area of inquiry. While the alter-globalization framework draws attention to the efforts of social actors to reform the meanings and values of society itself, it remains the case that social movement organizations and actors connected to sport have to work amidst the interests of corporations and the state. How they negotiate and even integrate these powerful interests into their organizing and activism is worthy of further attention.

Sixth, the significance of the media should be of interest in understanding the relationship between sport and social movements. On the one hand, the symbiotic relationship between contemporary sport and the media clearly offers social movement actors a platform from which to work for change and reform. On the other hand, sport media tends to organize and disseminate content in a conservative fashion that is likely at odds with social movement goals and values. Is it possible, then, for social movement actors connected to sport to capitalize on the opportunities that sports media provide while challenging and even reforming the ways in which sports media perpetuates many of the structures that social movements oppose? Research is needed in this area.

Finally, and seventh, tensions, contradictions and opposing forces within sport itself likely pose a challenge for social movement organizations that coalesce in and through sport culture. For example, a focus on elite sport versus sport for all, private sport versus public sport, and individual, competitive versus cooperative and communitarian sport constitute notable tensions within the culture of sport itself. As such, there is likely no single sporting form or definition through which social movement actors definitively organize or advance their cause. How do social movement actors then reconcile such tensions?

In sum, this book has demonstrated that sport in its organization and culture connects to the history and dissemination of social movements in important ways and vice versa. At the same time, many of the challenges and intricacies of social movement formation, mobilization and success or failure in relation to sport remain under-examined and worthy of ongoing investigation and assessment.

References

Adams, C. (2002). Fighting for acceptance: Sigfrid Edström and Avery Brundage: Their efforts to shape and control women's participation in the Olympic Games. In K. B. Wamsley, R. K. Barney and S. G. Martyn (Eds), *The Global Nexus Engaged: Past, Present, Future Interdisciplinary Olympic Studies: Sixth International Symposium for Olympic Research*. London, Ontario: International Centre for Olympic Studies, University of Western Ontario, pp. 143–8.

Adams, D. (2000). Toward a global movement for a culture of peace. *Peace and Conflict*, 6(3), 259–66.

Alter Chen, M. (1995). Engendering world conferences: The international women's movement and the United Nations. *Third World Quarterly*, 16(3), 477–93.

Alvarez, S. E. (1998). Latin American feminisms 'go global': Trends of the 1990s and challenges for the new millennium. In S. E. Alvarez, E. Dagnino and A. Escobar (Eds), *Cultures of Politics/Politics of Cultures: Re-Visioning Latin American Social Movements*. Boulder, CO: Westview, pp. 293–316.

Amnesty International (2012). *Amnesty International Report, 2012*, London: Amnesty International.

Anderson, J. (2003). Turned into taxpayers: paraplegia, rehabilitation and sport at Stoke Mandeville, 1944–1956. *Journal of Contemporary History*, 38(3), 461–75.

Andriotis, K. (2008). Integrated Resort Development: The Case of Cavo Sidero, Crete. *Journal of Sustainable Tourism*, 16, 428–44.

Anon (1996). Surfers Against Sewage. *Environmental Health Perspectives*, 104(7), 684–5.

Anti-Golf Movement (2010). *Manifesto*: http://www.antigolf.org/english.html [Last accessed 15 October 2012].

Antrobus, P. (2004). *The Global Women's Movement: Origins, Issues and Strategies*. Black Point, NS: Fernwood Publishing.

Antrobus, P. and Sen, G. (2006). The personal is global: The project and politics of the transnational women's movement. In S. Batliwala and L. D. Brown (Eds), *Transnational Civil Society: An Introduction*. Bloomfield, CT: Kumarian Press, pp. 142–58.

Appadurai, A. (2006). *Fear of Small Numbers: An Essay on the Geography of Anger*. Durham and London: Duke University Press.

Arnaud, P. (1994a). *Les origines du sport ouvrier en Europe*. Paris: Éditions L'Harmattan.

—(1994b). Le sport des ouvriers avant le sport ouvrier (1830–1908): le cas français. In Arnaud, P. (1994). *Les origines du sport ouvrier en Europe*. Paris: Éditions L'Harmattan, pp. 45–85.

Atwood, M. (2012). Rachel Carson's *Silent Spring*, 50 years on. *The Guardian*, 7 December. [Last accessed online 20 December 2012]: http://www.guardian.co.uk/books/2012/dec/07/why-rachel-carson-is-a-saint.

Bailey, S. (2008). *Athlete First: A History of the Paralympic Movement*. Chichester: John Wiley.

Baird, V. (2004). *Sex, Love and Homophobia*. London: Amnesty International.

Bale, J. (1994). *Landscapes of Modern Sport*. Leicester: Leicester University Press.

Bandyopadhyay, K. (2008). Feel Good, Goodwill and India's Friendship Tour of Pakistan, 2004: Cricket, Politics and Diplomacy in Twenty-First-Century India. *The International Journal of the History of Sport*, 25(12), 1654–70.

Bannerji, H., Mojab, S., and Whitehead, J. (Eds), (2001). *Of Property and Propriety: The Role of Gender and Class in Imperialism and Nationalism*. Toronto: University of Toronto Press.

Barkham, P. (2011). 'Anton Hysén: Anyone afraid of coming out should give me a call', *The Guardian*, 29 March, available at: http://www.guardian.co.uk/football/2011/mar/29/anton-hysen-afraid-coming-out [accessed 5 October 2012].

Barton, C. (2004). Global women's movements at a crossroads: Seeking definition, new alliances and greater impact. *Socialism and Democracy*, 18(1), 151–84.

Barton, S. (2009). *A Sporting Chance: The History of Special Olympics Great Britain*. Leicester: Leicester City Council and Special Olympics Great Britain.

Barton, S., Carter, N., Holt, R., and Williams, J. (2011). *Learning Disability, Sport and Legacy. A Report By the Legacy Research Group on the Special Olympics GB National Summer Games Leicester 2009*, available at: https://www.dora.dmu.ac.uk/bitstream/handle/2086/5323/Learning%20Disability,%20Sport%20and%20Legacy%20A%20Report%20by%20the%20Legacy%20Research%20Group%20on%20the%20Special%20Olympics%20GB%20National%20Summer%20Games%20Leicester%202009.pdf?sequence=1 [Last accessed 4 October 2012].

Bastian, K. (1986). *Moscow'86 Goodwill Games*. Atlanta, Ga.: Pelican Publishing Company.

Basu, A. (Ed.), (1995). *The Challenge of Local Feminisms: Women's Movements in Global Perspective*. Boulder, CO: Westview Press.

—(2000). Globalization of the local/localization of the global: Mapping transnational women's movements. *Meridians*, 1(1), 68–84.

Beaudet, P., Canet, R., and Masicotte, M.-J. (2010). *L'altermondialisme: forum sociaux, résistances et nouvelle culture politique*. Montreal: Écosociété.

Beck, U. and Sznaider, N. (2006). Unpacking cosmopolitanism for the social sciences: A research agenda. *The British Journal of Sociology*, 57(1), 1–23.

Bennett, T., Grossberg, L., and Morris, M. (Eds), (2005). *New Keywords*. Oxford: Blackwell.

Bezanson, K. and Luxton, M. (Eds), (2006). *Social Reproduction: Feminist Political Economy Challenges Neo-Liberalism*. Montreal and Kingston: McGill-Queen's University Press.

Blackburn, R. (2011). 'Reclaiming Human Rights'. *New Left Review*, 69, 126–38.

Blühdorn, I. (2009). Locked into the politics of unsustainability. *Eurozine.com*. *Retrieved from* http://www.eurozine.com/articles/2009-10-30-bluhdorn-en.html. Last accessed 8 September 2013.

Blumer, H. (1971). Social Problems as Collective Behaviour. *Social Problems*, 18, 298–306.

Booth, D. (2004). 'Book review of D. Hartmann (2003) *Race, Culture and the Revolt of the Black Athlete*'. *Olympika* XIII, 93–8.

Borrel, M. (1999). *Sociologie d'une métamorphose: La fédération sport et gymnique du travail entre société communiste et mouvement sportif (1964–1992)*. Unpublished PhD Thesis, Institut d'études politiques de Paris.

Bourdieu, P. (1984). *Distinction: A Social Critique of the Judgement of Taste*. London: Routledge.

Boykoff, J. (2011). The Anti-Olympics. *New Left Review*, 67, 41–59.

Brackenridge, C. (1995). Think global, act global: The future of international women's sports organizations. *International Council for Health, Physical Education, Recreation, Sport and Dance Journal*, 31(4), 7–11.

Briassoulis, H. (2010). 'Sorry Golfers, This Is Not Your Spot!': Exploring Public Opposition to Golf Development. *Journal of Sport and Social Issues*, 34(3), 288–311.

Briggs, R., McCarthy, H., and Zorbas, A. (2004). *16 Days: the Role of the Olympic Truce in the Toolkit for Peace*. London: Demos.

Brindle, D. (2012). Disability movement at a crossroads as Paralympic arrives *The Guardian*, 21 August, pp. 1 and 10–11.

Brittain, I. (2012). *From Stoke Mandeville to Stratford: A History of the Summer Paralympic Games*. London: Common Ground.

—(2010). *The Paralympic Games Explained*. London: Routledge.

—(2008). The Evolution of the Paralympic Games. In R. Cashman and S. Darcy (Eds), *Benchmark Games. The Sydney 2000 Paralympic Games*. Sydney: Walla Walla Press, pp. 19–34.

Brock, P. (1998). *Varieties of Pacifism: A Survey from Antiquity to the Outset of the Twentieth Century*. New York: Syracuse University Press.

Broderick, T. (Thursday 11 August 2011). Jets Logo Militaristic? Absurd, *Winnipeg Sun*.

Brownell, S. (2012). Human rights and the Beijing Olympics: imagined global community and the transnational public sphere. *The British Journal of Sociology*, 63(2), 306–27.

Bunch, C. and Fried, S. (1996). Beijing'95: Moving women's human rights from margin to center. *Signs*, 22(1), 200–4.

Burawoy, M., Blum, J., George, S., Gille, Z., Gowan, T., Haney, L., Klawiter, M., Lopez, S., O'Riain, S., and Thayer, M. (2000). *Global Ethnography. Forces, Connections and Imaginations in a Postmodern World*. Berkeley, CA: University of California Press.

Burleson, C. (2012). The ancient Olympic Truce in modern-day peacekeeping: revisiting Ekecheiria. *Sport in Society*, 15(6), 798–813.

Butterworth, M. L. (2012). Militarism and Memorializing at the Pro Football Hall of Fame. *Communication and Critical/Cultural Studies*, 9(3), 241–58.

Cabrera, L. (2011). *The Practice of Global Citizenship*. Cambridge: Cambridge University Press.

Camilleri, J. A. (1990). Rethinking sovereignty in a shrinking fragmented world. In R. B. J. Walker and S. H. Mendlovitz (Eds), *Contending sovereignties – Redefining political community*. Boulder, CO: Lynne Rienner, pp. 13–44.

Cantelon, H. and Letters, M. (2000). The Making of the IOC Environmental Policy as the Third Dimension of the Olympic Movement. *International Review for the Sociology of Sport*, 35(3), 294–308.

Cariou, K. (2011). Kimball Cariou: My beef with Stephen Harper and Don Cherry, *The Georgia Straight*. 7 January [Last accessed from http://www.straight.com/article-367600/vancouver/kimball-cariou-my-beef-stephen-harper-and-don-cherry].

Carlos, J. and Zirin, D. (2012). *The John Carlos Story: The Sports Moment that Changed the World*. Chicago, IL: Haymarket Books.

Carson, R. (1962/2002). *Silent Spring*. Boston, CT: Houghton Mifflin/Mariner Books.

Cashman, R. and Darcy, S. (Eds), (2008). *Benchmark Games. The Sydney 2000 Paralympic Games*. Sydney: Walla Walla Press.

Castells, M. (1996). *The Information Age: Economy, Society and Culture, Volume 1: The Rise of Network Society*. Oxford: Blackwell.

Caudwell, J. (2011). 'Does your boyfriend know you're here?' The spatiality of homophobia in men's football culture in the UK. *Leisure Studies,* 30(2), 123–38.

—(2012). Review of C. Symons (2010). *The Gay Games, Sport in History,* 32(2), 330–3.

Centre on Housing Rights and Evictions (COHRE). (2007). *Fair Play for Housing Rights: Mega-Events, Olympic Games and Housing Rights.* Geneva: COHRE.

Chappelet, J.-L. (2008). Olympic Environmental Concerns as a Legacy of the Winter Games. *International Journal of the History of Sport,* 25(14), 1884–902.

Charlton, J. (2000). *Nothing About Us Without Us. Disability Oppression and Empowerment.* Berkeley, CA: University of California Press.

Chernushenko, D. (1994). *Greening our Games.* Ottawa: Centurion Publishing & Marketing.

Chesters, G. and Welsh, I. (2006). *Complexity and Social Movements: Multitudes at the Edge of Chaos.* London: Routledge.

—(Eds), (2011). *Social Movements – The Key Concepts.* London: Routledge.

Coalter, F. (2007). *A Wider Social Role for Sport: Who's Keeping the Score?:* London: Routledge.

Comeau, G. S. and Church, A. G. (2010). A comparative analysis of women's sport advocacy groups in Canada and the United States. *Journal of Sport and Social Issues,* 34(4), 457–74.

Cornelissen, S. (2012). Our struggles are bigger than the World Cup: civic activism state-society relations and the socio-political legacies of the 2010 FIFA World Cup. *British Journal of Sociology,* 63(2), 328–48.

Coy, P. G., Woehrle, L. M., and Maney, G. M. (2008). Discursive Legacies: The US Peace Movement and 'Support the Troops'. *Social Problems,* 55(2), 161–89.

Crossley, N. (2002). *Making Sense of Social Movements.* Philadelphia, PA: Open University Press.

Cunningham, G. B. and Regan, M. R. (2012). Political activism, racial identity and the commercial endorsement of athletes: Athlete activism. *International Review for the Sociology of Sport,* 47, 657–69.

Curran, G. (2007). Making Another World Possible? The Politics of the World Social Forum. *Social Alternative,* 26(1), 7–38.

Cushion, D. S. (2007). Protesting their apathy? An analysis of British press coverage of young anti-Iraq war protestors. *Journal of youth studies,* 10(4), 419–37.

Dalby, S. (1996). Reading Rio, writing the world: the *New York Times* and the 'Earth Summit'. *Political Geography,* 15(6/7), 593–613.

Dallmayr, F. R. (1999). Globalization from below. *International Politics,* 36, 321–34.

Darby, P. (2012). 'Gains versus Drains': Football Academies and the Export of Highly Skilled Football Labor. *Brown Journal of World Affairs,* 18(2), 265–77.

Darnell, S. C. (2012). *Sport for Development and Peace: A Critical Sociology.* London: Bloomsbury Academic.

Davidson, J. (2012). 'Racism against the abnormal? The twentieth century Gay Games, biopower and the emergence of homonational sport'. *Leisure Studies.* Available online at: http://www.tandfonline.com/doi/full/10.1080/02614367.2012.723731#. UfZNCRYhxHg.

Davis, K. (1993). 'On the movement'. In J. Swain, V. Finkelstein, S. French and M. Oliver (Eds), *Disabling Barriers – Enabling Environments.* London: Sage, pp. 285–92.

Davis-Delano, L. and Crosset, T. (2008). Using Social Movement Theory to Study Outcomes in Sport-Related Social Movements. *International Review for the Sociology of Sport,* 43(2), 115–34.

van Deburg, W. (1992). *New Day in Babylon: The Black Power Movement and American Culture, 1965–1975*. Chicago: University of Chicago Press.

de Jong, W., Shaw, M., and Stammers, N. (Eds), (2005). *Global activism, global media*. Ann Arbor, MI: Pluto Press.

Della Porta, D. and Diani, M. (2006). *Social Movements: An Introduction*, 2nd edn. Oxford: Blackwell.

De Rivera, J. (2004). Assessing the basis for a culture of peace in contemporary societies. *Journal of Peace Research*, 41(5), 531–48.

de Sousa Santos, B. (2006). Globalizations. *Theory, Culture and Society*, 23(2–3), 393–9.

Diani, M. (1992). The concept of social movement. *Sociological Review*, 40(1), 1–25.

Diani, M. and Bison, I. (2004). Organizations, coalitions, and movements. *Theory and Society*, 33, 281–309.

Donnelly, P. (1993). Democratization revisited: Seven theses on the democratization of sport and active leisure. *Loisir et Société/Leisure and Society*, 16(2), 413–34.

—(1996). Prolympism: Sport monoculture as crisis and opportunity. *Quest*, 48(1), 25–42.

—(2008). Sport and Human Rights. *Sport in Society*, 11(4), 381–94.

—(2011). From war without weapons to sport for development and peace: The Janus-face of sport. *SAIS Review*, 31(1), 65–76.

Donnelly, P. and Donnelly, M. (2013). *The London 2012 Olympic Games: A Gender Equality Audit*. Centre for Sport Policy Studies Research Report. Toronto: Centre for Sport Policy Studies, University of Toronto.

Donnelly, P., Atkinson, M., Boyle, S. and Szto, C. (2011). 'Sport for Development and Peace: a public sociology perspective', *Third World Quarterly*, 32(3), 589–601.

Dudziak, M. (2011). *Cold War Civil Rights: Race and the Image of American Democracy*. Princeton, NJ: Princeton University Press.

Dyck, C. B. (2011). Football and Post-War Reintegration: exploring the role of sport in DDR processes in Sierra Leone. *Third World Quarterly*, 32(3), 395–415.

Earth First! (2012). *About Earth First!*: URL: http://www.earthfirst.org/about.htm [Last accessed on 23 April 2012].

Edelman, R. (2006). 'Moscow 1980. Stalinism or Good, Clean Fun?' In A. Tomlinson and C. Young (Eds), *National Identity and Global Sports Events. Culture, Politics and Spectacle*. Albany, NY: State University of New York Press, pp. 149–61.

Edwards, B. and Marullo, S. (1995). Organizational mortality in a declining social movement: The demise of peace movement organizations in the end of the cold war era. *American Sociological Review*, 60, 908–27.

Edwards, H. (1969). *The Revolt of the Black Athlete*. New York: The Free Press.

Einwohner, R. L., Hollander, J. A., and Olson, T. (2000). Engendering social movements: Cultural images and movement dynamics. *Gender & Society*, 14(5), 679–99.

Engstrom, K. (2011). Jets Logo Incites Anti-war Zealots, *Winnipeg Sun*. Last accessed from http://www.winnipegsun.com/2011/07/27/jets-logo-incites-anti-war-zealots.

Enloe, C. (1995). The globetrotting sneaker. *Ms. Magazine*, 11–15 March-April.

—(2000). Daughters and generals in the politics of the globalized sneaker. In P. S. Aulakh and M. G. Schecter (Eds), *Rethinking Globalization(s): From Corporate Transnationalism to Local Interventions*. London: Macmillan Press, pp. 238–46.

Eriksen, L. (2009). 'Gay "olympics" kick off in Copenhagen', *The Guardian*, 25 July, p. 24.

Eschle, C. and Maiguashca, B. (2010). *Making Feminist Sense of the Global Justice Movement*. Plymouth, UK: Rowman & Littlefield Publishers Inc.

Evans, D. (1996[1992]). *A History of Nature Conservation in Britain*. London: Routledge.

Fallows, J. (2002). The Military-Industrial Complex. *Foreign Policy*, 133, 46–8.

Fantasia, R. and Stepan-Norris, J. (2004). The Labor Movement in Motion. In Snow, D., Soule, S., and Kriesi, H. (Eds), *The Blackwell Companion to Social Movements*. Oxford: Blackwell Publishing, pp. 553–75.

Fédération sportive et gymnique du travail (FSGT) (2011). Plaidoyer pour une compétition formatrice, éducative émancipatrice à quelles conditions?, *Sport et plein air*, April, p. 15.

Ferree, M. M. and Roth, S. (1998). Gender, class, and the interaction between social movements: A strike of West Berlin day care workers. *Gender & Society*, 12(6), 626–48.

Ferree, M. M. and Mueller, C. M. (2007). Feminism and the women's movement: A global perspective. In D. A. Snow, S. A. Soule and H. Kriesi (Eds), *The Blackwell Companion to Social Movements*. Malden, MA: Blackwell Publishing, pp. 576–607.

Field, R. (In Press). The New 'Culture Wars': The Vancouver 2010 Olympics, Public Protest, and the Politics of Resistance. In R. Field (Ed.), *A Tribute to Bruce Kidd*. Toronto: Toronto University Press.

Fifield, D. (2012). Police look into McClean death threat, *The Guardian*, Sport, 19/11/12, p.1.

Fleischer, D. and Zames, F. (2011). *The Disability Rights Movement: From Charity to Confrontation*, 2nd edn. Philadelphia: Temple University Press.

Fonow, M. M. (1998). Protest engendered: The participation of women steelworkers in the Wheeling-Pittsburgh strike of 1985. *Gender & Society*, 12(6), 710–28.

Ford, L. (2011). Transnational actors in global environmental politics. In G. Kütting (Ed.), *Global Environmental Politics*. London: Routledge, pp. 27–42.

Fraser, N. (1997). *Justice Interruptus: Critical Reflections on the 'Postsocialist' Condition*. London: Routledge.

Freeman, M. (2011). *Human Rights: An Interdisciplinary Approach*, 2nd edn. Cambridge: Polity Press.

Galtung, J. (1969). Violence, peace, and peace research. *Journal of Peace Research*, 6(3), 167–91.

—(1988). The Peace Movement: An Exercise in Micro-Macro Linkages. *International Social Science Journal*, 40(3), 377–82.

Gamble, S. (Ed.), (2001). *The Routledge Companion to Feminism and Postfeminism*. London: Routledge.

Gasser, P. K. and Levinsen, A. (2004). Breaking post-war ice: Open fun football schools in Bosnia and Herzegovina. *Sport in Society*, 7(3), 457–72.

Gender & Society. (1998 December). *Special Issue on Gender and Social Movements (Part 1)*. 12(6), 621–769.

—(1999 February). *Special Issue on Gender and Social Movements (Part 2)*, 13(1), 5–152.

Germain, R. D. and Kenny, M. (Eds), (2005). *The Idea of Global Civil Society*. London: Routledge.

Giddens, A. (1991). *Modernity and Self-Identity*. Cambridge: Polity.

Giulianotti, R. (2006). Human Rights, Globalization and Sentimental Education. In D. McArdle and R. Giulianotti (Eds), *Sport, Civil Liberties and Human Rights* London: Routledge [originally published in 2004 in *Sport in Society*, 7(3), 355–369].

—(2011a). Sport, Transnational Peacemaking, and Global Civil Society: Exploring the Reflective Discourses of 'Sport, Development, and Peace' Project Officials. *Journal of Sport & Social Issues*, 35(1), 50–71.

—(2011b). Sport, peacemaking and conflict resolution: a contextual analysis and modeling of the sport, development and peace sector. *Ethnic and racial studies*, 34(2), 207–28.

Gitersos, T. (2011). The sporting scramble for Africa: GANEFO, the IOC and the 1965 African Games. *Sport in Society*, 14(5), 645–59.

Gottlieb, R. (1994). *Forcing the Spring: The Transformation of The American Environmental Movement*. Washington, D.C.: Island Press.

Gounot, A. (1994). Sport réformiste ou sport révolutionnaire? Les débuts des Internationales sportives ouvrières. In Arnaud, P. (Ed.), *Les origines du sport ouvrier en Europe*. Paris: Éditions L'Harmattan, pp. 219–45.

—(1999). Jacques Doriot: l'impact sportif d'un homme politique. In J-M. Delaplace (Ed.), *L'histoire du sport, l'histoire des sportifs*. Paris: Harmattan, pp. 61–76.

Greenpeace. (2000). *A Guide to Sustainable Events*. Greenpeace Australia.

—(2008). *China After the Olympics: Lessons from Beijing (Executive Report)*. Greenpeace: http://www.greenpeace.org/eastasia/news/stories/climate-energy/2008/green/ (Last accessed on 12 December 2012).

—(2012). *Chemistry for Any Weather*. Greenpeace: http://www.greenpeace.de/fileadmin/gpd/user_upload/themen/chemie/gp_outdoor_report_2012_engl_fol_fin_neu_02_es.pdf (Last accessed on 12 December 2012).

Griffin, P. (2012). LGBT Equality in Sports: Celebrating our Successes and Facing our Challenges. In G. Cunningham (Ed.), *Sexual orientation and gender identity in sport: Essays from activists, coaches and scholars*. College Station, TX: Center for Sport Management Research and Education, pp. 1–12.

Griffiths, J. (2009). The Transition Initiative. *Orion Magazine*, http://www.orionmagazine.org/index.php/articles/article/4792 *(Last accessed 25 April 2012)*.

Gruneau, R. (In Press). Sport, Development and the Challenge of Slums. In R. Field (Ed.), *A tribute to Bruce Kidd*. Toronto: Toronto University Press.

—(1983). *Sport, Class and Social Development*. Amherst, University of Massachusetts Press.

Grzybowski, C. (2006). The World Social Forum: Reinventing global politics. *Global Governance*, 12(1), 7–13.

Güldenpfennig, S. (1985). Sport in the Peace Movement—A Challenge for the Sport Science. *International Review for the Sociology of Sport*, 20(3), 203–13.

Hall, M. A. (1996). *Feminism and Sporting Bodies: Essays on Theory and Practice*. Champaign, IL: Human Kinetics.

—(2002). *The Girl and the Game: A History of Women's Sport in Canada*. Toronto: University of Toronto Press.

Hardt, M. and Negri, A. (2000). *Empire*. Cambridge: Harvard University Press.

Hargreaves, J. (1985). 'Playing like gentlemen while behaving like ladies': Contradictory features of the formative years of women's sport. *International Journal of the History of Sport*, 2(1), 40–52.

—(1994). *Sporting Females: Critical Issues in the History and Sociology of Women's Sports*. London: Routledge.

—(1999). 'The 'women's international sports movement': Local-global strategies and empowerment. *Women's Studies International Forum*, 22(5), 461–71.

—(2001). *Heroines of Sport: The Politics of Difference and Identity*. London: Routledge.

Hartmann, D. (1996). 'The politics of race and sport: resistance and domination in the 1968 African American Olympic protest movement'. *Ethnic and Racial Studies*, 19(3), 548–66.

—(2003). *Race, Culture and the Revolt of the Black Athlete: The 1968 Olympic Protests and Their Aftermath*. Chicago: University of Chicago Press.

Hartmann-Tews, I. and Pfister, G. (Eds), (2003). *Sport and Women: Social Issues in International Perspective*. London: Routledge.

Harvey, D. (2012). *Rebel Cities: From the Right to the City to the Urban Revolution*. London: Verso.

Harvey, J. (1988). Sport and the Quebec Clergy, 1930–1960. In J. Harvey and H. Cantelon (Eds), *Not Just a Game*. Ottawa: University of Ottawa Press, pp 69–87.

Harvey, J. and Houle, F. (1994). Sports, world economy, global culture and new social movements. *Sociology of Sport Journal*, 11(3), 337–55.

Harvey, J., Horne, J., and Safai, P. (2009). Alter-globalization, Global Social Movements and the Possibility of Political Transformation through Sport. *Sociology of Sport Journal*, 26(3), 383–403.

Hayes, G. and Karamichas, J. (Eds), (2012). *Olympic Games, Mega-Events and Civil Societies*. London: Palgrave Macmillan.

Hayhurst, L. M. C. (2011). Corporatising sport, gender and development: Postcolonial IR feminisms, transnational private governance and global corporate social engagement. *Third World Quarterly*, 32(3), 531–49.

Held, D. (2007). Reframing global governance: Apocalypse soon or reform. In Held, D. and McGrew. (Eds), *Globalization theory*. Cambridge: Polity Press, pp. 240–60.

Held, D. and McGrew, A. (2007). *Globalization/anti-globalization: Beyond the great divide*, 2nd edn. Cambridge: Polity Press.

Heywood, L. (2007). Producing girls: Empire, sport and the neoliberal body. In J. Hargreaves and P. Vertinsky (Eds), *Physical Culture, Power, and the Body*. London: Routledge, pp. 101–20.

Hoberman, J. (2011). 'The Myth of Sport as a Peace-Promoting Political Force'. *SAIS Review*, 31(1), 17–30.

Hobsbawm, E. J. (1969). *Industry and Empire: The Birth of the Industrial Revolution*. Harmondsworth: Penguin.

—(2011). *How to Change the World: Marx and Marxism 1840–2011*. London: Little, Brown.

Höglund, K. and Sundberg, R. (2008). Reconciliation through sports? The case of South Africa. *Third World Quarterly*, 29(4), 805–18.

Holden, M., MacKenzie, J., and VanWynsberghe, R. (2008). *Environment and Planning C: Government and Policy*, 28, 882–905.

Hollins, S. (2013). *The Intersections between Economy, Environment and Locality: The London 2012 Olympic and Paralympic Games*, Unpublished PhD Thesis, University of Central Lancashire, Preston, U.K.

Holton, R. (2005). *Making Globalization*. New York and Basingstoke: Palgrave Macmillan.

Hooks, Bell. (1984). *Feminist Theory: From Margin to Center*. Cambridge, MA: South End Press.

Horne, J. (1998). The Politics of Leisure in Japan. *International Review for the Sociology of Sport*, 33(2), 171–82.

Horne, J. and Whannel, G. (2012). *Understanding the Olympics*. London: Routledge.

Howe, P. D. (2008). *The Cultural Politics of the Paralympic Movement*. London: Routledge.

Hunt, L. (2007). *Inventing Human Rights: A History*. New York: Norton.

ISPO. (2012). Greenpeace criticizes outdoor industry on use of toxic chemicals. ISPO: http://www.ispo.com/newsblog/2012/10/30/greenpeace-criticizes-outdoor-industry-on-use-of-toxic-chemicals/ (Last accessed on 12 December 2012).

Jarvie, G. (2003). Internationalism and sport in the making of nations. *Identities*, 10, 537–51.

—(2006). *Sport, Culture and Society*. London: Routledge.

Jarvie, G. and Thornton, J. (2012). *Sport, Culture and Society*, 2nd edn. London: Routledge.

Jehlicka, P. (1994). Environmentalism in Europe: an east-west comparison. In C. Rootes and H. Davis (Eds), *Social Change and Political Transformation*. London: UCL Press, pp. 112–32.

Jenkins, C. J. and Perrow, C. (2003). Farmworkers' Movements in Changing Political Contexts. In J. Goodwin and J. Jasper (Eds), *The Social Movements Reader: Cases and Concepts*. Malden, MA: Blackwell.

Jenkins, M. (November 2001). King of dirtbags. *Outside Magazine* (*http://www. outsideonline.com/outdoor-adventure/climbing/rock-climbing/King-of-the-Dirtbags.html?page=all* (Last accessed on 18 November 2012).

Johnston, J. and Laxer, G. (2003). Solidarity in the age of globalization: Lessons from the Anti-MAI and Zapatista struggles. *Theory and Society*, 32, 39–91.

Jones, S. (1996). British Workers' Sports Federation: 1923–1935. In Krüger, A. and Riordan, J. (Eds), *The Story of Worker Sport*. Windsor: Human Kinetics, pp. 97–116.

de Jong, W., Shaw, M., and Stammers, N. (Eds), (2005). *Global Activism, Global Media*. London: Pluto Press.

Kalant, A. (2004). *National Identity and the Conflict at Oka. Native belonging and Myths of Postcolonial Nationhood in Canada*. New York: Routledge.

Karamichas, J. (2013). *The Olympic Games and the Environment*. Basingstoke: Palgrave Macmillan.

Kay, J. (2007). 'No time for recreations till the vote is won'? Suffrage activists and leisure in Edwardian Britain. *Women's History Review*, 16(4), 535–53.

—(2008). It wasn't just Emily Davison! Sport, suffrage and society in Edwardian Britain. *International Journal of the History of Sport*, 25(10), 1338–54.

Keck, M. and Sikkink, K. (1998). *Activists beyond Borders: Transnational Advocacy Networks in International Politics*. Ithaca, NY: Cornell University Press.

Kelly, J. (2012). Popular Culture, Sport and the 'Hero'-fication of British Militarism. *Sociology*. Published online before print 5 November 2012. Available at: http://soc. sagepub.com/content/early/2012/11/02/0038038512453795.abstract [Last accessed 18 January 2013].

Kemp, S. and Squires, J. (Eds), (1997). *Feminisms*. Oxford: Oxford University Press.

Khan, N. S. (2002). The impact of the global women's movement on international relations: Has it happened? What has happened? In M. Braig and S. Wölte (Eds), *Common Ground or Mutual Exclusion? Women's Movements and International Relations*. London: Zed Books, pp. 35–45.

Kidd, B. (1996). *The Struggle for Canadian Sport*. Toronto: University of Toronto Press.

—(2008). A New Social Movement: Sport for Development and Peace. *Sport in Society*, 11(4), 370–380.

—(2010). Human Rights and the Olympic Movement after Beijing. *Sport in Society*, 13(5), 901–10.

Kidd, B. and Donnelly, P. (2000). Human Rights in Sports. *International Review for the Sociology of Sport*, 35(2), 131–48.

King, S. (2008). Offensive lines: Sport-state synergy in an era of perpetual war. *Cultural Studies ↔ Critical Methodologies*, 8(4), 527–39.

Kollman, K. and Waites, M. (2009). The global politics of lesbian, gay, bisexual and transgender human rights: an introduction. *Contemporary Politics*, 15(1), 1–17.

Krüger, A. (1996). The German Way of Worker Sport. In Krüger, A. and Riordan, J. (Eds), *The Story of Worker Sport*. Windsor: Human Kinetics, pp. 1–25.

Krüger, A. and Riordan, J. (Eds), (1996). *The Story of Worker Sport*. Windsor: Human Kinetics.

Kuumba, M. B. (2001). *Gender and Social Movements*. Walnut Creek, CA: Altamira Press.

Lange, J. I. (1990). Refusal to Compromise: The Case of Earth First!. *Western Journal of Speech Communication*, 54, 473–94.

Lapoix, F. (1976). *Les mouvements de défense de la nature*. Paris: Encyclopedia Universalis.

Leigh, M. H. and Bonin, T. M. (1977). The pioneering role of Madame Alice Milliat and the FSFI in establishing international track and field for women. *Journal of Sport History*, 4(1), 72–83.

Lenskyj, H. J. (1986). *Out of Bounds: Women, Sport and Sexuality*. Toronto: Women's Press.

—(1998). Sport and Corporate Environmentalism: The Case of the Sydney 2000 Olympics. *International Review for the Sociology of Sport*, 33(4), 341–54.

—(2000). *Inside the Olympic Industry*. New York: SUNY Press.

—(2002). *The Best Olympics ever*. New York: SUNY Press.

—(2005). 'Gay Games or Gay Olympics? Corporate sponsorship issues.' In J. Amis and T. B. Cornwell (Eds), *Global Sport Sponsorship*. Oxford: Berg, pp. 281–96.

—(2008). *Olympic industry Resistance*. New York: SUNY Press.

—(2012). *Gender Politics and the Olympic Industry*. London: Palgrave Macmillan.

Leopkey, B. and Parent, M. (2012). Olympic Games Legacy: From General benefits to Sustainable Long-Term Legacy. *The International Journal of the History of Sport*, 29(6), 924–43.

L'Etang, J., Falkheimer, J., and Lugo, J. (2007). Public relations and tourism: Critical reflections and a research agenda. *Public Relations Review*, 33(1), 68–76.

Light Shields, D. L. and Light Bredemeier, B. J. (1996). Sport, militarism, and peace. *Peace and Conflict: Journal of Peace Psychology*, 2(4), 369–83.

Loland, S. and Selliaas, A. (2009). The Olympic truce – the ideal and the reality. In K. Georgiadis and A. Syrigos (Eds), *Olympic Truce. Sport as a Platform for Peace*. Athens: International Olympic Truce Centre, pp. 57–69.

Macgilchrist, F. and Böhmig, I. (2012). Blogs, genes and immigration: Online media and minimal politics. *Media, Culture & Society*, 34(1), 83–100.

McArdle, D. and Giulianotti, R. (Eds), (2006). *Sport, Civil Liberties and Human Rights*. London: Routledge.

McDonald, K. (2006). *Global Movements: Action and Culture*. Oxford: Blackwell.

McEvoy, J. and Foisy, P.-V. (2011). *Le scandale du gaz de schiste*. Montréal: VLB.

McQuarrie, F. A. E. (2010). The Struggle over Worker Leisure: An Analysis of the History of the Workers' Sports Association in Canada. *Canadian Journal of Administrative Sciences*, 27(4), 391–402.

McRae, D. (2013). 'In football it's impossible to come out', *The Guardian*, 30 March, Sport section, pp. 1–4.

Majumdar, B. and Mehta, N. (2010). It's not just sport: Delhi and the Olympic torch relay. *Sport in Society*, 13(1), 92–106.

Maraniss, D. (2008). *Rome 1960. The Olympics that changed the world*. New York: Simon and Schuster.

Marullo, S. (1996). Frame Changes and Social Movement Contraction: US Peace Movement Framing After the Cold War. *Sociological Inquiry*, 66(1), 1–28.

Mayo, M. (2005). *Global Citizens: Social Movements and the Challenge of Globalization*. Toronto: Canadian Scholars' Press Inc.

Mayor, F. (2004). A global culture of peace: Transmission and ethical dimensions. *Higher Education in Europe*, 29(4), 491–94.

Melchers, R. (1988). Sport in the workplace. In J. Harvey and H. Cantelon (Eds), *Not Just a Game*. Ottawa: University of Ottawa Press, pp. 51–68.

Mertes, T. (2003). *A movement of movements: Is another world really possible*. Brooklyn, NY: Verso Press.

Meyer, D. S. (1993). Protest cycles and political process: American peace movements in the nuclear age. *Political Research Quarterly*, 46(3), 451–79.

—(1999). Civil disobedience and protest cycles. *Waves of protest: social movements since the sixties*, 101, 267.

Meyer, D. S. and Whittier, N. (1994). Social movement spillover. *Social problems*, 41, 277–98.

Millington, R. (2010). Basketball with (out) borders: Interrogating the intersections of sport, development, and capitalism. Unpublished Master's Thesis. Queen's University, Kingston Ontario.

Millington, R. and Darnell, S. C. (2012). Constructing and Contesting the Olympics Online: The Internet, Rio 2016 and the politics of Brazilian development. *International Review for the Sociology of Sport*. Published online before print 9 September 2012. Available at: http://irs.sagepub.com/content/early/2012/09/07/101 2690212455374.abstract [Last accessed 18 January 2013].

Mills, S. (1998). Post-colonial feminist theory. In S. Jackson and J. Jones (Eds), *Contemporary Feminist Theories*. Edinburgh: Edinburgh University Press, pp. 98–112.

Moghadam, V. M. (2000). Transnational Feminist Networks: Collective Action in an Era of Globalization. *International Sociology*, 15(1), 57–85.

—(2005). *Globalizing Women: Transnational Feminist Networks*. Baltimore: Johns Hopkins University Press.

—(2009). *Globalization and Social Movements: Islamism, Feminism and the Global Justice Movement*. Lanham, MD: Rowman & Littlefield Publishers.

Mohanty, C. T. (1985). Under Western eyes: Feminist scholarship and colonial discourses. *Boundary*, 2(3), 333–58.

—(1997). Women workers and capitalist scripts: Ideologies of domination, common interests, and the politics of solidarity. In M. J. Alexander and C. T. Mohanty (Eds), *Feminist Genealogies, Colonial Legacies, Democratic Futures*. London: Routledge, pp. 3–29.

—(2002). 'Under western eyes' revisited: Feminist solidarity through anticapitalist struggles. *Signs*, 28(2), 499–535.

—(2003). *Feminism without Borders: Decolonizing Theory, Practicing Solidarity*. Durham, NC: Duke University Press.

Mol, A. P. J. (2000). The environmental movement in an era of ecological modernisation. *Geoforum*, 31(1), 45–56.

Monbiot, G. (2012). 'After Rio, we know. Governments have given up on the planet'. *The Guardian*, 25 June. http://www.guardian.co.uk/commentisfree/2012/jun/25/rio-governments-will-not-save-planet [Last accessed 12 November 2012].

Morgan, R. (Ed.), (1996/1984). *Sisterhood is Global: The International Women's Movement Anthology*. New York: The Feminist Press at The City University of New York.

Morris, A. D. and McClurg Mueller, C. (Eds), (1992). *Frontiers in Social Movement Theory,* New Haven, Connecticut: Yale University Press.

Moyn, S. (2010). *The Last Utopia: Human Rights in History.* Cambridge, MA: Harvard University Press.

Muir, H. (2012). 'Disability is about human rights, not sob stories', *The Guardian,* 1 October, available at: http://www.guardian.co.uk/uk/2012/sep/30/hideously-diverse-britain-disability-human-rights [Last accessed 9 October 2012].

Munck, R. (2007). *Globalization and Contestation: The New Great Counter-Movement.* New York: Routledge.

Narayan, U. (1997). *Dislocating Cultures: Identities, Traditions, and Third-World Feminism.* London: Routledge.

Nash, K. (2012). Human Rights, Movements and Law: On Not Researching Legitimacy. *Sociology,* 46(5), 797–812.

Nash, R. (1967 [2001]). *Wilderness and the American Mind,* 4th edn. New Haven: Yale University Press.

Neier, A. (2012). *The International Human Rights Movement: A History.* Princeton, N. J.: Princeton University Press.

Nelson, D. (2002). Globocracy. *International Politics,* 39, 245–50.

Nisbet, R. (1983). *Prejudices: A Philosophical Dictionary.* Boston: Harvard University Press.

Oliver, M. (1990). *The Politics of Disablement: A Sociological Approach.* London: Macmillan.

—(1965). *The Logic of Collective Action; Public Goods and the Theory of Groups.* Cambridge: Harvard University Press.

Omond, R. (1985). *The Apartheid Handbook. A Guide to South Africa's Everyday Racial Policies.* Harmondsworth: Penguin.

Organizing Committee 2006 FIFA World Cup (2006). *Green Goal Legacy Report.* Frankfurt: Organizing Committee 2006 FIFA World Cup.

Pelak, C. F. (2002). Women's collective identity formation in sports: A case study from women's ice hockey. *Gender & Society,* 16(1), 93–114.

—(2005). Athletes as agents of change: An examination of shifting race relations within women's netball in post-apartheid South Africa. *Sociology of Sport Journal,* 22(1), 59–77.

—(2006). Local-global processes: Linking globalization, democratization, and the development of women's football in South Africa. *Africa Spectrum,* 41(3), 371–92.

Pelak, C. F., Taylor, V., and Whittier, N. (1999). Gender Movements. In J. S. Chafetz (Ed.), *Handbook of the Sociology of Gender.* New York: Plenum Publishers, pp. 147–75.

Perelman, M. (2012). *Barbaric Sport. A Global Plague.* London: Verso.

Pfister, G. (2010). Women in sport – gender relations and future perspectives. *Sport in Society,* 13(2), 234–48.

Pickerill, J. and Webster, F. (2006). The anti-war/peace movement in Britain and the conditions of information war. *International Relations,* 20(4), 407–23.

Pike, E. C. J. and Matthews, J. J. K. (July 2012). A postcolonial critique of the development and diversity of groups advocating the advancement of women and sport. Paper presented at the annual World Congress of the International Sociology of Sport Association. Glasgow: Scotland.

Pivato, S. (1994). Le socialisme anti-sportif: le cas italien. In Arnaud, P. (Ed.), *Les origines du sport ouvrier en Europe.* Paris: Éditions L'Harmattan, pp. 129–39.

Play Fair (2012). Fair Games? Human rights of workers in Olympic 2012 supplier factories. A report available from http://www.playfair2012.org.uk/2012/05/fair-games-human-rights-of-workers-in-olympic-2012-supplier-factories/ [last accessed 20 December 2012].

Pleyers, G. (2010). Alter-Globalization: Becoming Actors in the Global Age. Cambridge: Polity.

Polenberg, R. (1980). *One Nation Divisible. Class, Race and Ethnicity in the United States Since 1938*. Harmondsworth: Penguin.

Price, M. E. (2008). On seizing the Olympic platform. In M. E. Price and D. Dayan (Eds), *Owning the Olympics: Narratives of the New China*. Ann Arbor, MI: University of Michigan Press, pp. 86–114.

Pronger, B. (2000). 'Homosexuality and Sport. Who's winning?'. In J. McKay, M. Messner and D. Sabo (Eds), *Masculinities, Gender Relations and Sport*. Thousand Oaks, CA: Sage, pp. 224–40.

Pujadas, X. and Santacana, C. (1994). Le mythe des Jeux populaires de Barcelone. In Arnaud, P. (Ed.), *Les origines du sport ouvrier en Europe*. Paris: L'Harmattan, pp. 267–77.

Quanz, D. (1993). Civic pacifism and sports-based internationalism: Framework for the founding of the International Olympic Committee. *Olympika. The International Journal of Olympic Studies*, 2, 1–23.

Quanz, D. R. (1995). Formatting Power of the IOC: Founding the Birth of a New Peace Movement. *Citius, Altius, Fortius*, 3(1), 6–16.

Ramsamy, S. (1982). *Apartheid: The Real Hurdle. Sport in South Africa and the International Boycott*. London: International Defence and Aid Fund for Southern Africa.

—(1984). 'Apartheid, boycotts and the Games'. In A. Tomlinson and G. Whannel (Eds), *Five Ring Circus. Money, power and politics at the Olympic Games*. London: Pluto Press, pp. 44–52.

Rao, A. (1996). Engendering institutional change. *Signs*, 22(1), 218–21.

Reiger, J. F. (1975 [2000]). *American Sportsmen and the Origins of Conservation*, 3rd edn. Corvallis: Oregon State University Press.

Renou, X. (2012). 'Resisting the Torch'. In G. Hayes and J. Karamichas (Eds), *Olympic Games, Mega-Events and Civil Societies. Globalization, Environment, Resistance*. Basingstoke: Palgrave, pp. 236–46.

Riegel, R. E. (1963). Women's Clothes and Women's Rights. *American Quarterly*, 15(3), 390–401.

Riordan, J. (1996). Worker Sport Within a Worker State: The Soviet Union. In Krüger, A. and Riordan, J. (Eds), *The Story of Worker Sport*. Windsor: Human Kinetics, pp. 43–65.

Ritchie, I. (2003). Sex tested, gender verified: controlling female sexuality in the age of containment. *Sport History Review*, 34(1), 80–98.

Rivenburgh, N. K. (2009). Seeking discursive spaces for peace in media-sport narratives. *Conflict and Communication Online*, 8(2). Available at: http://www.cco.regener-online.de/ [Last accessed 18 January 2013].

Roberts, S., Secor, A., and Sparke, M. (2004). Neoliberal geopolitics. *Antipode*, 35(5), 886–97.

Robertson, B. (1998). 'Disability Community and Pride'. In L. Schlesinger and D. Taub (Eds), *Syllabi And Instructional Materials for Teaching Sociology of Disabilities*. Washington, DC: American Sociological Association, pp. 30–5.

Robertson, R. (1992). *Globalization*. London: Sage.

Rochon, T. R. (1990). The West European peace movement and the theory of new social movements. In R. J. Dalton and M. Kuechler, (Eds), *Challenging the political order: New social and political movements in Western democracies*. Cambridge: Polity Press, 105–21.

Rome, A. (2003). *Conservation, Preservation, and Environmental Activism: A Survey of the Historical Literature*: National Park Services (url: http://www.cr.nps.gov/history/hisnps/NPSThinking/nps-oah.htm [Last accessed on 17 April 2012].

Rootes, C. (2007). Environmental Movements. In Ritzer, G. (Ed.), *Blackwell Encyclopedia of Sociology*. Chichester: Wiley.

—(2008). Environmental Movements. In D. A. Snow, S. A. Soule and H. Kriesi (Eds), *Blackwell Companion to Social Movements*. Chichester: Wiley, pp. 608–40.

Rose, F. (2000). *Coalitions across the Class Divide: Lessons from the Labor, Peace, and Environmental Movements*. Ithaca, NY: Cornell University Press.

Rowe, D. (2012). 'The bid, the lead-up, the event and the legacy: global cultural politics and hosting the Olympics'. *The British Journal of Sociology*, 63(2), 285–305.

Rupp, L. J. and Taylor, V. (1999). Forging feminist identity in an international movement: A collective identity approach to twentieth-century feminism. *Signs*, 24(2), 363–86.

Ruppert, U. (2002). Global women's politics: Towards the 'globalizing' of women's human rights? In M. Braig and S. Wölte (Eds), *Common Ground or Mutual Exclusion? Women's Movements and International Relations*. London: Zed Books, pp. 147–59.

Sabatier, F. (2011). Combats pour l'émancipation: Une histoire des organisations sportives « communistes » de France (1923–2010). *Hommes et migrations*, 1289, 28–36.

Sabo, D. and Veliz, P. (2012). *The Decade of Decline: Gender Equity in High School Sports*. Ann Arbor, MI: SHARP Center for Women and Girls.

Sage, G. (1999). Justice do it! The Nike transnational advocacy network: organization, collective actions, and outcomes. *Sociology of Sport Journal*, 16(3), 206–35.

Salomon, K. (1986). The Peace Movement-An Anti-Establishment Movement. *Journal of Peace Research*, 23(2), 115–127.

Sandoval, C. (2000). *Methodology of the Oppressed*. Minneapolis: University of Minnesota Press.

Schendler, A. (2011). The Cold Revolution. http://www.outsideonline.com/blog/the-cold-revolution.html [Last accessed 5/11/2012].

Scherer, J. and Koch, J. (2010). Living with war: sport, citizenship, and the cultural politics of post-9/11 Canadian identity. *Sociology of Sport Journal*, 27(1), 1–29.

Schimmel, K. S. (2012). Protecting the NFL/militarizing the homeland: Citizen soldiers and urban resilience in post-9/11 America. *International Review for the Sociology of Sport*, 47(3), 338–57.

Scholte, J. A. (2005). *Globalization: A critical introduction*, 2nd Edn. New York, NY: Palgrave Macmillan.

Schultz, J. (2010). The physical is political: Women's suffrage, pilgrim hikes and the public sphere. *International Journal of the History of Sport*, 27(7), 1133–53.

Schwebel, M. (1996). Sports, peace, and conflict. *Peace and Conflict: Journal of Peace Psychology; Peace and Conflict: Journal of Peace Psychology*, 2(4), 297.

Schweinbenz, A. (2000). Not just early Olympic fashion statements: bathing suits, uniforms, and sportswear. In K. B. Wamsley, S. G. Martyn, G. H. MacDonald and R. K. Barney (Eds), *Bridging Three Centuries: Intellectual Crossroads and the Modern Olympic Movement: Fifth International Symposium for Olympic*

Research. London, Ontario: Centre for Olympic Studies, University of Western Ontario, pp. 135–41.

Scott, J. (2012). *Sociological Theory: Contemporary Debates*. Cheltenham: Edward Elgar.

Scraton, S. and Flintoff, A. (Eds), (2002). *Gender and Sport: A Reader*. London: Routledge.

Scupham-Bilton, T. (n.d.). *Olympic Pride. The History of LGBT Participation in the Olympics*. http://gaygames.org/wp/wp-content/uploads/2012/07/lgbtolympics.pdf [Last accessed 20 September 2012].

Seckel, H. (2012). Le football est un sport qui se joue à 7. *Le Monde*, 28 April, p. 7.

Seghezzo, L. (2009). The five dimensions of sustainability. *Environmental Politics*, 18(4), 539–56.

Sen, G. and Grown, C. (1987). *Development, Crises, and Alternative Visions: Third World Women's Perspectives*. New York: Monthly Review Press.

Sherpas Cinema. (2011). *ALL I CAN*. British Columbia, Canada: Sherpas Cinema (url: http://sherpascinema.com/news/now-playing-allican [Last accessed: 11/10/2012].

Sherry, E. (2010). (Re)engaging marginalized groups through sport: The Homeless World Cup. *International Review for the Sociology of Sport*, 45(1), 59–71.

Sherry, E., Karg, A., and O'May, F. (2011). Social capital and sport events: spectator attitudinal change and the Homeless World Cup. *Sport in Society*, 14(1), 111–25.

Shipley, T. (2011). Save our Jets: New Winnipeg Jets logo sacrifices nostalgia for militarism. Retrieved from: http://rabble.ca/news/2011/07/save-our-jets-new-winnipeg-jets-logo-sacrifices-nostalgia-militarism [Last accessed 24 March 2012].

Siebers, T. (2008). *Disability Theory*. Ann Arbor: University of Michigan Press.

Silveira, S. (2001). The American Environmental Movement: Surviving Through Diversity. *Boston College Environmental Affairs Law Review*, 28, 497–532.

Sluiter, L. (2009). *CleanClothes: A Global Movement to end Sweatshops*. London: Pluto Press.

Smith, J. (2004). Transnational Processes and Movements. In Snow, D., Soule, S., and Kriesi, H. (Eds), *The Blackwell Companion to Social Movements*. Oxford: Blackwell Publishing, pp. 311–35.

Smith, M. (1999). *Lesbian and Gay Rights in Canada: Social Movements and Equality-Seeking 1971–1995*. Toronto: University of Toronto Press.

Smith Page, J. (2001). The International Year for the Culture of Peace: Was it Worth It? *International Journal of Cultural Studies*, 4(3), 348–51.

Snow, D., Soule, S., and Kriesi, H. (Eds), (2004). *The Blackwell Companion to Social Movements*. Oxford: Blackwell Publishing.

Snyder, M. (2006). Unlikely godmother: The UN and the global women's movement. In M. M. Ferree and A. M. Tripp (Eds), *Global Feminism: Transnational Women' Activism, Organizing, and Human Rights*. New York: New York University Press, pp. 24–50.

Spears, B. (1972). Women in the Olympics: An unresolved problem. In P. Graham and H. Ueberhost (Eds), *The Modern Olympics*. New York, NY: Leisure Press, pp. 62–83.

Spivak, G. C. (1988). Can the subaltern speak? In C. Nelson and L. Grossberg (Eds), *Marxism and the Interpretation of Culture*. Basingstoke: Macmillan Educational, pp. 271–313.

—(1996). *The Spivak Reader: Selected Writings of Gayatri Chakravorty Spivak*. D. Landry and G. Maclean (Eds). London: Routledge.

Staggenborg, S. (1998). Social movement communities and cycles of protest: The emergence and maintenance of a local women's movement. *Social Problems*, 45(1), 180–204.

Stammers, N. (2009). *Human Rights and Social Movements*. London: Pluto.

—(2007). Local Social Movements and Mesoamerican Cultural Resistance and Adaptation. *Social Movement Studies*, 6(2), 161–75.

Sugden, J. (2006). Teaching and playing sport for conflict resolution and co-existence in Israel. *International review for the sociology of sport*, 41(2), 221–40.

Surfers Against Sewage. (2012). *SAS Background*: SAS (http://www.sas.org.uk/sas-background/ [Last accessed 18/11/2012].

Surfrider Foundation. (2010). *Surfrider Foundation Joins Force with Protect Our Winters*: Surfrider Foundation (URL: http://www.surfrider.org/press-center/entry/surfrider-foundation-joins-forces-with-protect-our-winters [Last accessed 18/11/2012].

Swiebel, J. (2009). Lesbian, gay, bisexual and transgender human rights: the search for an international strategy. *Contemporary Politics*, 15(1), 19–35.

Symons, C. (2010). *The Gay Games*. London: Routledge.

Tarrow, S. (1998). *Power in Movement: Social Movements and Contentious Politics*. Cambridge: Cambridge University Press.

—(2003). *Scale Shift in Transnational Contention*. Paper presented at the Transnational Process and Social Movements Conference in Bellagio, Italy.

Tartakowski, D. (1994). Organisations et cultures ouvrières dans l'Europe du XIXème siècle. Les premières formes de solidarité ouvrières. In Arnaud, P. (Ed.), *Les origines du sport ouvrier en Europe*. Paris: Éditions L'Harmattan, pp. 29–43.

Taylor, V. (1999). Gender and social movements: Gender processes in women's self-help movements. *Gender & Society*, 13(1), 8–33.

Taylor, V. and Whittier, N. (1996). Analytical approaches to social movement culture: The culture of women's movement. In H. Johnston and B. Klandermans (Eds), *Social Movements and Culture: Social Movements, Protest, and Contention*. Minneapolis, MN: University of Minnesota Press, pp. 163–87.

Taylor, V., Whittier, N. and Pelak, C. F. (2001). Women's Movement: Persistence through Transformation. In V. Taylor, L. Richardson and N. Whittier (Eds), *Feminist Frontiers*, 5th edn. New York, NY: McGraw-Hill., pp. 559–74.

Teeple, G. (2005). *The Riddle of Human Rights*. Amherst, NY: Humanity Books.

Therborn, G. (2011). *The World. A Beginner's Guide*. Cambridge: Polity.

Thériault, J.-Y. (1991). Individualisation, universalisation, démocratisation: le temps de l'histoire. *Possibles*, 15(2), 127–40.

Thompson, E. P. (1968). *The Making of the English Working Class*. Harmondsworth: Penguin.

Thörn, H. (2007). Social Movements, the Media and the Emergence of a Global Public Sphere: From Anti-Apartheid to Global Justice. *Current Sociology*, 55(6), 896–918.

Thorpe, H. and Rinehart, R. (2012). Action Sport NGOs in a Neo-Liberal Context: The Cases of Skateistan and Surf Aid International. *Journal of Sport & Social Issues*. Published online before print 25 September 2012. Available at: http://jss.sagepub.com/content/early/2012/09/28/0193723512455923 [Last accessed 18 January 2013].

Tilly, C. (2004). *Social Movements, 1768–2004*. Boulder, CO: Paradigm Publishers.

Tilly, C. and Wood, C. (2009). *Social Movements, 1768–2004*, 2nd edn. Boulder, CO: Paradigm Publishers.

Timms, J. (2012). The Olympics as a platform for protest: a case study of the London 2012 'ethical' Games and the Fair Play campaign for workers' rights. *Leisure Studies*, 31(3), 355–72.

Tinker, I. (Ed.), (1990). *Persistent Inequalities: Women and World Development*. New York: Oxford University Press.

Touraine, A. (1977). *The Self-Production of Society*. Chicago: Chicago University Press.

—(1981). *The Voice and the Eye*. Cambridge: Cambridge University Press.

—(1983). *Solidarity: The Analysis of a Social Movement: Poland 1980–1981*. Cambridge: Cambridge University Press.

—(1988). *Return of the Actor*. Minneapolis, University of Minnesota Press.

Travers, A. (2008). The sport nexus and gender injustice. *Studies in Social Justice*, 2(1), 79–101.

Triesman, D. (1984). The Olympic Games as a political forum. In A. Tomlinson and G. Whannel (Eds), *Five Ring Circus. Money, Power and Politics at the Olympic Games*. London: Pluto, pp. 16–29.

Tripp, A. M. (2006). Challenges in transnational feminist mobilization. In M. M. Ferree and A. M. Tripp (Eds), *Global Feminism: Transnational Women' Activism, Organizing, and Human Rights*. New York: New York University Press, pp. 296–312.

United Nations (1948/2012). 'The Universal Declaration of Human Rights' available at http://www.un.org/en/documents/udhr/index.shtml [accessed 12 November 2012].

United Nations Human Rights Council (UN HRC) (2012). *Born Free and Equal. Sexual Orientation and Gender Identity in International Human Rights. Law* Geneva: UN Human Rights Council.

Vanhala, L. (2011). *Making Rights a Reality? Disability Rights Activists and Legal Mobilization*. Cambridge: Cambridge University Press.

Walker, P. and Holman, Z. (2012). Now everyone wants a piece of the Paralympic action. *The Guardian*, 3 October, p. 11.

Waller, S., Polite, F. and Spearman, L. (2012). Retrospective reflections on the Black American male athlete and the 1968 Olympics: an elite interview with Dr Harry Edwards. *Leisure Studies*, 31(3), 265–70.

Wamsley, K. and Schultz, G. (2000). Rogues and bedfollows: The IOC and the incorporation of the FSFI. In K. B. Wamsley, S. G. Martyn, G. H. MacDonald and R. K. Barney (Eds), *Bridging Three Centuries: Intellectual Crossroads and the Modern Olympic Movement: Fifth International Symposium for Olympic Research*. London, Ontario: Centre for Olympic Studies, University of Western Ontario, pp. 113–8.

Wapner, P. K. (1995). *Environmental Activism and World Civic Politics*. New York: State University of New York Press.

War on Want. (2003). *Waging the War on Want*. London: War on Want.

Ward, N. (1996). Surfers, Sewage and the New Politics of Pollution. *Area*, 28(3), 331–8.

Wassong, S. and Muller, N. (2007). Jules Simon: A Prominent Person in Pierre de Coubertin's Early Network. *Sport in History*, 27(1), 110–26.

Wheaton, B. (2007). Identity, Politics, and the Beach: Environmental Activism in Surfers Against Sewage. *Leisure Studies*, 26(3), 279–302.

Wheeler, K. and Aright, J. (2006). A Global Perspective on the Environmental Impact of Golf. *Sport in Society*, 9(3), 427–43.

White, A. (1997). The growth of the international women and sport movement. In the proceedings of the *Second Scientific International Conference for Woman's Sport: Woman and Child, A Future Vision from a Sport's Perspective*. Alexandria, Egypt: University of Alexandria, pp. 3–11.

Wieviorka, M. (2005). After new social movements. *Social Movement Studies*, 4(1), 1–19.

Williams, R. (1977). *Marxism and Literature*. Oxford: Oxford University press.

Wilson, B. (2002). The 'anti-jock' movement: Reconsidering youth resistance, masculinity, and sport culture in the age of the Internet. *Sociology of Sport Journal*, 19, 206–33.

—(2007). New media, social movements and global sport: A revolutionary moment and the sociology of sport. *Sociology of Sport Journal*, 24(4), 457–77.

—(2012). *Sport and Peace: A Sociological Perspective*. Don Mills and Oxford: Oxford University Press.

Wilson, B. and Hayhurst, L. (2009). Digital activism: Neoliberalism, the Internet, and sport for youth development. *Sociology of Sport Journal*, 26(1), 155–81.

Winter, J. (2003). The Development of the Disability Rights Movement as a Social Problem Solver. *Disability Studies Quarterly*, 23(1), 33–61.

Woody, T. (2009). Surf's Up, Waste's Down. *The New York Times*, 19 November, p. F4.

Worden, M. (Ed.), (2008). *China's Great Leap. The Beijing Games and Olympian Human Rights Challenges*. New York: Seven Stories Press.

Wright Mills, C. (1956). *The Power Elite*. New York: Oxford University Press.

Wrynn, A. (2004). The Human Factor: Science, Medicine and the International Olympic Committee, 1900–70. *Sport in Society*, 7(2), 211–31.

Yulia, Z. (2010). Social movements through the gender lens. *Sociology Compass*, 4(8), 628–41.

Zirin, D. (2005). *What's my name, fool? sports and resistance in the United States*. Chicago, IL: Haymarket Books.

Selected Internet Sources

N. B. Some of the following sources are not directly cited in this book but are useful resources for research.

Brighton Declaration on Women and Sport. (1994). Brighton, UK: Sports Council. Retrieved from http://www.iwg-gti.org/@Bin/22427/Brighton+Declaration_EN.pdf. Last accessed 15 August 2012.

Brown, S. (10 August 2012). *London 2012: The Women's Olympics?* Retrieved from http://edition.cnn.com/2012/08/10/sport/london-olympics-women/index.html. Last accessed 5 September 2012.

China's Olympic Human Rights Challenges: http://fora.tv/2008/06/18/Chinas_Olympic_Human_Rights_Challenges#fullprogram [Last accessed 19 September 2012].

CSIT (2012). About us. Available online: http://www.csit.tv/en/menu_main/about-us. Last accessed 4 October 2012.

Disability Rights and Independent Living Movement (University of California, Berkeley): http://bancroft.berkeley.edu/collections/drilm/index.html [Last accessed 21 September 2012].

The Disability Rights Movement (The Smithsonian Institution, National Museum of American History): http://americanhistory.si.edu/disabilityrights/welcome.html [Last accessed 21 September 2012].

Dorsey, J. (10 April 2012). *Egyptian feminists challenge militant soccer fan chauvinism*. Retrieved from http://mideastsoccer.blogspot.ca/2012/04/egyptian-feminists-challenge-militant.html. Last accessed 7 August 2012.

Federation of Gay Games: http://gaygames.org/wp/ [Last accessed 20 September 2012].

FSGT (2012). Fédération sportive et gymnique du travail. Available online: http://www.fsgt.org/ Last accessed 11 October 2012.

Kluka, D. A. (2008). *The Brighton Declaration on Women and Sport: A Management Audit of Process Quality*. Unpublished doctoral dissertation. University of Pretoria, South Africa. Retrieved from http://upetd.up.ac.za/thesis/available/etd-05262009-160707/unrestricted/thesis.pdf. Last accessed 15 July 2012.

Laboratory for Diversity in Sport (Texas A & M University): http://www.diversityinsport.com [Last accessed 20 September 2012].

Matthews, J. and Pike, E. C. J. and White, A. (2012 February). *Analysis and Review of International Working Group on Women and Sport Progress Reports 1994–2010*. Retrieved from https://iwg--gti-org-bin.directo.fi/@Bin/fa89b0d1ac161abdc9704 7ec02e54058/1350653733/application/pdf/129727/AWF_IWG%20Progress%20 Reports%201994–2010.pdf. Last accessed 15 August 2012.

Play Fair. (2004). Play Fair at the Olympics. Press release. Available online: http://www.fairolympics.org/countries/PLAYFAIRpress.pdf (Accessed 20 November 2012).

Play Fair. (2012a). *Fair Games? Human rights of workers in Olympic 2012 supplier factories*. Available online: www.play-fair.org Last accessed 20 September 2012.

Scupham-Bilton, T. (n.d.). *Olympic Pride. The History of LGBT Participation in the Olympics*: http://gaygames.org/wp/wp-content/uploads/2012/07/lgbtolympics.pdf [Last accessed 20 September 2012].

Short History of CEDAW Convention (n.d.). Retrieved from www.un.org/womenwatch/daw/cedaw/history.htm. Last accessed 13 December 2012.

United Nations (2007). *Women 2000 and Beyond: Women, Gender Equality and Sport*. Retrieved from http://www.un.org/womenwatch/daw/public/Women%20 and%20Sport.pdf. Last accessed 15 August 2012.

UN Daily News. (13 August 2012). UN envoy on sport for peace praises 'exemplary' Summer Olympics. Retrieved from http://www.un.org/apps/news/story.asp? NewsID=42676&Cr=sports&Cr1=#.UHP5GI5CfRq. Last accessed 13 October 2012.

UNWomen.org (n.d.). Short history of the Commission on the Status of Women. Retrieved from http://www.un.org/womenwatch/daw/CSW60YRS/ CSWbriefhistory.pdf. Last accessed 13 December 2012.

War on Want. (2012b). Race to the bottom: Olympic sportswear companies' exploitation of Bangladeshi workers. Available online: http://www.waronwant.org/ attachments/Race%20to%20the%20Bottom.pdf. Last accessed 20 September 2012.

Wolff, A. (13 August 2012). Run the world, girls. *Sports Illustrated*. Retrieved from http://sportsillustrated.cnn.com/vault/article/magazine/MAG1204381/2/index.htm. Last accessed 5 September 2012.

Index

CPSIA information can be obtained at www.ICGtesting.com
Printed in the USA
LVOW10*1012060214

372622LV00007B/25/P